THE HUMAN GEOGRAPHY OF IRELAND

James H. Johnson

JOHN WILEY & SONS

New York · Chichester · Brisbane · Toronto · Singapore

Copyright © 1994 J.H. Johnson

Published 1994 by John Wiley & Sons Ltd,
Baffins Lane, Chichester,
West Sussex PO19 1UD, England
Telephone National Chichester (0243) 779777
International (+44) 243 779777

Other Wiley Editorial Offices

John Wiley & Sons, Inc., 605 Third Avenue,
New York, NY 10158-0012, USA

Jacaranda Wiley Ltd, 33 Park Road, Milton,
Queensland 4064, Australia

John Wiley & Sons (Canada) Ltd, 22 Worcester Road,
Rexdale, Ontario M9W 1L1, Canada

John Wiley & Sons (SEA) Pte Ltd, 37 Jalan Pemimpin #05-04,
Block B, Union Industrial Building, Singapore 2057

Library of Congress Cataloging-in-Publication Data

Johnson, James Henry, 1930–
  The human geography of Ireland / James H. Johnson.
    p. cm.
  Includes bibliographical references and index.
  ISBN 0-471-94832-2 (hb). —ISBN 0-471-94835-7 (pb)
    1. Human geography—Ireland. 2. Ireland—History. 3. Ireland—
Social conditions. 4. Ireland—Economic conditions. I. Title.
GF563.J64 1994
941.5—dc20
                                              93-5438
                                              CIP

British Library Cataloguing in Publication Data
A catalogue record for this book is available from the British Library

ISBN   0-471-94832-2 (hb)
        0-471-94835-7 (pb)

Typeset in 10/12pt Times from authors' disks by
Florencetype Limited, Kewstoke, Avon.
Printed and bound in Great Britain by Bookcraft (Bath) Ltd.

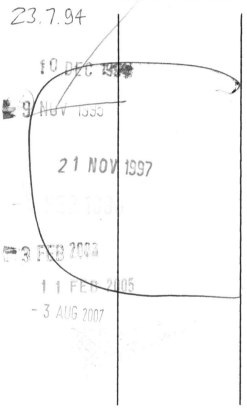

In memory of my parents

Contents

List of figures

List of tables

List of photographs

Preface

This book is in many ways a piece of personal indulgence, since its major aim is to convey to others some of the interest which the geography of Ireland has brought me, and to make some sense of fieldwork and other notes I have collected rather casually over the years. Its various chapters are better thought of as a series of fairly popular essays rather than as a scientific account of the total sum of geographical knowledge. In any case, to produce such a comprehensive account would now be an impossible task for an individual author because of the way geographical scholarship has flourished in Ireland over the past four decades.

Nevertheless, it is hoped that this book will provide a reasonably coherent account of some of the more interesting aspects of the human geography of Ireland. I have taken the view throughout that an understanding of the contemporary scene demands some knowledge of what has happened in the past, although I have not normally gone back beyond the nineteenth century. In order to provide a background to Ireland's human geography, I have also thought it appropriate to use an early chapter to summarize some of the relevant aspects of the island's physical geography; readers who know Ireland well will probably want to skip this, but others may welcome the chance to refresh their memories of the form of the land.

There are many things that this book is not. It is not a study in regional geography in the classic sense of the term. It does not presume to tell political leaders how geographers could run things so much better than they do. It does not seek to promote any special ideological position, nor espouse any particular nationalist stance. Although it may not always have been successful in avoiding the jargon of the geographer's trade, what it does try to offer is a book that is positively intended to be easily read by interested laymen as well as by students of geography.

Both my parents were Irish migrants, but neither fitted the usual stereotype. My mother started by following the typical pattern when she emigrated with her family to Canada; but untypically she later returned alone to Ireland. My father was also an emigrant, but moved to Ireland as a boy when my Yorkshire grandfather took a job as a railwayman in Ireland – in the context of the Irish diaspora it is sometimes forgotten that some movements of population also take place in the opposite direction. This book is dedicated to their memory. In a sense it was because of their untypical population movements that I grew up in Ulster, but 40 years ago the inexorable hidden hand of the economy (and also a feeling of mental claustrophobia which some other emigrants may identify with) led me to leave. As a result this book is essentially an outsider's view of Ireland, handicapped by distance but written with affection and, it is hoped, some detachment.

I am grateful to many people who, over the years, have sustained my interest in Irish geography. Estyn Evans was for me, as for many others of his students, a vital stimulus, in particular for the model he provided through his elegant prose and his wide interest in all branches of geography, not just the distinguished studies of folklife and archaeology for which he is particularly remembered. For ideas, information and companionship in the field at various times I thank Fred Aalen, Fred Boal, Ronnie Buchanan, Mary Cawley, Breandan MacAodha, Bruce Proudfoot, Desmond McCourt, Peter Humphreys, Anngrit Simms, Willie Smyth, Seamus Smyth, and many others too numerous to list. I am grateful to Matthew Ball of the cartographic unit in the Geography Department of the University of Lancaster for his assistance with the maps and diagrams. The failings of this book are, of course, mine, not theirs.

As always, I am indebted to my wife, not only for her comments on the text, but also for her insistence that I should maintain my personal interest in the geography of Ireland, even when the paths of my major research and writing led elsewhere.

St Patrick's Day
1993

James H. Johnson
Dolphinholme, Lancaster

Acknowledgements

The Author wishes to thank the following for permission to redraw illustrations from their published copyright work: N. Stephens, Fig. 2.3; R.K. Rohan, Fig. 2.4; An Foras Taluntais, Fig. 2.8; V.B. Proudfoot, Fig. 3.5; D.A. Gillmor, Fig. 3.7; D. McCourt, Fig. 4.1; P. Flatrès, Fig. 4.7; M. Murray, Fig. 4.8; The Royal Geographical Society, Fig. 6.1; J. Walsh and the Geographical Society of Ireland, Figs. 6.2, 6.3 and 6.4; M. Cawley and the Geographical Society of Ireland, Fig. 6.6; A. Simms, Fig. 7.1; P. Doherty, Fig. 8.4; K. Hourihan, Fig. 9.2; P. Duffy, Fig. 9.3; D. Fulton, Publishers, Figs. 10.1, 10.2 and 10.3.

For providing information on which illustrations were based the author wishes to thank L. Hanna (Fig. 3.2), G. Eogan (Fig. 3.4) and R. Breen (Fig. 5.3).

For permission to reproduce photographs the author is grateful to: Bord Faile for Photos 1, 3, 4, 7, 8, 11, 12, 13, 14, 16, 17, 19 and 25; Industrial Development Board, Northern Ireland, for Photos 15 and 22; Industrial Development Authority, Dublin, for Photos 21 and 23; the Controller, HMSO for Photo 10; and Mrs Jean Johnson for Photos 6, 18 and 24.

Chapter One

Introduction

This book is concerned with the geography of Ireland, but it does not seek to be a formal textbook or research monograph. Its aim is to provide a selective account of the human geography of Ireland, presented in a manner which, it is hoped, will be of interest to the general reader as well as to those who have a specific interest in discovering more about Irish geography. As a result it does not attempt to be a comprehensive description. Rather, it is more of a personal selection of what seem to be important themes, predominantly concerned with human geography.

The task of writing about the geography of Ireland is made more difficult by the speed at which change is taking place. Aspects of Irish rural life have survived from various periods in the past, as Estyn Evans in particular was able to demonstrate so eloquently in his many writings, but the pace of development is rapid. In 1957, when Evans published the first edition of possibly his best-known book, *Irish Folkways*, he was only too well aware of the degree to which traditional life was being obliterated by the spread of modern attitudes and artifacts. Nevertheless, a repetitive theme in his book was a concern with why so much of the past lived on in Ireland; and his search for the origins of some features of Irish life took him back as far as the earliest settlers in Ireland, some 8000 years ago.

The past still remains firmly embedded in the Irish present, but a selective quest for the origins of the modern situation, as opposed to an interest in relicts from the past, must now realistically begin much later, although continuity from previous times is still more important in Ireland than in many other parts of the modern world. This present book looks back no further than the nineteenth century; and the contemporary pace of change is such that even to delve back into the last century may seem unbalanced to some. The justification, apart from the personal predilections of the author, is that although geographers must have spatial awareness, they will miss much without an appropriate consideration of the past social and economic processes which have been influential in the formation of the geography of the present.

It also still remains true that although the island of Ireland held a pivotal location in the prehistory of Atlantic Europe, in more recent times Ireland has been remote from the main currents of European intellectual life and economic change, which were often filtered through Britain. Membership of the European Community has changed that situation in terms of Irish awareness of the outside world, but the island still remains a geographical outpost in terms of immediate access to the heartland of European economic growth.

In the new communications environment of the modern world the marginal location of Ireland has not been preventing quite rapid change; but the future geographical development of Ireland will still differ in detail from that found in other parts of Europe. One contributory factor to those differences will be the distinctive manner in which the human geography of modern Ireland has evolved in the past, as well as the more obviously unique assembly of physical, environmental and locational factors found in this particular outlier of western Europe.

Contrasts within Ireland

The political division of Ireland has left its mark on its evolving geography, since agricultural subsidies, population change, industrial development, investment in transport and energy policy (among other things) have all been influenced strongly by sometimes divergent policies of the two governments. Seventy years of two independent political approaches to often similar problems have left a not inconsiderable mark on the landscape of modern Ireland. But the immediate visibility of political division distracts attention from even more relevant geographical contrasts within Ireland.

At a broad scale the most outstanding feature is the contrast between eastern and western Ireland. As will be shown later, the physical environment allows much greater flexibility in agricultural production in the east; and both export and internal markets are also more accessible. Similarly, the economic pressures for urban growth are much stronger on the east coast, facing Great Britain. As a result, both in Northern Ireland and the Irish Republic, the population of the east is favoured in terms of income and alternative economic opportunities. These contrasts also operate at a more detailed scale. The intimate association of bleak uplands and more fertile lowlands in many parts of Ireland has brought a great level of geographical variety within short distances. Areas where traditional life has been conserved by agricultural poverty or relative remoteness lie close to other regions in which the pace of social and economic change is much more rapid.

Problems of terminology

Any discussion of Irish matters soon runs into problems of terminology, since the stresses of Irish politics seem to encourage remarkable sensitivities about names. For example, reference to the 'British Isles' is often avoided in the Republic of Ireland, although the locally preferred substitute, 'these islands', dodges the issue rather than provides a scientifically useful alternative. As a result, in this book *British Isles* will be used for that archipelago off the north-west coast of Europe in which Ireland is the second largest island and which is dominated by Great Britain; but it is used as a geographical description, not as a political statement.

The term *Ireland* itself is not without difficulties for political purists, since it is the official name in English for the independent republic governed from Dublin, with the implicit implication that its writ should run over the whole island. In the past this has lead to mental gymnastics in Irish official statistics with widely scattered footnotes to indicate that 'Ireland' in the published figures only referred to the 26 independent counties. In this book, however, common sense will prevail and the term will simply be used to refer to the whole island of Ireland with *The Republic of Ireland* (or simply *The Irish Republic*) being employed for the 26 counties which form an independent state. *Eire* is simply the Irish for Ireland, and although colloquially in Britain and Northern Ireland the term is used as an alternative for the Republic of Ireland it will be avoided here.

Northern Ireland refers to the six counties in the north-east which are currently under direct British rule, but which from 1922 to 1972 formed a partially self-governing province of the United Kingdom with its own parliament. Until relatively recently government publications in the Irish Republic frowned on the term 'Northern Ireland' and simply referred to the area as the 'Six Counties', although a greater willingness to face the reality of the longer-term political division of Ireland has gradually made 'Northern Ireland' acceptable as a politically correct usage.

At the same time, to the despair of someone wishing to write dispassionately about the area, unionists in Northern Ireland frequently speak of 'Ulster' to refer to their territory. In fact the historic province of *Ulster* is formed of nine Irish counties and includes Donegal, Cavan and Monaghan, as well as the six counties which form Northern Ireland. In this book the four provinces of Ireland – Ulster, Leinster, Munster and Connacht – will be given their historic boundaries, which have no political significance whatever in the modern world, but are sometimes useful as a means of identifying broad geographical contrasts and still also retain popular awareness as a result of their role in some sporting contests. Just to add to the complications, locally Northern Ireland is often referred to as *The Province*, although it is not clear whether this means a province of Ireland or of the United Kingdom. From time to time 'The Province' will be used here as a substitute for Northern Ireland, without attempting to answer this arcane question. Finally, there are two terms which are not strictly accurate geographically, but are convenient, widely used and inoffensive: the *North* is used to refer to Northern Ireland, and the *South* to the Republic of Ireland.

At a more local scale, for some imponderable reason political heat is currently generated by the use of the name 'Londonderry' or 'Derry', although in fact this sensitivity is of quite recent origin. In this book 'Derry' will be used for the urban settlement of that name and 'Londonderry' will be used for the county.

This usage helps to avoid geographical confusion and has some logic which is much too tiresome to justify here, except to say that it is not meant to have any political implication. Some placenames have changed since the independence of the Irish Republic and an attempt is made to use the names current at the period being described.

A book of this kind must largely be based upon the work of others and those who know the geographical literature will find many debts here to many other students of Irish geography. I have thought it undesirable in a book of this kind to encumber the text with an elaborate system of footnotes or with over-enthusiastic academic name-dropping. References in the text have only been used to identify specific quotations and to cite detailed pieces of research which it would have been confusing to include in the short general reading lists. Lists of selected further reading are provided with each chapter and these include the most important works that has been drawn upon if they have not already appeared as footnotes.

Some further reading

Two recent textbooks which give useful overviews of Irish geography are B. Brunt, *The Republic of Ireland* (Chapman, London, 1988), which is concerned with the contemporary social and economic geography of rural and urban life; R. Carter and A.L. Parker (eds), *Ireland – a Contemporary Geographical Perspective* (Routledge, London, 1989) which examines some geographical aspects of all Ireland in a multi-authored collection of specialist essays.

E.E. Evans, *Irish Folkways* (Routledge and Kegan Paul, London, 1957) is an extended and fully documented development of his earlier and popular *Irish Heritage* (Tempest, Dundalk, 1942) and records an Ireland that is rapidly disappearing. The same author's eloquently written *The Personality of Ireland: Habitat, Heritage and History* (University Press, Cambridge, 1973) examines in particular continuities in Irish life, some of which he sees as surviving from prehistoric times, although he is perhaps somewhat unkind to some historians. This appealing book has recently been reissued in paperback.

A recent, particularly well-illustrated description of the landscape of the countryside is D.A. Gillmor (ed.), *The Irish Countryside: Landscape, Wildlife, History, People* (Wolfhound Press, Dublin, 1989a). An unrivalled reference book to the geography of Ireland is the *Atlas of Ireland* (Royal Irish Academy, Dublin, 1979).

Chapter 2

Environmental aspects of Irish life

For many years geographers have been firmly distancing themselves from the view that the physical geography of an area determines an inevitable human response. Nevertheless, although physical factors are unfashionable among human geographers, it must still be said that they provide an inescapable framework for many aspects of life. It is in agricultural activities that the physical geography of Ireland makes its clearest impact and the account which follows is biased towards implications for farming. It is also designed to provide some indication of the diversity of the Irish physical landscape.

Morphological regions

A quick glance at any atlas map will show that the classic portrayal of the physical morphology of Ireland as being like a saucer, with a ring of uplands forming an outer rim around an undifferentiated central plain, owes more to over-simple exposition than to precise description. It is really not much better than the depiction of Ireland by a schools examination candidate, no doubt well-versed in food and nutrition, who described it as 'an island with a soggy centre'. It remains true that the major upland areas lie around the periphery of Ireland, although they are very far removed from forming a continuous rim, and each upland region shows considerable differences in its form and orientation (Figure 2.1). This should be viewed alongside Figure 2.2 which provides a classification of the broad morphological regions of Ireland, essentially based on the underlying geological structures.

The North-West

The oldest rocks in Ireland, often associated with mountainous terrain, are found in the *Caledonian Province of the North-West*. Two factors have guided the broad outlines of relief and drainage in this morphological region. One is the differential resistance of the rocks to erosion; the other is the tendency for

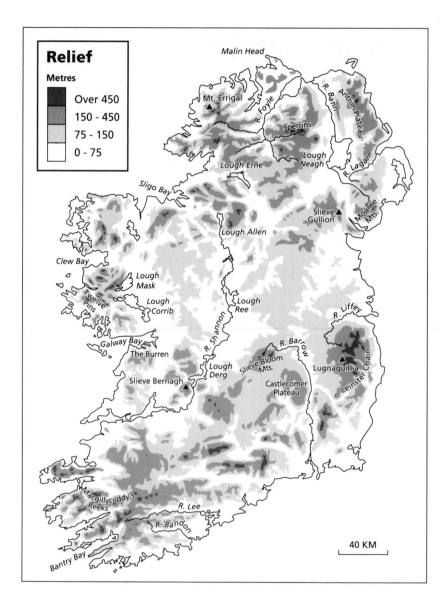

Figure 2.1 Relief

rivers to pick out lines of weakness, which characteristically run in a roughly south-west/north-east direction and reflect the folding of the pre-Cambrian rocks of this region during the Caledonian mountain-building period. Metamorphic rocks and granites form extensive upland areas with the sharpest peaks, like Mount Errigal in Donegal and the Twelve Pins in Galway, being formed of quartzites which protrude above the lower upland surfaces, often formed of schists. This area of ancient rocks stretches from Malin Head in north Donegal

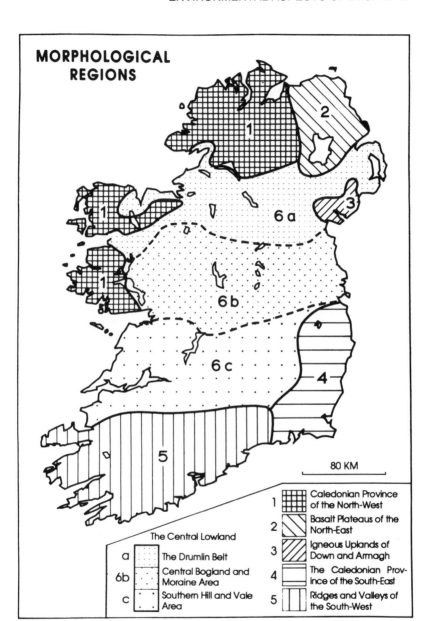

Figure 2.2   Morphological Regions

to the shores of Galway Bay in the south; but it is not a continuous zone, as it is broken by the broad embayments formed by Donegal, Sligo and Clew Bays, where Carboniferous limestone extends from central Ireland to the shores of the Atlantic. The region has also been further diversified during the Glacial Period by ice sheets which radiated out from Donegal and the highest parts of Connacht

Photo 1 Muckish Mountain in north-west Donegal. Among the ridges which contribute to the south-west–north-east Caledonian trend of the topography in this region the most pronounced are those developed on quartzites which have proved particularly resistant to erosion. Surrounding quartzite uplands like Muckish and Errigal are lower erosion surfaces developed on schists and now often covered by upland bog. (Courtesy of Bord Failte)

or was overrun by ice from Scotland, scraping soil from the uplands and depositing various forms of glacial drift on the lowlands.

This region is notable not so much for its height as for its bleakness, with thin soils, frequent strong winds and very high humidity making agriculture difficult. As a result the limited areas of lowland in the coastal areas of the north-west, often found on raised beaches, have had particular significance in supporting a dense concentration of population in past times when subsistence agriculture was dominant. However, the most significant lowland area associated with the Caledonian Province of the North-West is located further east, where a broad lowland is occupied by the basin of the river Foyle, lying between the uplands of west Donegal and the Sperrin Mountains of Tyrone and Londonderry. In particular around Omagh the river Foyle and its tributaries have eroded lines of weakness in sandstones and shales to form a broad lowland basin, coated with glacial drift, characterized by larger farms and more ploughed land than usual in the region.

The South-East

The theme of local diversity is repeated in the Leinster Chain in the south-east, which also shows the influence of the Caledonian period in its main orientation

Photo 2 Looking towards the Twelve Pins, north-east Galway. Here quartzite uplands have again been left upstanding, surrounded by undulating lowland covered by blanket bog, with only very small patches of cultivable land. (Photo: J.H.Johnson)

and forms the *Caledonian Province of the South-East*. The rocks involved in this period of folding are more recent than in the north-west, but what makes this region most distinctive is its extensive granite core, which has been exposed by denudation and represents the largest exposure of granite in the British Isles. This outcrop is some 112 kilometres long from south-west to north-east, but it is only approximately 24 kilometres wide, so that good agricultural land (and suburban Dublin at its northern limits) are brought into close proximity with the upland mass. The northern part of this granite area is a rolling upland, reaching its highest point of 934 metres in the dome-shaped peak of Lugnaquillia. Much of the upland is over 400 metres high and is often covered by blanket bog, forming the largest continuous area of upland in Ireland, but it is surrounded on either side by Ordovician rocks, mostly shales and slates, producing topographic diversity. Further south erosion has reduced the granite outcrop to a lower undulating zone about 150 metres above sea level. Here the Leinster Chain becomes a very narrow range of hills which are the surface expression of the more resistant rocks found in the contact zone where the granite intrusion has metamorphosed the surrounding sedimentary rocks. Most of the higher parts of the Leinster Chain have been modified by glaciation: corries are often found on north-east slopes and the larger valleys are notable for their 'U' shapes and deposits of moraine.

Photo 3 Part of the Wicklow Mountains from Powerscourt Gardens, Enniskerry. The topography in the Wicklows is normally rounded, but at the edge of the granite more resistant schists have created sharper hills like those in this picture. In the foreground is part of the Powerscourt demesne; the terraces seen here were designed by Daniel Robertson in the middle of the nineteenth century. (Courtesy of Bord Failte)

The South-West

A third major area of upland is found in south-west Ireland and is again diversified within itself. This *Ridge and Valley Province of the South-West* has been made distinctive by the manner in which the rocks have been pressed into large, rather simple folds during American times and given a roughly west–east orientation. On first inspection the form of the land surface appears to have been a direct result of the process of folding, with the uplands being formed of the Devonian mudstones, sandstones and, occasionally, quartzites which are found in the cores of the anticlines; but with Carboniferous limestones, shales and slates preserved in the synclines underlying the major valleys. In fact it is thought that these folds were completely covered by later deposits, which provided a cover on which a drainage system developed with the dominant streams flowing north–south. As erosion continued the more recent deposits were removed and the rivers progressively adjusted their courses to the underlying structure. Here and there the rivers maintained small parts of their original north–south courses, where they cut down through the sandstone ridges as superimposed streams, but their east–west tributaries became progressively more important as they developed along the more easily eroded Carboniferous deposits, most notably in the rivers Lee and Bandon. Hence in the South-West, as elsewhere in Ireland, the differential resistance of rocks to erosion has been of considerable importance in shaping the form of the land, since the chance fact that Carboniferous limestone was underlain by more resistant Devonian rocks has been a critical factor in the re-emergence of the cores of the anticlines to form more resistant upland ridges in the modern landscape.

In east Cork and west Waterford the east–west valleys are broad and the intervening ridges narrow and relatively low. Further west the synclinal valleys grow progressively narrower and the intervening ridges form much higher, more continuous and more barren mountains, with considerable areas over 600 metres high. Still further west, the east–west valleys widen out again; but here the lowlands have been flooded by the sea to create rias, like Bantry Bay, which together form the famous discordant coastline of south-west Ireland. These rias lie between bleak sandstone ridges, an example of which being the exotically named Macgillycuddy's Reeks, which include the highest mountain in Ireland, Carrauntoohil (1120 metres). The coastal plain here is very narrow, if present at all; and in this maritime location the surrounding uplands experience some of the heaviest rainfall in Ireland. Although unglaciated areas occur in nearby lowlands, the mountains of the South-West have been etched by numerous corries and in many valleys erosion by ice has added greater drama to a landscape already deeply dissected in pre-glacial times.

The North-East

The upland areas of north-east Ireland are also close to the coast. County Antrim and much of eastern Londonderry are dominated by the basalt outpourings which occurred in Tertiary times. The highest areas of the basalt *Antrim Plateau* lie quite close to the north-eastern coast of Antrim, where short streams have bitten deep into the basalt edge to form the Glens of Antrim; and sombre, peat-covered hills dominate the landscape close to this broken coastal escarpment. Further south, at a somewhat lower altitude, grassland and rough pasture characterize the agricultural scene to the north of Belfast. Streams flowing west from the Antrim plateau to join the lower Bann have more gentle profiles; their broad, open valleys form good agricultural land, particularly where glacial sands alleviate the heavy soils commonly found on the basalts.

To the west of the Antrim plateau the basalts have sagged to form a long north–south depression, which is occupied by Lough Neagh and by the lower Bann river, which flows north from the lake. In this lowland area glacial deposits again have special significance, providing well-drained agricultural land in a region where a high water-table is commonly present. Immediately to the west the basalts reappear as uplands in Londonderry, where they form a continuous hill mass with the schists of the Sperrins. The land use of these uplands is dominated by government forestry plantations.

South Down and South Armagh

A contrasting landscape is provided in the *Igneous Region of South Down and South Armagh* which also extends into the Carlingford peninsula in the Irish Republic. The underlying geology is complex. Slieve Croob is formed of Devonian granite and associated metamorphic rocks and its upland moorland links with the foothills of the Mourne Mountains, which are formed of more recent Tertiary granites. The rounded summits of the Mournes are often over 600 metres high. They provide extensive sheep pastures but are probably more important as a recreation area for the city of Belfast, which also draws much of its water supply from catchment areas in the Mournes.

The area of igneous uplands continues into South Armagh, but here the mass of Slieve Gullion, the highest mountain, consists of an intrusion of gabbro, not granite. Surrounding the central upland is a ring of lower but barren hills, often formed of dolerite. This is a bleak area, with small, poor farms on the lower lands. Among the farmers of this region ancient traditions have survived, in an area where, in spite of its location in eastern Ireland, poverty has protected it from change.

Central Ireland

The various contrasting upland areas lie around the periphery of the *Central Lowland*, where underlying Carboniferous limestone is often masked by glacial drift and lowland peat deposits. Rather than forming a featureless plain, much of this central region probably represents the remains of an extensive erosion surface lying between 60 metres and 120 metres above sea-level. The Shannon and its tributaries dominate the drainage system and for much of its tortuous course this river has only a slight gradient: in over 300 kilometres downstream from Lough Allen it drops only 18 metres, but then the low plateau character of the region is indicated by the river's much more rapid fall of 33 metres over the 24 kilometres between Lough Derg and tide-level at Limerick, notably exploited by the large hydro-electric power station at Ardnacrusha, which marked the first important step after the establishment of the Irish Free State to use local resources for widespread electrification.

In detail, the Central Lowlands contain important internal contrasts, which owe something to the presence of isolated areas of upland and also to variations in the nature of superficial deposits. South of a line between Galway Bay and Dublin the topography is characterized by isolated uplands between 300 metres and 600 metres in height to form a southern hill and vale area. Here older rocks emerge through the Carboniferous limestone, sometimes showing evidence of Amorican folding (for example, in Slieve Bernagh) and sometimes revealing Caledonian elements in their trend (as in Slieve Bloom). In this area, too, more resistant, horizontally-bedded Carboniferous rocks have been left upstanding to form higher plateau areas, notably to the west of the river Barrow (where the Castlecomer Plateau lies at about 300 metres) and in the Burren of county Clare.

Photo 4 Part of the Burren, county Clare. This area of Carboniferous limestone provides a region of barren scenery distinguished by karst features of various kinds. One possibility is that the limestone in this region was formerly covered by glacial drift, but that overgrazing has resulted in extensive soil erosion which has exposed the underlying rocks. (Courtesy of Bord Failte)

But lying between these various uplands are broad, fertile vales, and these relatively well-drained lowlands form some of the best agricultural land in Ireland, especially in Limerick and Tipperary. Part of the character of this hill-and-vale zone is provided by glacial deposits. In particular, end-moraine deposits wind their way eastwards from the Shannon estuary around the various uplands before reaching the Irish Sea just north of the Leinster Chain.

Further north the outcrop of limestone is continuous but here the character of the Central Lowlands owes much more to its cover of glacial drift and bogland, although west of the Shannon discontinuous patches of bare limestone pavement appear from beneath the drift. In the central segment of the Central Lowlands glacial deposits take the form of long sweeping ridges of sandy moraine, roughly orientated east–west (Figure 2.3). These eskers and kame moraines provide lines of easier communication through the extensive, ill-drained lowlands which lie between them, where peat has accumulated in the form of large patches of so-called 'raised' bog. The well-drained soils of the sandy glacial deposits also provide islands of relatively good grazing and arable land. It is this central zone which most closely fits the stereotype commonly attributed to central Ireland of a dull landscape in which brown bogland is interdigitated between low green hills.

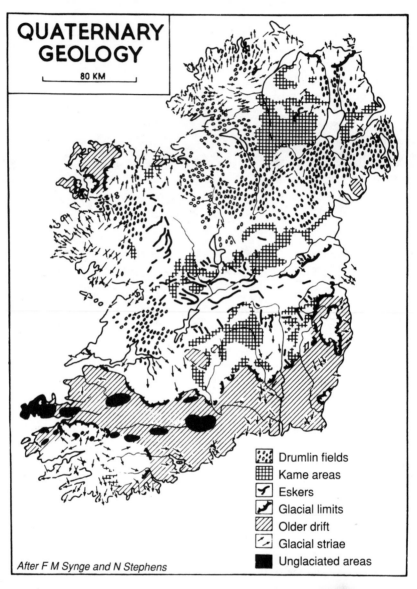

Figure 2.3 Quaternary geology. The map, based on the work of Synge and Stephens (1960) illustrates some of the larger-scale features of Ireland's glacial geomorphology.

In the northern segment of the Central Lowlands a belt of country stretches across Ireland from Sligo Bay to the north-east coast, consisting of swarms of low hills or drumlins, largely made up of boulder clay, although in the west of this northern region the limestone is capped by other Carboniferous rocks like Millstone Grit and emerges to form higher plateaus which reach 600 metres in places, for example in county Sligo. Between the drumlins are ill-drained areas, often bogland, which originally broke the farmland into small cultivable patches. Before the era of modern drainage and properly surfaced roads this zone provided a significant barrier to longer-distance communication.

The drumlin belt extends off the Carboniferous Limestone to the north-east, across into Northern Ireland. Here there are contrasts in the underlying rocks, as this area of Armagh and Down is a geological continuation of the Southern Uplands of Scotland, but the underlying metamorphic rocks have been reduced in height by earlier periods of erosion and are in any case largely masked by glacial drift, usually in the form of drumlins. To the east of this region in Northern Ireland rainfall amounts are relatively low by Irish standards, making the often tenacious soils of the drumlin belt more easily workable for arable crops.

Similarities and Contrasts

This summary has indicated that in geological terms Ireland is in a very real sense an outpost of Britain, with similar geological provinces occurring in both islands. Both the Caledonian trend of the north-west and the underlying rocks of Antrim and Down extend to Scotland, the rocks of the Wicklows are found in Wales, the Amorican province extends to south-west England, and Carboniferous limestone also shapes the landscape of northern England. But, as even this short account will have indicated, although the rocks are replicated in Britain and Ireland, the suites of landforms associated with these similar geological regions often contrast sharply. In many ways this paradox is also reflected in other aspects of the geography of Ireland. Socially, historically and economically, Ireland and Britain have been intimately linked since prehistoric times, but these close connections have often produced remarkably different results in the human geography of the two islands.

The contrasting morphological regions of Ireland which have just been described introduce variety into Irish land use, in particular by creating various scattered negative areas where farming is greatly impeded or absent. But although detailed contrasts are frequently the result of local topography, the explanation of major geographical variations in regional types of farming must often be sought in other factors.

Climate and agriculture

The climate of Ireland is often quickly dismissed as a more 'maritime' version of the so-called cool temperate west marginal type found in western Europe and in particular throughout the British Isles. In comparison with Great Britain there are more days with rain, higher humidity and fewer hours of sunshine; and the cool, damp climate with few extremes of temperature has encouraged an agricultural system in which grass has taken a dominant role and in which rural wealth, traditionally at least, was measured in terms of the number of cattle

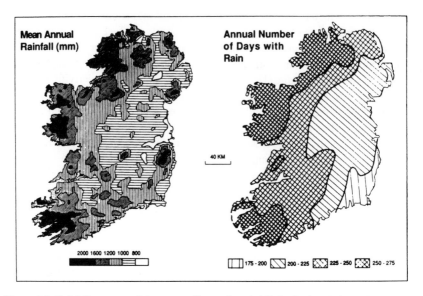

Figure 2.4 Rainfall amount and frequency. (Source for rainfall distribution: Rohan, 1975)

which were owned. Such a situation has been long-standing: the twelfth century monk Geraldus Cambrensis was moved to observe that Ireland is 'richer in pastures than in crops, and in grass than in grain' (Gerald of Wales, 1982, 34).

Rainfall

In spite of the universal stereotype of excessive dampness given to the Irish climate, there are important regional differences in the amount of rainfall and in its seasonal distribution (Figure 2.4). Certainly the range of annual average rainfall totals is somewhat less than in Britain, since Ireland, at one extreme, is without extensive high uplands comparable with the Scottish Highlands and, at another, lacks the more continental rainfall regime associated with south-east England. Nevertheless, the great majority of rain-producing atmospheric systems move across Ireland from west to east and the major areas of upland are also in the west, so that in the western peninsulas an average annual rainfall of between 1200 and 2500 mm (50–100 ins) has been recorded, and higher figures are likely to go unrecorded in some of the more remote, mountainous areas. The other extreme is found in a small area around Dublin, where the annual average rainfall is less that 800 mm (about 30 ins). In an average year the rest of Ireland (which represents some 80 per cent of the country and most of the area where farming is made possible by soil and temperature conditions) receives between 800 and 1200 mm (approximately 30–50 ins) of rain – an amount that is not outstandingly high in comparison with many other parts of western Europe.

But rain makes a bigger impact on Irish landscape and on the daily life of the countryside than annual totals might suggest. An important element in this is

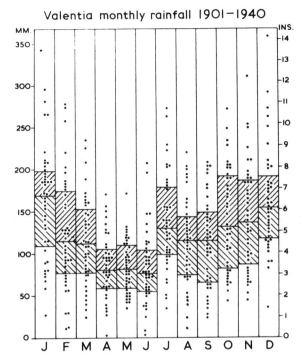

Figure 2.5 Valentia: rainfall dispersion graph. The graph illustrates the rainfall regime typical of south-west Ireland and commonly thought to apply throughout the island, although in fact there are east–west contrasts.

the frequency with which rainfall occurs (Figure 2.4). On the west coast, for example, measurable amounts of rain are recorded on an average of more than 250 days a year; and over much of the remainder of the island rainfall occurs on over 225 days. Only in the south-east is the average frequency of rainfall reduced to a minimum of 190 days and even if this figure is low by Irish standards, it is relatively high when compared with eastern Britain.

Associated with these many days on which rain falls are a large amount of cloud cover and restricted levels of sunshine. The south-east again stands out from the rest of Ireland with higher than average sunshine amounts, and not surprisingly this is the region with a greater emphasis on growing wheat and malting barley. In much of Ireland the cool summers, the presence of much cloud and the absence of sunshine combine to produce increased humidity. Given a similar synoptic situation, relative humidity can be as much as 20 per cent higher than in eastern England, with the result that the dampening effect of the rain is consistently greater.

The importance of humidity for Irish agriculture is heightened by its seasonal distribution. In the west rainfall totals are high in all months, but reach a maximum in winter, the textbook rainfall regime for the Atlantic fringe of Europe (Figure 2.5). To the east the winter maximum is much less clearly marked, so

Photo 5 Farms in Iar-Connacht. This line of farms is located on a low glacial ridge in west Galway between the barren low hills behind them and the peat bog in the foreground. In this region such patches of relatively good agricultural land are extremely scarce and on viable farms in this damp environment are devoted to grass rather than arable crops. (Photo: J.H. Johnson)

that in Dublin, in the driest part of Ireland, August is often the wettest month, to the distress of summer visitors. A late summer or early autumn maximum is commonly found throughout eastern Ireland, with the result that the east–west contrast in the amount of rain that falls during the main growing and harvesting seasons is less than might be expected. As a result the problems of dealing with a damp harvest season are greater for a farmer in eastern Ireland than the annual rainfall totals would suggest. Not only is grass everywhere a climatically favoured crop but there are often inherent difficulties in ripening cereals on a reliable and profitable basis.

Temperature

Temperatures in Ireland also reflect a maritime influence (Figure 2.6). The annual range is small. In summer very hot spells are rare and average temperatures relatively low. In July the warmest area is in the south-east, averaging just over 15.5°C (60°F), decreasing to 13.8°C (57°F) in Donegal. The maritime influence on temperature is equally strong in winter, although the distribution of average winter temperatures contrasts with summer conditions: January isotherms in western Ireland largely trend north–south, but also curve around to follow the north and south coasts. Temperatures fall below freezing point on fewer than 50 days in an average winter, with the south-west and the sea-coasts escaping the greatest frequency of frosts.

The resulting extensive frost-free period allows agricultural tasks to be spread

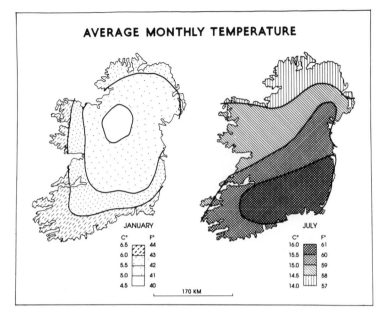

Figure 2.6 Winter and summer temperatures

over a relatively long period of the year for the latitude: the gathering of potatoes can continue well into December, and Spring sowing often commences in early March. Winter temperature variations may be small, but the critical isotherm of 5.5°C (42°F) – the temperature below which the growth of grass is halted – runs across the country in January. As a result grass ceases to grow for only a short period in much of Ireland; and in the south-west, the great dairying region of the country, the growth of pasture is merely retarded rather than completely halted. In practice farmers still withdraw their cattle from the fields during the winter, but this is largely because of the damage that the animals could do by trampling damp pastures and soils (or poaching, as it is called). More generally, there is a contrast in the length of the growing season between the northern interior of Ireland and the southern coastal regions: in the northern interior the commencement of the growing season is retarded by about three to four weeks, and overall the total growing season is several weeks shorter than in the south (Burke, 1968).

Wind

Even this summary account of the Irish climate would be incomplete without some mention of wind (Figure 2.7). Calm days are rare and strong winds are not uncommon in most parts of Ireland. It is on the exposed parts of the west coast that wind takes on its most important role. The few surviving traditional houses on the west coast still have a distinctive form of thatched roof, with the straw

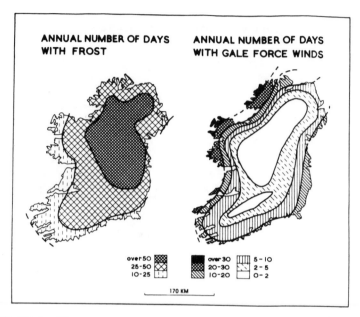

Figure 2.7 Wind and frost

being held down by ropes pegged into the gables to resist the effects of strong winds; but it is on plant life that the influence is most important, since in exposed locations the wind is a more serious inhibitor of plant growth than frost.

This influence is particularly effective on trees. In winter, when the ground is relatively cold and the amount of water that can be absorbed by the roots is restricted, desiccation by the ever-present wind limits tree growth in exposed localities and deforms tree shapes, even where trees can establish themselves. Indeed, one of the most impressive features of the semi-natural vegetation of the frost-free west coast of Ireland is its almost subtropical luxuriance in those few, favoured localities where shelter from the wind is found. For example, in the Killarney area of the south-west, where an equable, damp and sheltered environment is available, the famous oak woods are enriched by climatically more exacting species like arbutus.

The west coast and the more exposed uplands experience gale force winds up to 40 times in an average year and, as a result, direct physical damage to established woodlands can be brought about by storms. Forestry plantations of conifers have been damaged on a number of recent occasions, particularly where these trees have been established on peat covered uplands, since here tree anchorages are more easily weakened by storms and in exceptional years many trees on exposed sites have been completely destroyed. But the wind should not merely be interpreted as a negative force in Irish land use. The frequent presence of fresh breezes and the relative absence of completely calm days are on balance a positive advantage for the Irish farmer. The drying effect

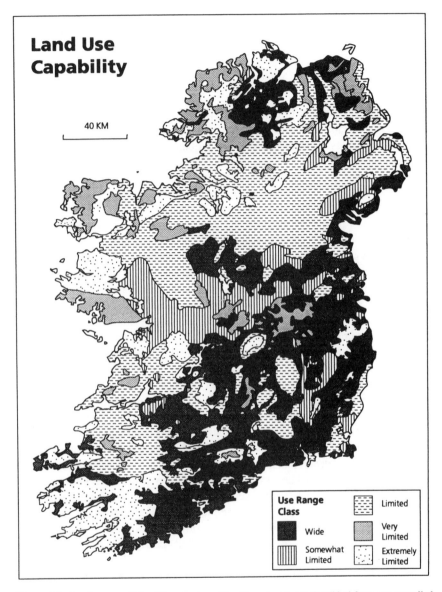

Figure 2.8 Land use capability. The map (considerably reduced and simplified from one compiled by M.J. Gardiner in *Atlas of Ireland*, 1979) is based on combinations of various different soil associations and indicates the varying strength of the physical limitations imposed by natural conditions on agricultural activities.

of breezy conditions often provides an important aid to the harvesting of grain and grass in the face of the high humidity and lack of sunshine that is characteristic of the Irish climate.

Soils

Throughout Ireland the nature of the underlying parent materials strongly affects the soils that are formed upon them, since the two factors which help to produce mature soil profiles – sufficient time and adequate aeration for their development – are not often found in Ireland. But when the complications associated with the variation in local parent materials are put on one side, the inherent drainage characteristics of the soil emerge as the dominant feature, both for practical farmers as well as for soil scientists (Figure 2.8).

As a result of high water-tables, gleys and peat gleys are common everywhere in Ireland, but they are particularly characteristic of those areas where soils have developed on glacial till with a high clay content. These soils are particularly important in the Midlands, especially to the west where heavier rain produces damper conditions and glacial deposits not only provide clayey parent materials, but also impede natural drainage. These poorly drained gley soils have a limited range of agricultural uses, being best suited for forestry and summer grass production. Some could be improved by careful management and the application of appropriate fertilizer but the output from the grasslands which they support tends to be comparatively low, since the grazing season must be curtailed to prevent poaching by livestock. Extensive drainage, which is essential for the improvement of these soils, is difficult and expensive to implement, partly because of their impervious and compacted subsoils, but also because of the organizational problems presented by the relatively small, owner-occupied holdings typical of Irish farming (Bruton and Convery, 1982). Yet integrated arterial drainage schemes have been developed in both the Republic and Northern Ireland, involving engineering work on the lower courses of rivers, with these improvements being extended up tributaries and eventually linking with field drains. The result is that where these works have been completed growing seasons are longer and fertilizers are less rapidly leached out of the soil (Wilcock, 1979).

Where drainage is good, as for example on soils derived from granites, coarse sandstones and from glacial sands and gravels, the leaching of soluble mineral salts proceeds very rapidly. This process produces fully developed podsols in the uplands where rainfall is higher and acid parent materials, derived from granite, are available. Such upland podsols are only suitable for extensive hill grazing and forestry.

On the lowlands deep ploughing and fertilization will allow podsols to be used for arable cultivation, but in the agricultural lowlands brown podsolic soils are much more frequent than pure podsols and present fewer problems for the farmer. In favourable locations the brown podsolic soils grade into brown earths which form discontinuous patches of still greater soil fertility. Both the brown earths and the brown podsolic soils are important in that they have numerous possible agricultural uses. They will support good grassland as well as a wide range of arable, fruit and vegetable crops. Those farmers who are endowed with these soils have much greater flexibility in choosing an economically viable form of agriculture because they can adapt more easily to the changing demands of the market. In the important tillage areas of Ireland these soils are particularly common. In Carlow, for example, 47 per cent of the surface area of the county is made up of these two soil groups and, indeed, 67 per cent of this county has been classified as having soils of the highest class for agriculture (Gardiner, 1979). Brown earths and brown podsolic soils are most frequently found in the east and the south of Ireland, where drier conditions and better-drained subsoils have encouraged their development. The brown soils are also more common in those areas (also in the south-east) where older glacial drift is found at the surface and where, as a result, there has been more time available for the processes of soil development.

The role of good drainage in the formation of the agriculturally more flexible soils of Ireland indicates why soil texture plays an important part in the Irish farmer's assessment of his land, particularly as other beneficial features follow from the presence of brown soils. For example, well developed brown earths have a deeper soil profile, which encourages the deeper rooting of crops; and this, linked with the frequent presence of a heavy-textured subsoil, gives these soils a good moisture-holding capacity, in spite of their better drained surface layers. Perhaps surprisingly, their resulting ability to resist occasional droughts is not without importance for farming in eastern Ireland. These soils, also, tend to be less afflicted by phosphate deficiency, which is a major chemical problem in Irish farming.

An interesting special case, with a highly localized distribution, is provided by the so-called Plaggen soils of the western and southern coasts of Ireland (Conry, 1971). These are man-made and are found only in coastal districts not more than one mile from the sea. They have been created by the addition to the original land surface of large quantities of sea-sand, often used in conjunction with stable manure or composted seaweed. These soils, which are traditionally devoted to growing potatoes, are an indication of the intensive cultivation formerly found in the densely-settled coastal strip in the high rainfall areas of the south and west. Here locally available sand was used to counteract soil acidity and to improve soil drainage, a technique that also has a long tradition elsewhere in Europe and was continued in a few areas of Ireland until the 1950s. The resulting soils are highly calcarious, with a very sandy texture and a deep surface horizon. They are considered to offer superior productivity, giving higher yields and supporting a wider range of crops than other local soils, although eel-worm infestation is a considerable problem where inferior crop rotations have been adopted and potato crops have been taken off them too frequently.

Environmental concerns for future development

The physical environment which provides the context for agriculture has been summarized, but in the modern world environmental worries about pollution of various kinds are frequently advanced from non-agricultural points of view.

These environmental concerns, which are particularly important for the health of the tourist industry, for the attraction of new industry, for the provision of recreation, and for the quality of urban life, often owe as much to the perception of environmental conditions as to their actual scientifically assessed characteristics. Yet by general European standards Ireland currently poses relatively few problems of pollution and environmental degradation.

The industrial revolution has certainly left its impact on the urban landscape of Belfast, but the production of toxic chemical wastes was not one of its major by-products. Certainly air quality in the Belfast region has been a problem, but smoke concentrations have been greatly reduced by the decline of traditional manufacturing industries and the spread of new methods of home heating, coupled with the introduction in 1964 of legislation instituting smoke-free areas. Sulphur dioxide levels have not fallen as much as smoke concentrations because of the absence at present of natural gas for domestic heating. In Dublin mean winter smoke concentrations have been worse than in Paris and substantially worse than in London; and it seems likely that domestic coal burning is also the source of sulphur dioxide concentrations which are similar to those in London (Sweeney, 1982; 1989). However, the general impact of the problem is reduced by the location of these two large cities on the east coast of Ireland, the frequency of westerly winds and by the rapidly increased use of natural gas for domestic heating in Dublin.

Water quality overall is much better than in Britain and major problems of water quality are being attacked. There are, however, potential problems, particularly in rural areas, because of the more intensive use of agricultural fertilizers, intensive pig production, inefficient septic tanks which are unable to cope with the higher demands made on them as a result of the provision of rural piped water supplies, and the greater use of household detergents (Patrick, 1987). Similar problems are associated with urban sewage.

As a result it appears that water quality in many areas is deteriorating. Two per cent of rivers in the Republic are classified as seriously polluted; and in Northern Ireland (where the classification system is somewhat different) 2.7 per cent are deemed to be of poor quality although none are seen as suffering gross pollution. Some lakes are already a cause for concern because of nutrient enrichment, with adverse consequences for their use for drinking water. This also reduces their attraction for boating of various kinds and for recreational fishing, posing problems for the tourist industry.

In spite of these indications of unsatisfactory developments Ireland still remains one of the least polluted areas of Europe. Those who are concerned about environmental problems in Ireland see greater potential difficulties, particularly because environmental protection legislation has been put in place only relatively slowly. For example no emission controls have been applied to the power station at Moneypoint on the Shannon estuary, although it is a major emitter of acid-rain pollutants. Again there are worries in the Cork Harbour area which is the site for much of the Irish chemical industry. The extensive cutting of peat bog and its replacement by exotic coniferous forest has more commonly been seen as source of national pride in the use of local resources than as the important conservation issue it has become in Britain, although doubts are now being raised.

The Irish do not seem to have the same sensitivity to litter as the Swiss. Although some might argue that this is merely a matter of surface appearance, it is an important environmental concern for those interested in the development of an up-market tourist industry. Environmentalists have noted that Ireland has some of the lowest recycling rates in Europe, with few appropriate facilities or even collection points. Indeed, one Irish company which recycles plastic bottles into fibres has to import the necessary waste from overseas.

Membership of the European Community is, of course, putting pressure on the Irish government to attack these matters more urgently, and in Northern Ireland the British government is under a similar influence. In both parts of Ireland, however, there is an inevitable stress between the parallel needs to encourage economic development and also to preserve the environment. Given contemporary levels of unemployment it is not surprising that the need to create jobs takes precedence over the more arcane environmental concerns. Yet for many of the developments that may make Ireland an attractive place for new employment – for example, in encouraging tourism and in providing a base for more sophisticated employment in research and development – a general concern with environmental issues is of critical importance. This is not least in agriculture, where a reputation for a healthy environment, in which food of high purity is produced, represents an important marketing image to be developed, exploited and maintained.

Further reading

A very well documented study which links the evolution of the natural landscape with its later modification by people is F.H.A. Aalen, *Man and the Landscape of Ireland* (Academic Press, London, 1978). A somewhat different, more popular but highly scholarly presentation of the same broad theme is F. Mitchell, *The Irish Landscape* (Collins, London, 1976) and his lavishly illustrated *Shell Guide to Reading the Irish Landscape* (Country House, Dublin, 1986). The most accessible study of the geomorphology of Ireland is J.B. Whittow, *Geology and Scenery in Ireland* (Penguin Books, Harmondsworth, 1973). A more technical exposition is provided by G.L.H. Davies and N. Stephens, *The Geomorphology of the British Isles: Ireland* (Nelson, London, 1978).

Useful soil and climate maps are included in the *Atlas of Ireland* (Royal Irish Academy, Dublin, 1979), and an informative survey of Irish climate is P.K. Rohan, *The Climate of Ireland* (Stationery Office, Dublin, 1975). For an informative survey of Irish soil types and their potential see M.J. Gardiner and T. Radford, *Soil Associations of Ireland and their Land Use Potential* (An Foras Taluntais, Dublin, 1980).

A particularly useful summary of environmental problems associated with water is D. Wilcock, 'Water resource management' in R. Carter and A.L. Parker (eds), *Ireland – a Contemporary Geographical Perspective* (Routledge, London, 1989), 359–93. Problems over the actual implementation of environmental legislation in the Republic of Ireland are discussed in D. Cabot, *The State of the Environment* (An Foras Forbartha, Dublin, 1985). For a much more polemical statement see G. Greenwood, 'The state of the environment in Ireland', *European Environment* 2 (1992), 8–9.

Chapter 3

Human dimensions in agriculture

The quite subtle variations in the physical environment in which Irish farming is undertaken produce regional variations in the emphasis of agriculture which are discussed later in this chapter and are illustrated in Figure 3.8. In the light of the climatic differences already discussed, the greater importance of cereal crops in the south-east is scarcely a matter for surprise, nor is the emphasis on milk production in the south-west. Yet an explanation of the regional contrasts in farming which relies solely on differences in the physical environment is clearly incomplete, since farm size, the organization of agricultural production and market location are all relevant considerations.

Farm size

The size of holdings and the nature of land-tenure are two linked factors, which have a profound influence on Irish agricultural practice. The break-up of large estates and the transfer of ownership to their tenants began in the last two decades of the nineteenth century and had been essentially completed by the First World War. The holdings that were converted from occupation by tenants, often with uncertain tenure, to owner-occupation are often small, although a distinction must be made between the sizes of farms as legally owned and the areas actually cultivated by farmers as working holdings, since these are not necessarily the same and are often a source of confusion in interpreting official statistics.

Figure 3.1 attempts to deal with this problem in a number of ways. Holdings that are too small to be effective units of agricultural production have been excluded; then, on a county basis, the remaining number of holdings has been divided into the total acreage of crops and pasture. Clearly a small holding in an agriculturally favourable area provides a more acceptable income than a farm of a similar size in a region of difficulty. But bearing this limitation in mind the map gives some indication of regional contrasts in farm size.

The smallest holdings are found on small patches of cultivable land often on the western coasts. These offer only meagre subsistence, producing potatoes

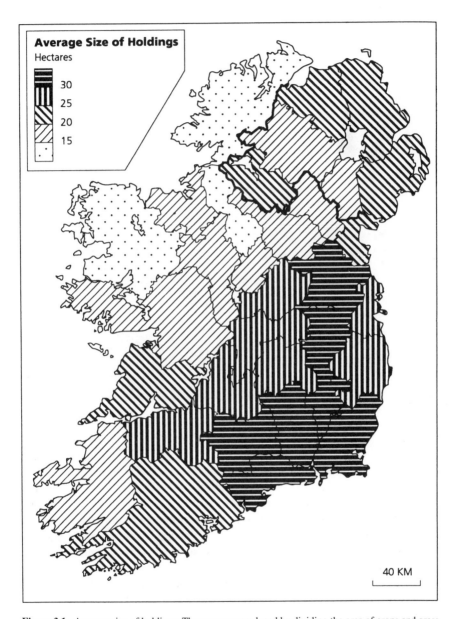

Figure 3.1 Average size of holdings. The map was produced by dividing the area of crops and grass in each county by the number of holdings. Rough grazing is excluded from this calculation. In Northern Ireland holdings of less than six hectares are excluded and statistics for 1988 have been used; and in the Irish Republic the map excludes holdings of less than four hectares and is based on statistics for 1980.

Photo 6 Whitehill Farm, Killygordon, county Donegal. Donegal shows remarkable contrasts between its eastern and western parts. Here, in the valley of the river Finn (a tributary of the Foyle), more substantial, although still relatively small, farms contrast with the minute holdings common on the west coast. The farm in this picture is no longer involved in milk production but is now concerned with rearing livestock, both cattle and sheep. The large barn at the rear of the dwelling was constructed in the 1940s. (Courtesy of Jean Johnson)

and a few vegetables for their owners; but as the twentieth century has proceeded these small holdings have increasingly been farmed in a less systematic manner. In an era in which the population has been decimated by emigration and characterized by a growing proportion of more elderly people, overseas remittances and government assistance are providing a more reliable means of support than traditional methods of cultivation, which in this region used the spade rather than the plough. In fact, as expectations of what constitutes an acceptable standard of living have risen, many holdings are of a size which makes it inappropriate to consider them as 'farms' in any normal sense of this term (Figure 3.2).

Dominating a greater expanse of the country and forming a much more integral part of the functioning pattern of Irish farming is a zone of small farms, each averaging 30–50 acres (12–20 hectares), which stretches across Ireland, north of a line between Galway Bay in the west and Dundalk Bay in the east. Figure 3.3

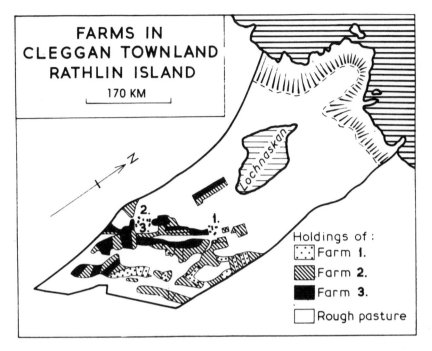

**FARMS IN
CLEGGAN TOWNLAND
RATHLIN ISLAND**

170 KM

Holdings of :

Farm 1.

Farm 2.

Farm 3.

Rough pasture

Figure 3.2 Farm holdings in a townland on Rathlin Island. Although Rathlin lies off the north-east coast of Ireland its farming in this marginal area possesses similar features to those common on the western coasts of Ireland, although here not yet modified by the impact of tourism. I am grateful to Lewis Hanna for providing the information on which this map was based.

provides an example of such a farm. This region of small farms is roughly coincident with the drumlin belt which also stretches across the country and offers small patches of cultivable land, similar in size to the average size of holdings.

Although it is tempting to see some connection between these two phenomena, it would be too simple an exercise in physical determinism to look for a direct correlation. Such historical factors as the tradition of greater security of tenure for small farmers in Ulster and the possibility in the eighteenth and early nineteenth century of enhancing rural incomes through the domestic linen industry must have had some role in preserving this region of small farms, if not causing it in the first place. Yet these historical factors can hardly offer sufficient explanation on their own, since the region of small farms, the area where the Ulster custom of tenant right flourished, and the districts where the domestic linen industry brought a substantial rural income did not coincide in any precise way. Whatever its cause, this belt of small farms represents a distinctive feature of the agricultural geography of Ireland.

Farms over much of the rest of the south and east of Ireland are larger, with an average size of 50–75 acres (20–30 hectares). This is the region where soils are more adaptable to a variety of agricultural activities, where commercial farming and good cultivation practices have been longest established. Not

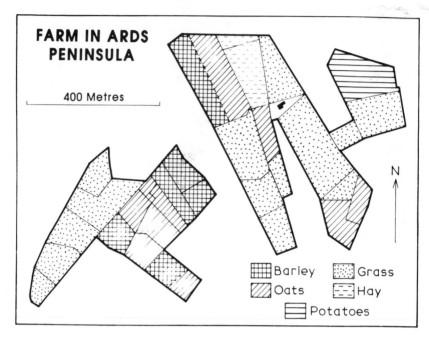

FARM IN ARDS PENINSULA

400 Metres

N

Barley Grass
Oats Hay
Potatoes

Figure 3.3 Farm from the small farm belt, county Down. Although still a small farm this holding has been enlarged by the purchase of a neighbouring, but not contiguous farm, involving some inconvenience in farming operations.

surprisingly it is also the broad region where farmers' cash incomes compare more favourably with the average levels which are achievable by small businessmen in urban areas. Within this region an area dominated by the largest farms is found immediately to the west and north-west of Dublin, where the final preparation of fat cattle for market is a characteristic agricultural activity (Figure 3.4).

Inflexibility and other structural problems

This broad description of farm sizes requires some further elaboration. Discussions of regional contrasts based on average sizes of farms should not be allowed to hide the fact that holdings of a variety of sizes are found everywhere. Very small farms are found in all districts, even in the south and east. It should also be recalled that by international standards nearly all Irish farms can be objectively described as 'small'. As a result there are obvious pressures encouraging farm amalgamation. What is surprising is not the degree to which this is taking place but, on the contrary, the relative slowness of farm enlargement given the remarkable decline in rural population year after year, the social pressures on rural people to attain higher standards of living, and the pace with which other agricultural changes have been taking place in recent decades.

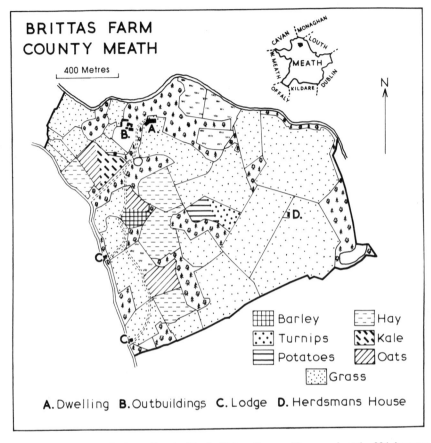

BRITTAS FARM COUNTY MEATH

400 Metres

N

Barley   Hay
Turnips   Kale
Potatoes Oats
Grass

A. Dwelling B. Outbuildings C. Lodge D. Herdsmans House

Figure 3.4 Large cattle farm, County Meath. Brittas Farm, with approximately 224 hectares (560 acres), is an example of the larger cattle-fattening farms found in Meath and nearby areas. I am grateful to George Eoghan for providing the information on which this map was based.

Part of the explanation rests with the almost universal system of owner-occupation which dominates farm holding in Ireland, in which most agricultural land is owner-occupied and probably nearly all the rest is rented by owner-occupiers to enlarge their working holdings. Because of the political and financial struggle by their grandparents and great-grandparents to obtain possession, Irish farmers are loath to allow land which they now own to slip out of their control. Even some of those small farmers who have emigrated or moved to an urban life elsewhere in Ireland keep ownership of their holdings, presumably hanging on to the possibility of eventually returning to their original homes. One result is that considerable inflexibility has been introduced into land transactions, with enterprising farmers who wish to buy more fields finding that the relatively little land that comes on the market is likely to sell at inflated prices. As a result an important check is imposed on the rationalization of the pattern of land holding.

There are a number of ways in which this problem is obviated to some extent. One method – a continuation of long-held practices – is by cooperation among kin. Although farms may be owned by individual families some economies of scale can be obtained by sharing machinery and labour between neighbours, often relatives. Sometimes this can take a more elaborate form. One example is provided by a farmer in Tyrone who operates a creamery and a number of milk rounds as well as his own dairy farm. In addition this farmer obtains additional milk from a farmer brother who himself diversifies his activities by supplying beef to his own butcher's shop in a nearby town. Finally he acquires milk from a third brother who devotes all his energies to his dairy farm, as well as purchasing milk from other suppliers when needed. Such an example is, of course, not typical, but it serves to indicate that individual farm size is not necessarily a reliable guide to the scope of a farming enterprise.

A further outcome is the distinctive system of renting land on very short leases, generally known in Ireland as conacre (MacAodha, 1967). Traditionally these leases are auctioned or otherwise rented for a year at a time. This system, or something very like it, is found in many parts of Ireland, but it is most important in the small farm belt of the north, particularly in those areas which

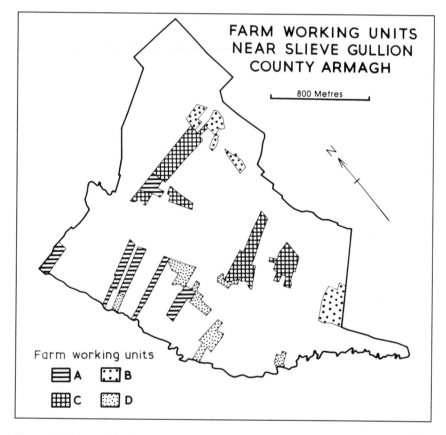

Figure 3.5 Farm working units near Slieve Gullion. Simplified from a map by Bruce Proudfoot (1956), based on field work by members of the Queen's University Geographical Society.

have experienced most rural depopulation, but it is not completely restricted to this zone. The conacre system is convenient for those owners who for one reason or another have given up cultivating the land themselves. A widow who requires an income, a farmer who wishes to retire from farming and has no heir, or an emigrant who does not want to cut irrevocably his links with Ireland by selling the small farm he may have inherited – these are some examples of the kind of people who rent out their land in this way, since it is a form of tenure which does not involve any long-term loss of control.

At the same time a more enterprising farmer who cannot find additional land to purchase may decide that renting conacre land will temporarily meet his requirements. Or a less prosperous farmer may find this a useful strategy if he cannot afford to buy more fields but needs a larger holding to support a growing family. One unfortunate result is that farmers who lease land in this temporary manner often have little incentive to use the highest standards of land management. A further problem is illustrated by Figure 3.5, which shows a number of farm working units in an area close to Slieve Gullion in County Armagh, a region in which the conacre system is widely practised (Proudfoot, 1956). This map reveals the scattered pieces of land that are worked by individual farmers, thus implying that some of their working time is wasted and hence imposing limitations on the intensity of cultivation that is possible. Figure 3.6 provides a further example, in this case looking outwards from a farm that has been divided between six different conacre tenants, only one of which farms an adjoining farm.

This fragmented structure of holdings can also be found where extra land is acquired by purchase on a piecemeal basis, field by field. Whatever the precise mechanism, however, fragmented holdings are most common in those areas

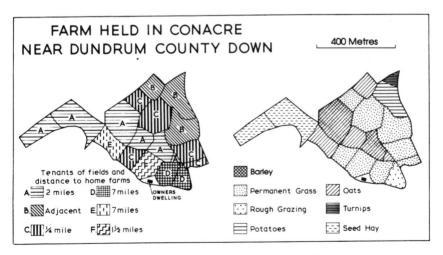

Figure 3.6 Farm held in conacre, Dundrum, county Down. The map illustrates the distance to the farms which are renting the various fields of this holding and indicates one of the penalties associated with the conacre system.

dominated by small farms, precisely the situation in which structural handicaps of this kind are likely to have the strongest adverse effects and are linked with a situation in which farmers with the smallest holdings are often older than average, are more frequently unmarried or alternatively are without heirs wishing to inherit their farms (Fennell, 1968).

The cattle trade and the market

Farms of various sizes are often linked, both locally and regionally, by the well-established trade in cattle at the various stages in their cycle of development from calves to finished animals ready for slaughter. Because this trade operates at a number of different scales it is difficult to describe its geographical manifestations simply, but basically it reflects the fact that small farms can only handle a limited number of animals at any one time and may lack the resources to withhold animals from the market for more than a limited time. The trade in cattle is a long-standing feature of Irish life. The traditional fair was based on this activity, although today the role of the fair has been taken over very largely by auction marts, some operated cooperatively by groups of farmers, but the majority being privately owned. The rise in transport by motor lorry has also meant that private sales to dealers who visit farms periodically have also become more common (Gillmor, 1967).

At its simplest level the cattle trade involves the smallest farmers selling off young cattle surplus to requirement to medium-sized farmers. In turn, after keeping them for a year or so, these farmers sell their animals as store cattle to larger farmers who finish them for the domestic market. Many of these sales are at a local scale, but because contrasts in farm size exist at the regional as well as the local level, they also produce inter-regional movements of cattle at various stages in their development and produce regional emphases in the nature of cattle farming.

Figure 3.7 illustrates some examples of the moves which took place in a sample period, based on the research of David Gillmor, who used the records of auction marts in preparing these maps (Gillmor, 1969; 1970). The dairying area of the south-west was an important source of young animals, since these were surplus to the requirements of dairy herds. Many of these animals were moved to the classic store cattle country of east Connacht; and then at a later stage they were transferred to the cattle fattening farms of Meath. Although this work was not extended to Northern Ireland, similar movements take place there also. As the map shows, the detailed pattern of cattle movements was much more complex than a simple description can convey, but the outlines are clear. What these movements indicate is the manner in which the cattle trade binds together the different agricultural regions of Ireland in spite of the land-use contrasts which exist. The various agricultural regions of the country are different, but they are certainly not economically independent of each other.

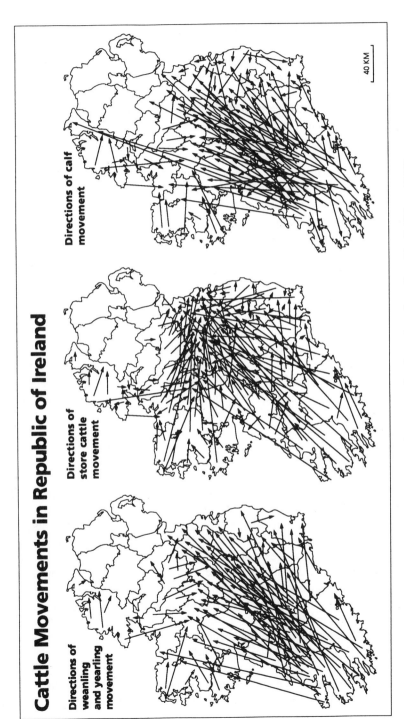

Figure 3.7 Cattle movements in the Republic of Ireland. Based on returns of cattle auction sales collected by D. Gillmor (1969).

Another relevant factor is the location of the market for agricultural production. Partly this is a product of the demands made by the two great cities of Ireland, Dublin and Belfast. Greater Belfast – that is, the city and subsidiary settlements immediately associated with it – has a population of about 600,000 people, nearly over half of the total population of Northern Ireland. Similarly, Greater Dublin consists of nearly one million people and, although not so dominant in the Irish Republic as Belfast is in Northern Ireland, Dublin remains the largest urban settlement in Ireland, north and south. As a result agriculture in areas close to these two cities has been strongly influenced by the local urban market, particularly for liquid milk and vegetables. In theory, modern methods of transport make immediate access to the market a less important factor in agricultural production than in the past; but its influence has been preserved by the clear, unrivalled dominance of these two cities and perhaps also by the fact that rural communities in Ireland are slower to change their accustomed agricultural activities than is the case in some other modern societies.

This factor is reinforced by the fact that much of Ireland's agricultural production is eventually destined for export, and by far the largest market for this production – in spite of efforts to diversify markets – is Great Britain. In this aspect of Irish life, as in many others, the most important human geographical factor is the nearby presence of Britain. The export of cattle to Great Britain, either ready for slaughter or for further preparation on British farms, has been a long-standing feature of Irish agriculture. As a result it is not surprising that the movement of animals is progressively towards the ports on the east coast, both in Northern Ireland and in the Irish Republic. This tendency has not been changed to any significant degree by the greater emphasis in recent times on the export of ready-prepared beef.

Farming regions

Figure 3.8 summarizes the various agricultural regions of Ireland. In looking at this map it must be recalled that negative areas, where agriculture is not practised, are omitted to simplify the map. The map can tell its own story, but some more general observations are appropriate.

To the south-west the area dominated by dairy farming blends imperceptibly into the region in the south-east where arable farming, with an emphasis on cereals, is more important. Although it is tempting to explain the nature of agriculture here in environmental terms, other factors also operate. The export market for butter through the city of Cork has been an important influence since at least the beginning of the eighteenth century; and contracts from brewers and distillers for malting barley have encouraged the growth of cereals in the south-east.

The western coastal fringe is an area of cottage farming which has already been discussed. In the late nineteenth century ancient farming practices lingered on here, with patches of good soil being cultivated intensively, and the sea and

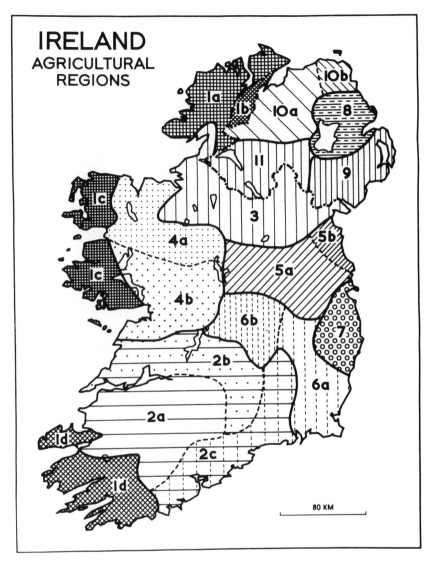

Figure 3.8 Agricultural regions. Note that negative areas beyond the limits of cultivation are omitted in order to simplify the map. The regions on the map are as follows:

1. Small farm belt of the western fringe
   a) west Donegal
   b) east Donegal
   c) Connacht
   d) Cork and Kerry

2. Dairying region of the south-west
   a) Intensive dairying zone of mid-Munster
   b) dairying with increased cattle rearing
   c) dairying with increased arable cultivation

3. Small dairying and cattle farms of the drumlin belt

4. Western sheep and cattle raising region
   a) with greater emphasis on sheep
   b) with greater emphasis on cattle

5. Midland cattle fattening region
   a) cattle-finishing predominant
   b) increased level of arable

6. Mixed arable region of the south-east
   a) greater emphasis on arable
   b) greater emphasis on cattle

7. Mixed agriculture area of the Dublin region

8. Milk production region of south Antrim

9. Small farm arable region of east Ulster

10. Arable and livestock region of north Ulster
    a) Foyle, Roe and lower Bann valleys: tillage and dairying
    b) north Antrim: greater emphasis on livestock

11. Small farm dairying and cattle rearing region of south-west Ulster

Photo 7 Inisheer, Aran Islands, county Galway. This aerial view of a corner of one of the Aran Islands gives a vivid impression of the windswept, treeless environment of these western islands. They are almost completely devoid of surface water in spite of their location in an area of high rainfall. Like the Burren, these islands are formed from the remains of gently dipping limestone rocks. The limestone pavement emerging through the sparse pasture suggests the struggle for existence which life on the islands implied before tourism brought some additional income, although this, inevitably, is modifying their traditional way of life. (Courtesy of Bord Failte)

moorland being exploited as well, to provide subsistence for a dense population in relation to the available resources. But these resources are much less meaningful for modern commercial farming, which has only lightly touched this area. Some possible activities, like the glasshouse cultivation of salad crops, which have been seen by some optimists as an appropriate development in a region like this, have not proved to be viable because of its relatively remote location and the continuing long-term decline in the number of active workers.

East Connacht is characterized by pastoral farming, with the rearing of sheep being somewhat more important to the north and cattle to the south, but with both types of animal being found throughout the region. Further east again lies the cattle-fattening region, although arable cultivation is also more important in this eastern region. The diversified area close to Dublin represents the variety of farming activities encouraged by the Dublin market.

Northern Ireland has been distinguished as a separate set of agricultural regions, although similarities of farming type extend across the Irish border. The justification for doing this is that, until both the Republic and United Kingdom joined the European Community, a separate financial regime for agriculture

Photo 8 Slane, county Meath. Here, on the banks of the river Boyne, is an example of some of the cattle-fattening country which is distinctive in this region of Ireland. Its landscape of large farms, grass and woodland contrasts with the bare terrain of the west. The abandoned rural textile mill provides an outlying reminder of the nineteenth-century industrial development of the north-east. (Courtesy of Bord Failte)

operated in the two parts of Ireland, with the result that levels of investment by Northern Ireland farmers in land improvement and in agricultural machinery was higher than in the South and the income produced by farms of similar size was also greater. Although there is convergence in the economic environment in which farmers are now operating, that difference has not been completely removed and past investment still has an influence on the productivity of farming.

One general feature, however, is repeated in both jurisdictions, since in Northern Ireland the contrasts between a more arable east and a more pastoral west still remain, although this underlying tendency is blurred by the dominance of milk production in the southern part of the Antrim Plateau, partly an expression of the Belfast market for liquid milk but also reflecting the environmental conditions of this region where pasture is the most sensible land use. Similarly, the lower Foyle and Roe valleys produce islands with greater emphasis on arable farming than might be expected, because of the pockets of more adaptable soil which are found there.

What emerges from these regional variations is the subtle combination of locational, physical, political, social and economic factors, which together shape the agricultural geography of Ireland. The discussion which is provided with

Figure 3.8 provides a brief general account of regional differences and the landscape of rural Ireland also provides parallel evidence of regional contrasts in farming, although less clear-cut than the hard-and-fast lines which have to be drawn on a map would suggest. In the real world agricultural regions often blend into one another, a product of cumulative change rather than obvious breaks.

Some current changes

Some of the contrasts in Irish farming spring from policy differences in the two jurisdictions under which farming has been undertaken. For much of the period since the Second World War farmers in Northern Ireland enjoyed much higher levels of government subsidy: in 1970–71, for example, government expenditure in Northern Ireland per male engaged in farming was more than three times greater than in the Republic. One clear-cut result was a much sharper increase in agricultural productivity in Northern Ireland, with, for example, the number of livestock units in the Republic increasing by about 50 per cent between 1926 and 1970, but by 130 per cent in Northern Ireland. This differential has been reduced in the last two decades, but one reputable estimate is that gross output per unit of cultivated land in the Republic was 75 per cent of that found in Northern Ireland in 1925, fell to as little as 32 per cent in 1960 and was still only 55 per cent in 1985 (Gillmor, 1989b). These figures should not be allowed to mask the fact that gross agricultural output in real terms doubled in the Republic of Ireland between 1960 and 1985.

The balance of farm incomes in the two areas, however, has changed greatly as the result of entry into the European Community and the 1970s were characterized by considerable increases in agricultural income in the Republic. Gains to farmers in Northern Ireland were much less striking, partly because of their more favourable situation to start with and also perhaps because agricultural policy in the United Kingdom was less strongly influenced by agricultural interests than in the Republic of Ireland. The net result has been that agricultural incomes are now very similar per person employed. In the 1980s European agricultural surpluses and high increases in the costs of agricultural support brought inevitable changes in EC policy, in particular, as far as Ireland was concerned, the introduction of a ceiling on milk production in 1984. This and other changes have brought a severe check to the rate at which farm incomes had been increasing in both parts of Ireland.

EC policy has also provided modest funds to encourage farm modernization and to assist agriculture in less-favoured areas. However, the Farm Modernization Scheme was aimed at those farmers who had some reasonable hope of raising their incomes to what were deemed to be appropriate levels: low-income farmers did not qualify for the highest levels of assistance and thus this policy did not strongly influence the west of Ireland where there was most need for restructuring. Although this restriction was lifted after a policy change in

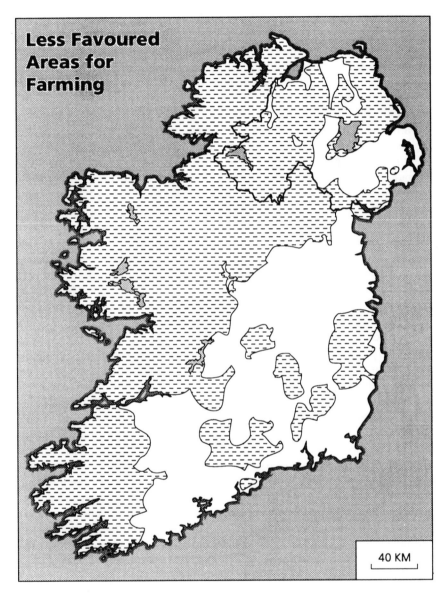

Less Favoured Areas for Farming

40 KM

Figure 3.9 Less-favoured areas for agriculture. The areas are those defined for the purpose of EC directives. The map shows the maximum extent and omits internal variations which refer to different types of agricultural activity.

1985, the high average age of farmers in the west and existence there of less enthusiasm for change has meant that relatively little alteration has taken place so far. For example, Seamus Grimes (1988) has shown in a detailed study of farming in Leitrim – the most marginal farming area in Ireland – that both EC and Irish government initiatives have met with little success and he argues that a dependency on welfare payments has reduced local initiative in exploiting either individual or community resources.

On the other hand farmers in the west have benefited in particular from the Less-Favoured Areas Scheme, which provides payments based on their numbers of cattle and sheep in areas of physical difficulty for agriculture. In detail there are various levels of difficulty recognized but in total 60 per cent of the Republic and 75 per cent of Northern Ireland are now classified as less-favoured areas (Figure 3.9). A broad region in the north and west of the Republic falls into this category, together with the more restricted upland areas in the south-east. In Northern Ireland, there is again an east–west contrast, complicated by the presence of the Antrim Plateau and the Mourne Mountains in the east. Whether this system is a sensible way of maintaining rural communities in European areas of environmental difficulty is a matter of some debate; there is no doubt that these are areas of relatively low average income, but headage payments bring greatest returns to those who are better off to start with and are least likely to leave the land in any case.

Overall, particularly in those eastern areas where farm incomes are highest, the activities of individual farmers have become less wide-ranging and there has been concentration on particular types of production on individual farms (Gillmor, 1987). Various factors have lain behind this change. The introduction of milk quotas has meant that some farmers have concentrated in other areas of production like raising beef cattle; but the trend to specialization pre-dates this development as Edwards (1974) has shown in a detailed study of east Londonderry. The pressure of the market has demanded more efficient production, so that larger units for the rearing of pigs and poultry have become more prevalent. The decline in the agricultural labour force has also demanded more investment in specialized plant in order to maintain production (Edwards, 1986). The growth of other forms of employment has encouraged the development of part-time farming, which in turn has also demanded the adoption of simpler, more specialized farming systems.

In terms of farm incomes a paradoxical situation has emerged from these changes. In the Republic of Ireland agricultural income per male member of family has grown most in recent decades in the southern and eastern counties and least in the west, particularly the north-west. Comparable statistics for Northern Ireland are not available, but it is likely that an east–west contrast also exists here, at least in so far as the better arable farming areas are concerned. The paradox is that, in spite of efforts to support the agricultural population, the greatest proportional increases in agricultural income have occurred in those areas where returns from farming were already highest. Added to that, the lowest increases have occurred in those regions where the importance of agriculture for the total economy is greatest, because of the scarcity of alternative occupations.

Regional contrasts may at present be sharpening, but if the more extreme variations are put on one side, what also emerges are the similarities which bind together Irish farming as well as the differences. The importance of cattle in the agricultural economy and of grass in the pattern of land use; the prevalence of the small farm and the inflexibility of farm structure; the dominance of the export market for Irish agricultural produce; the continued decline of the agricultural population and the high average age of many farmers – these are currently general features of the Irish agricultural scene. Some of these features may change in the future. The European Community is bringing more diversified markets – already both North and South are less dependent on the British market, although more than half the output of agriculture is still exported. A new generation of farmers, more youthful and more enterprising, may inherit the family farms and the process of farm amalgamation and specialization may gather further momentum. Yet the extent to which potential changes like these will have a substantial and lasting effect is far from clear since it is in the nature of Irish life that developments of this kind tend to be gradual rather than dramatic.

Further reading

Although now somewhat dated, the best comprehensive study of the agricultural geography of Northern Ireland is L. Symons (ed.), *Land Use in Northern Ireland* (University of London Press, London, 1963). An equivalent and more recent study of the Irish Republic, although unfortunately difficult to find in many libraries, is D.A. Gillmor, *Agriculture in the Republic of Ireland* (Akademiai Kiado, Budapest, 1977). However a briefer version is provided in D.A. Gillmor, 'Agriculture' in D.A. Gillmor (ed.), *Irish Resources and Land Use* (Institute of Public Administration, Dublin, 1979), 109–36.

Changing methods of marketing cattle are discussed in D.A. Gillmor, 'Cattle marketing in Ireland', *Administration* 15 (1967), 308–27. The useful data on recent changes in agriculture in all of Ireland is provided by D.A. Gillmor in his chapter 'Agricultural development', in R. Carter and A.L. Parker (eds), *Ireland – a Contemporary Geographical Perspective* (Routledge, London, 1989), 171–99. A slightly earlier account of the same topic, but providing a good cartographic presentation of the impact of the early years of the Farm Modernization Scheme, is J.A. Walsh, 'Agricultural change and development', in P. Breathnach and M. Cawley (eds), *Change and Development in Rural Ireland* (Geographical Society of Ireland, Special Publication 1, Maynooth, 1986), 11-33.

Finally, distributional patterns are presented in A.A. Horner, J.A. Walsh and J.A. Williams, *Agriculture in Ireland: a Census Atlas* (University College, Dublin, 1984).

Chapter 4

Rural settlement: fields and farms

To a visitor from overseas possibly the most striking feature of the rural landscape of modern Ireland is the apparent absence of the village in the European sense. What is meant here by 'village' is a nucleated settlement of long antiquity, which provides the location for what was originally a cluster of farm dwellings and also provides the day-to-day services used by the rural population, like for example the village shop, the local elementary school and the church.

That initial impression would not be completely accurate. In the south and east of Ireland those with sharp eyes might detect a few indications of villages that were probably founded by Norman settlers, for example Kilmessan in county Meath. These relics have survived in greatly degenerated form and are now rarely recognisable as villages in the European tradition. Here and there, too, a tidy planned village stands out in sharp contrast to the usually more informal Irish rural scene, where a settlement has been laid out by some improving landlord, probably in the eighteenth century, and now languishes beside his former demesne: Castlebellingham in Louth provides an example of a settlement of this kind. Or again, in the north-east, the traveller may come upon a moribund industrial village, where a cluster of houses had been erected by some nineteenth century manufacturer beside a now defunct linen mill, as for example in Mossley in county Antrim. Finally, there are chapel villages, usually dating from the early nineteenth century, when new Catholic chapels were constructed in large numbers and sometimes formed the nuclei around which small rural service centres were clustered, each with perhaps a school, a public-house, grocery shop, a forge, and a village hall (Whelan, 1983).

Yet in spite of these exceptions the first impression remains largely accurate, since most of the obvious departures from the normal are of relatively recent origin; and the inhabited rural landscape is one which is dominated by isolated farmhouses, located in the midst of their fields, and dispersed rather evenly over the cultivated land. This impression of a nearly universal and long-standing dispersed settlement pattern has often, in the past, encouraged over-simplified explanations (Johnson, 1958). Some have regarded it as a product of the pastoral emphasis of Irish agriculture, which necessitated a close relationship between a farmer's residence and his fields. Others interpreted dispersed farms as being the direct result of the Celtic heritage of the country. Still others preferred an environmental explanation and saw in the dispersed pattern the workings of the moist Irish climate, which was thought to demand no strong concentration of rural settlements on local sites where drinking water was easily available. All these ideas may have had some element of truth associated with them, although they cannot have acted independently of one another and in any case owe more to theory than to a careful analysis of the day-to-day life of the modern farmer.

Clachans, rundale and dispersed farmhouses

It is now clear that simple, unqualified explanations like these are not compatible with what is now known of the history of the landscape. Many isolated farmhouses were established, not in the distant past, but in the nineteenth century. In many parts of Ireland single farms were frequently preceded by clusters of farm dwellings and their associated outbuildings, usually grouped without any formal plan. These clusters varied in size from as few as three dwellings to as many as forty, but unlike a typical European village they lacked both an inn and a church. Nevertheless, in these settlements communal life and the exchange of services were characteristic, not least because their inhabitants were related by kinship.

Photo 9 Ballyhillin, county Donegal. These remnants of what was once a much larger clachan, located near Inishowen, reveal some of the features of an earlier settlement pattern. The infield is located on a raised beach lying below the settlement. Behind, evidence of outfield cultivation remains on the hillside. (Photo: J.H. Johnson)

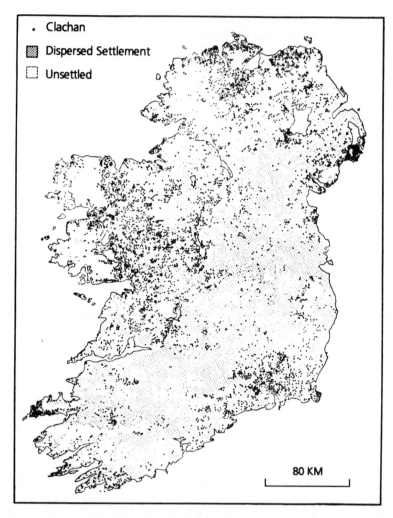

Figure 4.1 Clachans in the 1830s. The first edition of the Ordnance Survey maps of Ireland was used by Desmond McCourt to produce this map. It is not possible from this source to tell whether every large cluster of farm buildings was still operating as a clachan at this time; in some cases they were already relict features, but many must still have been functioning.

Geographers have generally employed the term *clachan* to refer to a group of farms of this kind. There are some linguistic problems with this word, as it is not found in modern spoken Irish, thus leading to the argument that its use is inappropriate. It is, however, a dialect word in the north of Ireland, where the early research on Irish rural settlement was undertaken. The term is also found in the Scottish Highlands, where it can be applied to settlements similar to the Irish farm clusters, also making the term 'clachan' convenient to use. As a result it is not surprising that it has become generally adopted. At the beginning of the nineteenth century clachans were not evenly spread throughout Ireland, but were concentrated in a number of distinct regions, commonly but not exclusively in the western peninsulas (Figure 4.1). Most clachans have now disappeared from the landscape; but, even today, occasional, partially functioning examples can be found in the more remote parts of Ireland.

When these clachans were being actively used they were commonly associated with a type of common-field cultivation, comparable with the Scottish infield-outfield system, often known in Ireland as *rundale*. In its fully developed form, rundale involved the land surrounding a clachan being worked as a joint farm by all the families who lived there, with the plots and strips of an individual household being scattered through the arable land, some on the fertile, constantly-tilled infield, and some on more temporary outfield patches reclaimed periodically from poorer land (McCourt, 1955). By tradition the land was redistributed from time to time among all the joint tenants to reflect the changing requirements of their families (hence the term *changedale* occasionally applied to the system), but by the early nineteenth century redistribution was a folk memory rather than a current agricultural practice.

On the other hand, the traditional practice of subdividing the individual family holding among all the male heirs of the household sometimes continued in those areas where emigration was not yet providing an alternative possibility and where landlords had not been exerting a tight grip on the farming practices of their estates. Particularly where rural population was still growing rapidly at the beginning of the nineteenth century, this process produced extremely

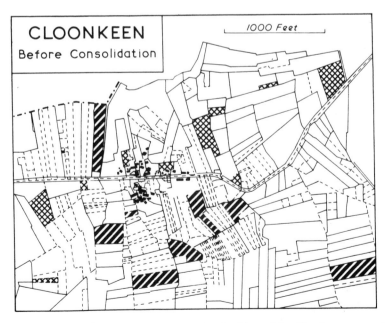

Figure 4.2 Complications of land-holding associated with rundale: Cloonkeen, county Mayo before consolidation. The shadings indicate the holdings of two sample farmers and the map should be compared with that in Figure 4.6.

complicated patterns of landholding (Figure 4.2). Lying alongside areas where clachan settlement was important were other regions where dispersed farms were already firmly established. Other districts showed a mixed pattern, and at the beginning of the nineteenth century this probably reflected more than anything else varying levels of landlord activity in estate management.

A notable feature of clachan settlement was its flexibility, as clachans are known to have expanded and contracted in size at various times, largely influenced, it is reasonably assumed, by fluctuations in population numbers. In theory a clachan and its associated field system could be produced by the subdivision of a single farm, stimulated by population growth. But this alone is not a sufficient explanation, since it would surely have been a grave break with established practice if people with compact farms were to subdivide their compact holdings into smaller farms, consisting of scattered strips.

Fact confirms that view: substantial farmers working compact holdings usually resisted any inclination to subdivide. What seems to have developed were two contrasting traditions. In one, small farmers, following what were probably more ancient practices in the remote parts of the country (particularly the west and close to the limits of cultivation), were prepared to subdivide their holdings to accommodate the needs of their children. The other tradition consisted of farmers who would not subdivide, possibly also reflecting long-established attitudes, but by the nineteenth century largely because these farmers usually formed part of a growing cash economy and were not prepared to reduce their holdings below a commercially viable size.

As a result, at the beginning of the nineteenth century an important contribution to this dualism in field systems and settlement forms was often found in the varying attitudes of landlords, some permitting peasant subdivision and others discouraging it. In those areas where ancient traditions survived the process was difficult to suppress if tenants were determined to carry it out, since it could easily be undertaken informally, unless landlords or their agents were prepared to act with ruthless vigour. In any case, given the agricultural techniques of many Irish farmers, it was often the case that more intensive agriculture and a higher rental income could be obtained in the early years of the nineteenth century by having more tenants on the land, rather than by resisting subdivision, although such a policy would create problems later when the emphasis of agriculture changed.

Yet underlying these varying attitudes to estate management were regional differences in the incidence of clachans, related in the last resort to the varying importance of the two agricultural traditions, one wedded to life in clachans and the cultivation of scattered common-field plots and the other favouring dispersed farmsteads with fields compactly arranged around them. In the south-east, for example, large individual farms had been established in the manorial districts of Leinster and Munster by late medieval times, although it is clear that village settlements with open fields and large regular strip holdings were introduced by the Normans. Commercial farming was important in favoured areas as early as the seventeenth century; and although relics of other nucleated patterns still remained in the south-east, the single farmstead was probably the most important form of rural settlement in much of this broad region by the early eighteenth century (Aalen, 1970).

Similarly, the early seventeenth-century plantation of Ulster had introduced many small towns and fortified villages to the north of Ireland, but already by the end of the seventeenth century many of the new settlers had abandoned the protection of their planted nucleated settlements to live in scattered individual farmsteads, set among their own compact fields, although clachans and common-field strips survived on the more marginal lands. On the other hand, in much of Donegal, in the more remote parts of Kerry and Cork, and in western Connacht, clachans were still much more commonly found during the eighteenth and early nineteenth century. Here subdivision remained a firmly rooted folk custom in an area where large landowners, culturally divorced from their tenants, had often become established in the seventeenth century, but had only succeeded in superimposing a thin veneer of new attitudes on much older ways of life.

Indeed, there are even hints in the prehistoric record that a dualism of this kind may have been a more ancient feature of Irish life. There is some place-name and documentary evidence that clustered rural settlements were found in at least those areas for which medieval documents exist, and that these were Irish as well as Anglo-Norman settlements. On the other hand, the only clear settlement forms that survive in the archaeological record from the first millenium A.D. are single, scattered farmsteads, each surrounded by an enclosing bank, and variously known as *ring-forts*, *raths* or *cashels*. It is tempting to seek the ancestors of clachan dwellers in the clustered settlement of pre-Norman Ireland and also to presume that dispersed farms in the forms of raths flourished at the same period, thus taking the dualism in the Irish settlement pattern back into prehistory (Proudfoot, 1959).

It would be dangerous to push this speculation too far because our knowledge of settlement patterns from the fourteenth to the eighteenth century is still extremely sketchy. What remains clear is that, for a variety of reasons, a dualism was still extant at the beginning of the nineteenth century. What also emerges is that the flexibility inherent in the clachan settlement pattern was to be of great importance in its gradual disappearance during the nineteenth century.

Stresses on the traditional system

It is often assumed that clachans and rundale farming did not exist independently, but during their period of decline remnants of clachans often survived after rundale farming had disappeared. Immediately after fields were recast farm buildings often remained where they were, although later relocation might well take place. In the same way, areas used as upland grazing or bogland remained held in common, long after the adjoining arable lands had been enclosed and their associated clachans dispersed (Johnson, 1963a).

The decline of the ancient system can be explained by its growing inefficiency and by the dissemination of new agricultural techniques, associated with the spread of commercial farming. These processes of change began to operate while clachans and their associated field system were still flourishing in some regions. Enclosure came first to the south-east, although the idea that there was an enclosed landscape in this region since at least medieval times must now be revised. Certainly enclosure was found here earlier than further north or west, but it is likely that many enclosed fields date from the eighteenth century. The background is complex, because of the existence of villages of medieval Norman colonial origin, compact holdings of Cromwellian planters, monastic granges and the later enclosure of formerly bare hillsides and bogland margins. Yet, in spite of this, it has been argued that there was no extensive pattern of enclosed fields until the latter half of the seventeenth century and that the process of enclosure was particularly active in the eighteenth century. Similar evidence comes from east Ulster, in the Barony of Lecale in county Down, where at the beginning of the eighteenth century two-thirds of the land was being farmed by groups of partners, presumably using some form of common-field system (Buchanan, 1970).

There are good reasons for thinking that the growth of commercial farming was an important force behind eighteenth-century enclosure in eastern Ireland. The cattle-fattening areas of Meath were well established at the beginning of the nineteenth century; and there is a correlation in the modern landscape between this agricultural region and the presence of larger, regular fields, which suggests that the nature of commercial farming in this area has shaped the form of its original enclosure. Elsewhere enclosed fields were smaller and more irregular but also associated with commercial influences. In those areas of southern and eastern Ireland where wheat and barley were adopted as important commercial crops in the second half of the eighteenth century, the growth of cereals interfered with traditional grazing rights on infield stubble, thus decreasing the relative importance of livestock in the farm economy and adding to the advantages of an enclosed farm, more directly under the personal control of an individual farmer.

In those areas where commercial farming of whatever kind was establishing its grip, there was a growing and spreading awareness that the old methods of farming were becoming unsatisfactory. It was not so much that production was inefficient in any absolute sense, but that more farmers began to count the cost of their labour and to measure the output of their farms in cash terms. The diffusion of these new commercial attitudes did not become effective throughout Ireland as a whole until the second half of the nineteenth century, but for a long period before this commercial attitudes were gradually being adopted in various parts of Ireland.

As elsewhere in the British Isles, the introduction of new crops and rotations gave a death blow to the traditional field system, since these innovations were difficult for an enterprising farmer to introduce into the common-field system and therefore agricultural improvement was retarded. Not only were there problems in integrating winter-sown cereals into the rundale system but (and perhaps in the long-run more important when Ireland as a whole is considered) improved breeds of stock were also difficult to introduce and maintain in a system which involved common grazing.

In the first decades of the nineteenth century strain was also being put on the rundale system in areas where subsistence farming still dominated the rural scene. This pressure was the result of the steady growth of population in rural areas, surging upwards towards the end of the eighteenth century and continuing until the Great Famine of the 1840s. One result of this increase was steady encroachment on uncultivated areas which were located around the edges of lowland bogland or at the upland margins of cultivation – a process in which the general adoption of the potato as a subsistence crop played an important part. But the so-called waste lands brought under cultivation had not been completely unused, since they were often grazed by livestock; and the availability of this grazing land was important, not least because it allowed the removal of animals from the unfenced strips of the infield during the growing season. The new situation made the easy working of the rundale system more difficult.

Population growth was important in another way. The rise in population numbers was associated with a remarkable increase in the size of many individual clachans, with some in county Clare, it is said, acquiring as many as 120 to 200 dwellings. The point was reached when day-to-day life in large huddles of dwellings like this became steadily more intolerable. Squabbles over rights-of-way and other petty affairs appear to have become more common, indicating the stresses involved in living in informally designed clachans that had swollen beyond a functionally desirable size. Similar difficulties arose in cultivating holdings that, for the same reason, were increasingly divided into minute, fragmented strips.

Nineteenth-century decline

Such pressures were preparing the way for drastic alterations to the traditional system of farms and fields, but the vital impetus behind the changes which eventually took place often did not come from the farmers themselves, but from their landlords. In areas where commercial farming was firmly established in the late eighteenth century, tenants and landlords appear to have cooperated in a mutual process of gradual change; but where rapid population growth was combined with more ancient farming practices little could be done unless a landlord was prepared to act drastically. Some landlords were willing to muster the necessary unscrupulous vigour to clear the surplus population off their estates and to recast the rural landscape, particularly after the collapse in market prices for cereals immediately following the Napoleonic Wars. Most landlords, however, were unable or unwilling to do much until after the Great Famine, when rapid population decline replaced increase and gave greater scope for action.

Whatever the precise date at which landlords began to remodel their estates, their activity placed a distinctive stamp upon the rural landscape. Large areas where traditional farming practices had survived into the nineteenth century were

Photo 10 Roe Valley, county Londonderry. This aerial view shows in the foregound the results of the reorganisation of holdings which was undertaken by the Fishmongers' company, the local land-lord, in the nineteenth century. (Courtesy of J.K. St Joseph, Crown copyright 1993/MOD)

put into the melting-pot, holdings were consolidated, and the surplus people were evicted, if they were not already in the process of emigrating. Frequently the new farms were arranged up and down the slope of the land, giving a characteristic 'striped' appearance to much of the modern Irish rural landscape (Figure 4.3). The resulting holdings have been called 'ladder' farms, because their fields were arranged like the rungs of a ladder; and although this long, thin shape was not the best possible from a functional point of view, it represented a compromise between the traditional system, in which each farmer's scattered strips provided a fair share of every quality of land, and the landlords' demand for a more efficient agricultural structure based on compact farms.

The reorganization of fields and farms was not simply the result of authoritarian action by landlords, since the changing landscape of rural Ireland was also a product of population change. Even in the 1830s some localized patches of

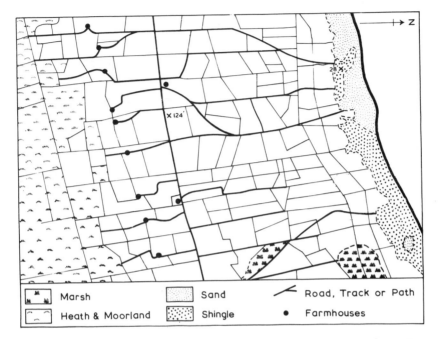

Figure 4.3 The landscape pattern produced by 'striped' or 'ladder' farms in county Kerry. Farms of this type were created during the process of enclosure to give each tenant access to land of varying qualities, and as a result stretched from river edge (or in this case from the coast) to upland moorland. In their classic form they were often one field wide, with their field boundaries arranged like the rungs of a ladder.

population decline were found in those areas where pre-Famine emigration was particularly important and was associated with the reorganization of holdings (Johnson, 1963b). But the effect of this influence became widespread after the Famine, when general rural population decline allowed landlords greater freedom to undertake comprehensive changes.

Population decline also encouraged more gradual, piecemeal alterations to the rural landscape, almost in the form of a natural process. For example, if a farmer and his family emigrated their fields would be added to those of a neighbour to form compact, but often irregular farms. If clachan settlements were found in these areas, sometimes they would be gradually abandoned, perhaps being inhabited by a single family rather than a group (Figure 4.4). Eventually when new homes were required these might be more conveniently located to give better access to their associated fields. However, in a few cases small groups of farmhouses still survive, with relatively compact but curious shaped holdings, which provide evidence of a process of piecemeal consolidation without relocation of farm buildings, as the number of farm families was reduced (Figure 4.5).

Emigration was not the only factor behind population decline, since rates of natural increase were also reduced for reasons which will be discussed in a later chapter. Careful fieldwork has shown how this had a direct effect on farm

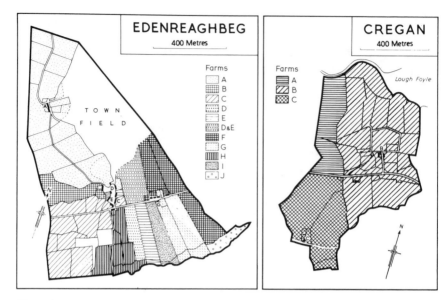

Figure 4.4 Holdings in two townlands on the Grocers' Estate, Londonderry, 1820. In Edenreaghbeg some rationalization of holdings had already taken place by 1820, but a clachan and a fairly complex field system still survived. Rental values suggest that the area marked 'town field' was the remnant of an outfield, on which area most farmers still had grazing rights. In Cregan, on the same estate, there was no trace of a clachan in the 1830s, but in 1820 there were some hints that one formerly existed (around farm B). By 1820, however, consolidation was complete and the townland was occupied by two compact farms and a third which extended over into another townland.

holdings in part of Lecale in county Down, since eventually in this area a number of farmers had no heirs to inherit their holdings, either because of celibacy or emigration, hence leading to further amalgamations of farms and the disappearance of clachans (Buchanan, 1958). It is highly likely that this was also a relevant factor elsewhere, although it must have been a relatively slow and haphazard process, often dependent on the ability of the population of an individual clachan to maintain itself in the face of demographic changes which severely affected the normal functioning of traditional society. Even if traditional settlement forms survived, the new demographic situation of emigration coupled with lower rates of natural increase (discussed in chapter 5) made it unlikely that former conditions would reassert themselves.

During this period of change the association between residence in clachans and the cultivation of common fields also became less clearly marked. On open moorland held by groups of partners, common grazing rights often survived because there was little, if anything, to be gained from enclosure, although in the long run, in upland areas like the Sperrins, traditional systems of allocating grazing rights have died out in recent times (MacAodha, 1956). On lower, more fertile lands the clachans and cultivated common fields disappeared much more rapidly. By and large, remnants of clachans tended to linger on longer than common arable fields because they did not interfere with the introduction of agri-

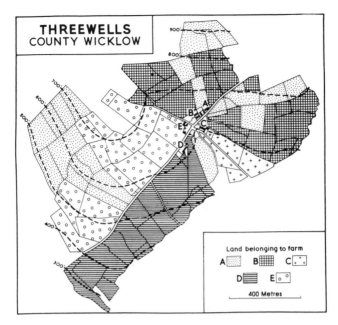

Figure 4.5 Threewells, county Wicklow. The map provides a contemporary example of the results of piecemeal consolidation, where the vestiges of a farm cluster has survived, although with somewhat curiously shaped compact holdings.

cultural innovations as directly as complexity of land-tenure and fragmentation of holdings. Sometimes, when clachans were large and complex, a landlord felt it worthwhile to subsidize the building of new dispersed farmsteads at the same time as he reorganized the field system. The presence of smaller clachans was not such a grave embarrassment. In these cases it was possible to reorganize fields and still keep the farm clusters, often in accordance with the local wishes of the tenants. In these cases the old buildings had a good chance of surviving for a while, if only as uninhabited out-buildings. Eventually, increased rural prosperity and the natural process of decay led to the need for replacement, at which time it was likely that the new farmsteads would be located more conveniently within their compact farms.

In spite of the operation of these various factors promoting change, at the end of the nineteenth century a number of areas still remained where the traditional farming system, or some modification of it, continued to flourish. This hard core was largely dispersed by government action, in particular by the Congested Districts Board, which was established by the British government in 1891. The Board was given responsibility for raising the standard of living in those areas of western Ireland where population continued to press hard on resources – hence its name. Craft industries were encouraged, new fishing harbours were constructed, and encouragement was given to agricultural improvements.

In the better-favoured areas of western Ireland the Board and its successor, the Irish Land Commission, which took over this work after Irish independence

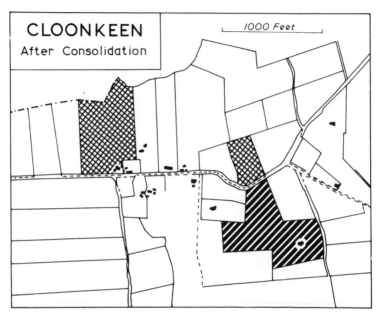

Figure 4.6 Cloonkeen, county Mayo: Land Commission Consolidation. Cloonkeen, which was located on the Lucan Estate, was rearranged by the Land Commission in October 1909. This map should be compared with Figure 4.2, which shows the same area before consolidation. The shading illustrates the holdings of a number of sample farmers.

in 1922, were able to make considerable changes to the structure of agriculture (Nolan, 1988). Clachans were dispersed, new houses were provided and complicated patterns of landholding were simplified (Figure 4.6), although, with the wisdom of hindsight, it is clear that even the reconstituted holdings were often smaller than was appropriate to produce an acceptable income. This was not the only governmental activity bringing change to the rural landscape. From 1883 to 1919, but particularly after 1906, local authorities took advantage of central legislation to demolish many one-roomed cabins inhabited by farm labourers and replaced them with simple, but solid, cottages located alongside the roads (Aalen, 1986). Although these local authority cottages were less common in Ulster and in Connacht, where hired labour was relatively less important for farmers, a total of 50,000 were built and represented the first major public housing initiative not only in Ireland, but in the British Isles.

In the more remote parts of the West, particularly in west Connacht, the resistance to change was especially strong. Holdings here were often minute and intricately fragmented, with cultivated plots the size of mere gardens. In these areas, many of them residual zones of native Irish speaking, the inhabitants may have also possessed an unusually strong respect for tradition. Although field boundaries were straightened and improvements to housing undertaken, the problem of making any real fundamental change defeated government officials, since the alterations to land holding and settlement that would have been neces-

Photo 11 Achill, county Mayo. This view in Achill island suggests the former pressure on cultivable land on the western fringe of Ireland and the regular field boundaries indicate that some reorganization of holdings has taken place here. Although the peat cuttings are still used above the houses (many of them quite recently rebuilt), the former infield in front of them is now far from intensively cultivated. (Courtesy of Bord Failte)

sary to make genuine economic sense would, at the same time, have destroyed the very society that efforts were being made to preserve.

In recent years, however, many clachans in this area have been gradually abandoned. As in the past, remittances from overseas and government grants and loans are providing the inhabitants of these more resistant areas with the means of building new homes; but there are pressures unconnected with agriculture which are encouraging the desertion of the old farm clusters. Sites that are better located for attracting tourist visitors are now being sought and, as a result, new homes are increasingly being located along coastal roads where there is access to transport and beaches. At these sites, too, electricity supplies and piped water are more easily available (MacAodha, 1965). What government influence could only lightly disturb, new social and economic forces are now altering more radically and more permanently.

The end result is that in most of rural Ireland the landscape is dominated by an even scatter of farmhouses and what appear to be compact holdings. In fact hints of past conditions are still retained in the landscape. The French geographer Pierre Flatrès (1957, separate Figure 1) has presented an intriguing summary of rural settlement forms in Ireland, based on the evidence of the contemporary landscape (Figure 4.7). Some of the features he recorded, like the irregular fields

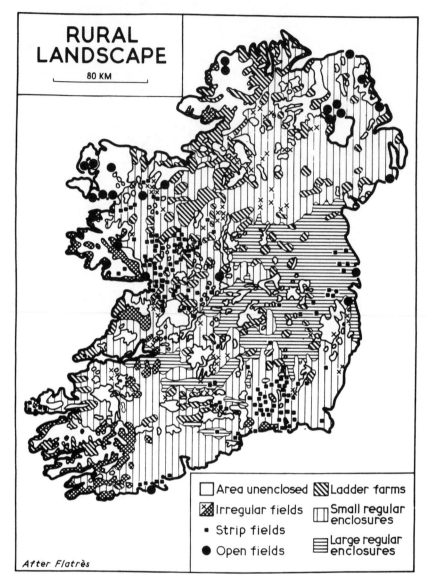

Figure 4.7 The rural landscape. This map was based on a survey of field evidence in the early 1950s by Pierre Flatrès (1957). Some of the survivals he recorded have now disappeared and a few examples of open fields and other features were missed, but the map gives a valuable impression of the underlying complexity of an apparently simple rural landscape.

in upland areas, may simply reflect a direct influence of the physical environment. But most are a product of human activity and, in particular, reflect the processes by which more ancient systems were removed. The ladder farms, the larger enclosures of the cattle-fattening areas of Meath, the survivals of old open fields – these and other features of his map have been discussed in this chapter. Indeed, the landscape itself is often the best indication that we have today of the process of change, since few comprehensive records of the pre-enclosure landscape have survived.

Contemporary rural settlement change

The landscape of rural Ireland is still undergoing change. That change is most marked in those areas where farming is most prosperous and there is most to gain from further adjustments to farms and fields. It is also most obvious where urban influences are strongest in the countryside, bringing commuters and their homes to the rural environment. Often these areas overlap in the hinterlands of Belfast and Dublin; but the forces of contemporary change extend more widely than this in modern Ireland as new employment is spread to smaller towns, with the encouragement which this also gives to part-time farming and investment in new houses in the countryside.

For those urban residents who can afford it, the building of their own house in the countryside often seems to offer the possibility of obtaining a more attractive lifestyle. Such an attitude is perhaps stronger in Ireland than it may be elsewhere because a greater proportion of Irish families have become urban dwellers more recently and still retain family contacts with rural areas. At the same time, a farmer who can sell off a modest site along a main road may welcome the much greater return that this will produce in comparison with its use for agriculture. It is clear that in Ireland, North and South, there has been less restraint than in Great Britain on residential building in the countryside, in spite of the fact that rural planning policy has given lip-service to the restriction of the building of new, scattered houses.

Around Belfast, for example, decentralization of employment, services and population has produced particular pressures for scattered urban fringe developments of this kind. In spite of restrictions to the outward spread of Belfast and the delimitation of an area of special control, 87 per cent of applications for housing development between 1973 and 1986 in a zone of 365 square kilometres around Belfast were for single dwellings: and planning permission was granted for 57 per cent of applications for sites located in the countryside (Murray, 1991). But this tendency can be seen in areas further away from the magnet of a large city, where a more relaxed planning regime has been operated. Some might see these as a visible expression of the process of counterurbanization, which has become more noticeable in recent censuses in many western countries, which show that in some areas, but not in all, the process of rural depopulation has been arrested, as more people for a variety of reasons choose to live in rural areas. In

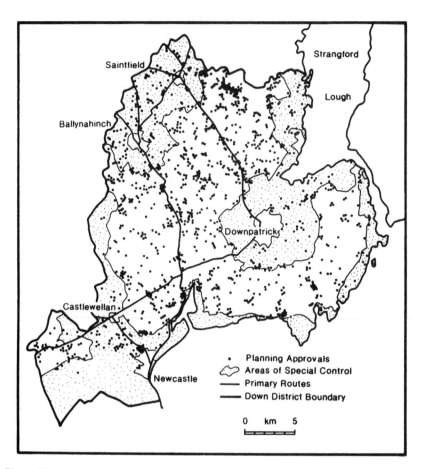

Figure 4.8 New houses in the countryside near Downpatrick. This data, from the Town and Country Planning Service of the Northern Ireland Department of the Environment, reveals the number of planning approvals for new rural dwellings between 1979 and 1986 in Down District, an area outside the immediate suburban pressures of Belfast. Murray (1991) shows that quite a number of the permissions granted fall in areas of special landscape control, with the pressures being greatest closer to Belfast.

Down District (around Downpatrick), for example, Murray (1990) has shown that 1943 applications were made for new houses and 74 per cent were permitted between 1979 and 1986 (Figure 4.8). Or again, in a contrasting environment, the growth of ribbon developments of tourist-generated housing in the treeless environment of some areas on the west coast of Ireland has made an adverse landscape impact in a region where the natural scenery itself provides an important economic resource.

In detail, these developments may be somewhat different in Northern Ireland and the Republic of Ireland because of the different legislative environments, but the basic situation is similar. Patrick Duffy (1986) has pointed out that, in his view, there are no really effective policies for the countryside; and although his remarks were directed at the Republic of Ireland they can reasonably be applied to Northern Ireland as well. One reason for this situation, he argued, is that because rural decline has been almost universal until recently, pressures for building in the countryside were largely unexpected. In addition, although there was a strong concern about the Irish countryside among influential people, it was often motivated by nostalgia rather than by a critical awareness of rural physical, social and economic planning problems. Finally, there was no real awareness of the considerable variety of problems and solutions at the local level – the problems of the 'West' were perceived (perhaps vaguely), but the urgency of the different pressures in those areas closer to the main centres of population were much less clearly appreciated.

These problems include the incremental effect of change, with each development in itself appearing insignificant, but with the process causing a substantial cumulative impact over a period of years. The problem is not limited to the landscape; most of these houses are not provided with main drainage, so that the coincidence of septic tanks, sumps and wells, all on half-acre sites, offers a cause for environmental alarm. The problems of pollution are not limited to residential developments. Technical changes in farming continue: for example, drainage from silage pits and slurry from more intensive animal keeping pose problems in some areas.

Other changes simply involve the gradual disappearance of the typical, and often highly regarded, rural landscape, popularly thought to date from time immemorial, even though it was often a creation of the nineteenth century. New scattered bungalows owe much more to Spanish haciendas than to traditional Irish cottages. Similarly, field boundaries are being removed and inconvenient archaeological structures quietly made to disappear in those farming regions where greater mechanization is possible, with these changes being greatest in the richer counties, like Meath, where the commercial gain from these changes is greatest, although in hilly areas like Monaghan they may be more noticeable to the passing visitor.

Planning restrictions may have been less firmly enforced because of fears of high compensation payments – certainly this has been argued both in Northern Ireland and in the Republic – but there is possibly a more fundamental underlying factor. The rights of ownership, only achieved by most Irish farmers at the beginning of this century, are still covetously prized; and in the minds of many people there is still a strongly rooted belief in the rights of individuals to use their own land as they see fit.

Unyielding resistance to rural landscape change is impossible and almost certainly unwise. To quote one simple example of potential change which might provide benefits, the dispersed pattern of settlement that has been created in rural Ireland has produced a dense network of roads, because of the need for access which farmers and others require to the regional road network. A study in part of county Antrim by Michael Barbour (1977) has compared the theoretical total length of surfaced roads required to service the rural community with those actually found. Depending on the ideal system adopted, he argued that a reduction of somewhere between 30 and 40 per cent in the length of roads would be possible; and such findings are of widespread relevance in many other parts of Ireland. Gradual relocation of dwellings along the main roads would go some way towards reaching that possible target, although it has to be said that the longer-term aesthetic results of the process might not be widely welcomed. In any case it could only be expected to occur if a taxation system were established which directly passed on the real costs of road provision to the farming population involved.

Further reading

A documented survey of earlier work in this area is provided in J.H. Johnson, 'The development of the rural settlement pattern of Ireland', *Geografiska Annaler* 43 (1961), 165–73. As well as providing a clear summary of his work in this field, for a discussion of the ability of the rural settlement pattern to adjust to changing conditions see D. McCourt, 'The dynamic quality of Irish rural settlement', in R. Buchanan, E. Jones and D. McCourt (eds), *Man and his Habitat* (Routledge and Kegan Paul, London, 1970), 128–64. A later survey, with a somewhat different emphasis, is R.H. Buchanan, 'Field systems of Ireland', in A. Baker and R. Butlin (eds), *Studies of Field Systems in the British Isles* (University Press, Cambridge, 1973), 580–618.

For enclosure in an area where the process often took place earlier than in those areas where the bulk of rural settlement studies have been concentrated see F.H.A. Aalen, 'The origin of enclosures in eastern Ireland' in N. Stephens and R.E. Glasscock (eds), *Irish Geographical Studies in Honour of E. Estyn Evans* (Queen's University, Belfast, 1970), 209–23.

Contemporary problems are discussed in P.J. Duffy, 'Planning problems in the countryside' in P. Breathnach and M. Cawley (eds), *Change and Development in Rural Ireland* (Geographical Society of Ireland, Maynooth, Special Publication 1, 1986), 60–68. For Northern Ireland see J.H. Caldwell and J.V. Greer, *Physical Planning in Rural Areas of Northern Ireland* (Occasional Paper 5, Department of Town and Country Planning, Queen's University, Belfast, 1984).

Chapter 5

Population in the nineteenth century

Ireland is commonly thought to have had a unique population history in much of the nineteenth and twentieth centuries, since various aspects of its demography do not appear to match very convincingly with what was happening in many other parts of western Europe. In particular, unlike most countries of the developed world, the second half of the nineteenth century and the early twentieth century were marked by a steady population decline; and although this was followed by a period of relative stability in total population, high levels of marital fertility were maintained in the mid-twentieth century, resisting the general trend elsewhere. But although the details of its evolving population geography may find few exact parallels elsewhere, developments in Ireland were a logical reflection of more general processes, like urbanization and rural depopulation, and in that sense were not as exceptional as might seem at first sight.

The total population of Ireland was increasing rapidly at the beginning of the nineteenth century; and although the amount of that increase may have been sometimes overstated, it is clear that substantial growth had been taking place since the 1780s if not earlier. In fact the rate of population increase was similar to that in England, but the peculiarity of Ireland was that by far the greater part of its growth was in rural areas and lacked the stimulus of the industrial revolution. Population increase ended in the mid-1840s when the Great Famine, associated with the failure of the potato crop, which started in 1845 and continued for a number of successive years without respite, inaugurated a sharp reduction in population (Table 5.1). In the second half of the century a continued fall in total population was recorded at every succeeding census, largely the product of a flood of emigration to North America and Britain, but also to Australia. Population continued to fall until the mid-1930s when a period of relative stability was initiated, with some hints of a changing situation in recent decades.

The Great Famine of the 1840s coincided with the critical turning point in the population of nineteenth-century Ireland, occurring as it did between a period of sharp population increase and one of decline. Hence a widely held view is that the Great Famine broke for ever the attachment of the rural Irish to their native soil. Throughout Ireland faith in an agricultural way of life, with the potato as

Table 5.1 Population of Ireland, 1821–1926

Date of census	total population ('000s)	percentage change
1821	6,802	
1831	7,767	+14.19
1841	8,175	+5.25
1851	6,552	−19.85
1861	5,799	−11.50
1871	5,412	−6.67
1881	5,175	−4.39
1891	4,705	−9.08
1901	4,459	−5.23
1911	4,390	−1.54
1926	4,229	−3.68

the key subsistence crop, was permanently destroyed, so that opportunities overseas were more eagerly seized by Irish emigrants. But there are problems in accepting that interpretation without some important qualifications, inspired by what was happening before the Famine, by the detailed impact of the Famine itself, and by the developments which occurred in the decades which followed it.

Geographical contrasts in pre-Famine Ireland

A popular impression of pre-Famine Ireland is that it was a land where rapid population increase had produced a uniform population of impoverished tenants, ekeing out a life of bare subsistence based on the potato – a population which was invariably crushed by the impositions of rapacious landlords. The problem with that view is that it makes no allowance for local and regional geographical contrasts. Descriptions of the demographic processes underlying this assumed situation also suffer from similar problems of over-generalization.

A standard interpretation, most eloquently presented by K.H. Connell (1950), has been that the potato became more generally adopted by peasant farmers sometime in the eighteenth century. With its high yields, its adaptability to acid soils, its suitability for breaking in uncultivated land, and its tolerance of the damp uncertainty of the Irish harvest, this crop expanded the ability of Ireland to feed its rapidly increasing population. That population was growing because of its high birth rates, encouraged by early marriage. Traditionally a man would not marry until he could obtain a home of his own, but the willingness of parents to subdivide their holdings in order to provide a source of livelihood for their adult children and the possibility of winning new plots from waste land at the margins of cultivation made it easier to obtain a patch of land sufficient to support a family on a diet dominated by the potato. It has also been argued that landlords were prepared to allow this process because, given the early nineteenth-century technology of Irish farming, to permit the growth of a larger labour force on their lands seemed the only plausible method of increasing agricultural production and hence rents.

There are problems with this interpretation, particularly in disentangling cause and effect; but from a geographical perspective the major difficulty is that the combination of circumstances which has just been described applied to some parts of Ireland much more than to others. One commentary on this is hidden away in what might seem an unlikely location – the history of Guinness's brewery written by P. Lynch and J. Vaisey (1960). These authors recognized the existence of two 'Irelands' at the beginning of the nineteenth century. In their view three-quarters of the population lived under a largely subsistence and rural economy, without money to purchase commercial products and with traditional life continuing almost unchanged. The rest operated in a 'maritime' economy, coupled to Great Britain by long-standing economic and social links. This maritime Ireland, they argued, formed a coastal strip in the east, stretching from Belfast to Cork, with outliers in the towns of Limerick and Galway, and with fingers of maritime Ireland penetrating from Dublin into the Irish midlands, along the routes of the then recently constructed Royal and Grand canals.

That description is perhaps more geographically realistic, but there are good reasons for wanting to elaborate it quite considerably. Even on a broad regional scale 'subsistence' Ireland was already deeply penetrated by external commercial influences at the beginning of the nineteenth century. Temporary migration of agricultural workers from the west to Britain and to south-eastern Ireland was becoming more important. Various ramifications of the linen industry, like the spinning of thread, were found beyond its domestic heartland, which in any case extended into what appeared to be classified as subsistence Ireland. The illicit distillation of poteen in the more remote parts of the country was not simply undertaken to assuage local cravings, but the product was also marketed surreptitiously in the cash economy of the east. Even small farmers in the more remote parts of the country had surplus cattle for sale which, sold from farmer to farmer at various stages in the rearing of beef animals, eventually found their way to the markets of the east. All of these activities brought some cash into the more remote areas of Ireland, although the impact of these commercial influences was not necessarily found in every family, community and local region.

At a yet more detailed scale there is plentiful evidence of considerable contrasts within quite small areas. For example there were important differences between the minute subsistence holdings of west Donegal and the larger, more commercial farms of the Laggan – the name given to east Donegal. Or again, there were obvious contrasts between farming at the upland limits of cultivation in the Leinster Chain and the lowlands of Wexford. West and east Kerry showed differences similar to those in Donegal. In eastern Galway, even within the lands held by one landlord, the situation varied between townland and townland.

This was also a socially differentiated rural population which did not simply consist of impoverished farmers and landlords (usually absentee). In nearly all rural areas there were landless labourers, cottiers holding only a patch of land, and small farmers; but there were also rural craftsmen and more substantial farmers. By no means all landlords were absentee, and many were working their own productive home farms. In addition there were clergymen, teachers, land-agents and traders. Cottiers and very small farmers, dependent on the potato for much of their subsistence, were found close to farmers who were much more commercially orientated. The numbers completely tied to subsistence cultivation were high – estimates vary but at least two million seems a reasonable figure based on the 1841 population census. Yet this implies that the majority of rural people were not in that extreme situation and although many were likely to be extremely badly affected by the failure of the potato crop, they were not exposed to complete disaster.

Economic and demographic changes in the pre-Famine period

Lynch and Vaisey were broadly correct in seeing a dualism within early nineteenth-century Ireland, but it was geographically much more complicated than they suggested, even at a local scale. This detailed variegated pattern is important in explaining the contrasting accounts that have been produced of pre-Famine conditions, particularly as these local differences were often an expression of the important changes that were already taking place in population and society in rural Ireland (Johnson, 1970a). Harvest migration, for example, was increasing in importance, as improved transport made the journey to Britain more feasible. The domestic linen industry was already decaying in its more marginal locations, but was developing into a more sophisticated semi-industrial activity in eastern Ulster. Agricultural change was widespread: traditional field systems and settlement forms were already being removed in diverse parts of Ireland, both 'maritime' and 'subsistence', and high food prices during the Napoleonic Wars had encouraged the spread of more commercially orientated farming in those areas of south-east Ireland where grain cultivation was a practical proposition. This evolving rural landscape implied that there were strong forces encouraging change in some parts of Ireland, whether the new ways of life were willingly accepted by the tenants themselves or were imposed by landlords for a variety of reasons, sometimes selfish, sometimes paternalistic.

What is clearly established is that the rural population was increasing in numbers, although there were considerable differences in the rate at which increase was taking place, particularly as the nineteenth century proceeded. It is also clear that the rate of increase was slowing down, particularly in the more commercially orientated parts of the countryside. It has often been thought that at this time the Irish rural population was becoming progressively poorer as an expanding population pressed more and more upon limited resources, but doubts have been cast on that proposition, at least in the decade before the Famine. Immediately before the Famine population pressure among the poorest may have been more strongly correlated with impoverishment than was the case a decade earlier, but this did not apply to all the population by any means and the reverse was more commonly the case. Areas with increased impoverishment were found in parts of north Leinster, north Connacht and west Ulster, but this was a result of the decline of hand spinning in these areas, as the domestic linen industry of the north-east underwent reorganization and concentration, not a product of direct agricultural change (Mokyr and O'Grada, 1988).

As a result it is less surprising to discover that, taking Ireland as a whole, life expectancy compared well with the average elsewhere in Europe; or that the average height of men (based on data from military recruits) was greater than in Britain and in at least six other European countries. Poverty varied by region and by class. Among the poorest (particularly in the West, at the limits of cultivation, and on badly managed estates) subdivision, early marriage, the rapid growth of population, poverty and increased reliance on the potato, all combined to produce a potential disaster if the basic subsistence crop were to fail; but the overall picture was of better health and a more diversified society than is commonly believed. The more conventional aspects of the human geography of Ireland tell a similar story. This was an Ireland in which public road transport in the 1830s linked all towns of any size and in which steam power had been applied to Irish Sea ferry services in the 1820s. It was a land in which agricultural output was rising substantially. This is perhaps unsurprising in the light of an increasing rural population, although perhaps more startling is O'Grada's calculation that the productivity of rural labour kept its existing level and perhaps even improved (O'Grada, 1988, especially pp. 46–77).

It is in this context that some of the population changes taking place in pre-Famine Ireland must be assessed. To start with, there is clear evidence that the rate of population increase was falling in the decade before the Famine. Part of that reduction was the result of a fall in fertility, possibly related to the fact that the average age of marriage was already increasing in the south-east – a topic to which it will be necessary to return later. Even more important, emigration was already well established at a relatively high level as a normal part of Irish rural life.

Every county in Ireland had some emigrants and those areas where emigration was important were not limited to the north where emigration to North America had been a well-established tradition among Presbyterian small farmers in the eighteenth century (Johnson, 1988). At a local level the parish reports to the Commission on the State of the Poorer Classes indicated that in 1834 a considerable number of local areas had 'many' emigrants, a similar number had 'some' emigrants and a wide scatter had 'a few' emigrants (Figure 5.1). Other information in these parish reports makes it clear that the existence of a few emigrants may be taken to indicate a process that was getting underway, rather than something of little fundamental importance. Even in areas where there was said to be no emigration in the mid-1830s many people were reported as being prepared to leave Ireland if they could raise the necessary money.

It seems likely that the term 'emigration' in these reports was being applied

Figure 5.1 Pre-Famine emigration, c. 1834. Based on the parish reports to the Commission of Enquiry into the Condition of the Poorer Classes in Ireland, 1834.

to those who were making long-distance moves. Limiting consideration to emigration across the North Atlantic, by far the most important destination, a conservative estimate is that about 30,000 people per annum were involved in the early 1830s. But, in addition, there were over 419,000 people listed in the 1841 census of Great Britain as having their place of birth in Ireland (and that was almost certainly an under-enumeration of the true figure and also makes no allowance for those who died before the date of the census). In total the level of emigration was comparable with that found in later decades of the century, after the immediate impact of the Famine.

The emigrants who went to the New World were not the poorest in the community, who could not afford the costs of moving across the Atlantic and who were less likely to have the flow of information about opportunities, without which the movement could not have taken place. They were sometimes rural craftsmen who were already leaving the countryside because of competition with urban-based manufacturers. Although they were frequently recorded as labourers or servants on the manifests of passenger ships, they were often the children of smaller farmers who were unable to envisage achieving the standard of living to which they aspired. At this time they were men rather than women, although nuclear families of husband and wife and probably children formed the most important single group of emigrants; and all religious groups were involved. The more general point is that before substantial amounts of emigration could take place appropriate developments in local society and economy were necessary to prepare the way. In pre-Famine Ireland important levels of emigration had already commenced in many areas and elsewhere society was being made ready for what was to come.

The impact of the Great Famine

It was in this changing context that the Great Famine made its dramatic impact during the period between 1845 and 1849, when the failure of the potato crop as a result of successive attacks of potato blight and subsequent shortages of seed potatoes brought hunger, disease and starvation to millions of people. Certainly there are problems in interpretation when details of the actual impact of the Famine are examined.

For a start there are severe technical problems in establishing the number of deaths caused directly or indirectly by the potato failure because of difficulties with the mortality statistics provided in the 1851 Irish census – the source of information on which it is necessary to rely. Death is a normal part of human experience, so the critical matter is the excess number of people who died during this period rather than the total; and to calculate this involves sometimes difficult assumptions about what would have been the normal expectation. The crude statistics themselves leave something to be desired, since they were taken some years after the event. For this reason, it is unlikely that all the deaths of very young children were reported to the census enumerators. In addition to this, complete households were wiped out or migrated away from their homes and thus were not available to have their experiences recorded in 1851. As a result it is highly likely that the published statistics understated the number of deaths which took place.

It has also to be remembered that infectious diseases, in particular cholera, played an important role in causing excess deaths, but in absolute terms these were more important in Dublin and Belfast. The impact of disease was certainly heightened by migration of distressed rural people into the cities, but a cholera epidemic was found in many other European cities during this period and it is unlikely that urban Ireland would have escaped unscathed, even if the potato failure had not occurred. Nor was the demographic effect of the Famine limited to deaths, since it is clear that starvation also brought temporary reductions in fertility which are very difficult to quantify convincingly. Even more important was the impact of emigration, directly stimulated by the Famine.

Bearing these qualifications in mind, a number of reputable estimates of excess deaths have been made which range from 800,000 to about one million – the most recent and probably the most authoritative settles for that latter figure (Boyle and O'Grada, 1986). This indicates that excess deaths from whatever cause represented approximately 12 per cent of the total population of Ireland at the time of the Famine. Such statistics confirm the Famine as a very grave disaster, which had a profound impact, not only on Ireland in the 1840s, but also on those retrospective perceptions of the Famine which shaped later political attitudes. Yet they also reveal that there were many people who escaped its worst effects.

In the light of the pre-Famine contrasts in the social geography of Ireland it is not surprising that there were considerable regional variations in the impact of Famine mortality. For example, perhaps only one per cent of the population of Carlow was involved, but in Mayo excess deaths may have represented over 25 per cent of the total population. To this must be added the sharply increased level of emigration associated with the Famine; and, although there are perhaps insuperable problems in calculating this accurately, what is certainly true is that the areas of highest mortality did not coincide exactly with the areas of heaviest emigration. Other indices of Famine suffering also show a far from complete correspondence with population change. It is possible to map spending on public works to relieve hardship and the amount of food being issued to ward off starvation; and these two indices may give some imperfect indication of the impact of the potato failure, although the crop was destroyed in nearly every part of Ireland. These produce a similar result. The information on population change can also be refined by focusing on the rural population and by assessing its reduction in relation to the amount of arable land, in order to get closer to local reality. Such a map shows some greater relationship between famine conditions and rural population decline, but it is far from perfect, particularly in the counties of west Ulster (Johnson, 1990).

A revisionist view of the Famine should not be pushed too far, since it is hard to overstate the suffering caused among the poorest in society. Infectious diseases which raged during the Famine years could cross class boundaries – and there is evidence of privileged families experiencing death and illness – but the effects of starvation were clearly concentrated on the poorest in the rural community. The overall effect was to decimate this group, which was most dependent on the potato, less informed about the possibilities of escape, and without the financial reserves to buffer them from the worst suffering. Many died, some managed to move as far as the slums of British cities – if this can be called an escape – and those who could afford to and were aware of the possibility joined the emigrant stream to North America which was greatly swollen as a result.

The longer-term political impacts of the disaster were also considerable, although it has to be said that long-surviving political attitudes were shaped by a mistaken perception that the Famine was the result of a plot by the British government to destroy the emerging Irish nation. The truth was that reality was much more messy, with the real culprits being bureaucratic incompetence, a lack of official comprehension in London about what was actually happening in the more remote parts of Ireland, and sheer bad luck (O'Grada, 1989).

Yet the lack of a convincing geographical fit between hardship and population change indicates that there were other longer-term influences operating on the Irish population, besides the Famine. Of course the immediate withdrawal of many rural people from the cultivated land was a major force in changing other aspects of the geography of Ireland, sweeping away the poorest houses and the traditional settlement patterns they formed from many areas. Population decline immediately brought about a sharp reduction in the importance of arable farming, allowing a considerable increase in agricultural productivity per worker, as well as providing a stimulus for many, but not all, landlords to act in a ruthless manner to institute these changes.

But in spite of these clear, short-term impacts, what also emerges clearly is that, even if the Great Famine had not occurred, many of these changes to the rural economy were inevitable at some point in the nineteenth century. Taking a step away from the horrors of the Famine years, the end product was, in effect, the spread of modernized commercial agriculture and its associated social and demographic changes. As has already been shown, this process was underway before the 1840s. Although stimulated by the Famine, it still had some way to go long after the impact of the Famine was over. In other words, it was a long, continuing process and, given Ireland's location, the technological and social changes of the nineteenth century and the massive expansion of the urban population of Great Britain, it was surely an inevitable outcome.

Population change in the aftermath of the Famine

The lack of a high correlation between the worst famine conditions and population decline in the 1840s has already been commented upon, although detailed observations pose many problems. In county Londonderry population was already declining in some northern parishes before the Famine (Figure 5.2). During the years of the potato failure increased levels of population decline were concentrated in those areas where rural population pressure was greatest. At first sight this might seem to have been a direct product of famine deaths, but in fact the decline was largely the result of out-migration. It appears that this loss of population was stimulated as much by the decline of the domestic linen industry as by the potato failure, which was the last straw rather than the ultimate cause

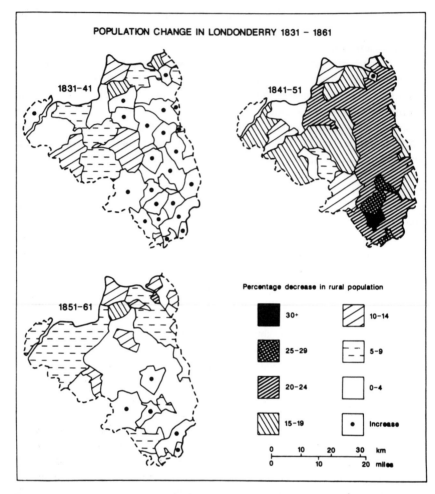

Figure 5.2 Population change in Londonderry, 1831–61. The regional pattern of population change in the inter-censal decade following the Great Famine bore greater similarities to pre-Famine patterns than during the period of the potato failure.

of emigration for many farmer-weavers. What is surprising, however, is the re-assertion of earlier trends after the immediate impact of the years of the potato failure, with population increase being highest in the areas of greatest population pressure and population decline continuing in the more prosperous parts of the county (Johnson, 1970b). This was no mere local phenomenon. Many Poor Law Unions in western Ireland showed some increase in population between 1851 and 1871 and a more restricted number also experienced population growth between 1861 and 1871, the result of lower emigration rates and higher levels of natural increase.

Underlying these demographic factors were other causes, related to the local nature of the agricultural economy. An interesting, if restricted, insight into these

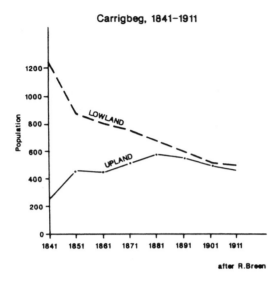

Carrigbeg, 1841–1911

after R.Breen

Figure 5.3 Population change in Carrigbeg, county Kerry, 1841–1911. These statistics, compiled by Richard Breen (1984), reveal local contrasts in the level of population change both during and immediately after the Famine.

is given by a study of two District Electoral Divisions in county Kerry, which together had a total population of about 1500 in 1841, which was reduced to just over 1000 in 1901 (Breen, 1984). The area could be divided into two sectors – an 'upland' region characterized by small holdings cultivated by family labour, and a 'lowland' region with predominantly larger farms which employed farm servants. Population change in each of these areas followed different paths (Figure 5.3).

Surprisingly in the light of overall population decline, during the 1840s there was an increase in population in the uplands, as a result of the creation of new farms at the margins of cultivation. These farms were occupied by newly created households. After 1851 population here continued to grow slowly for a couple of decades, presumably as these households produced more children. In the later 1870s and in the 1880s, a period of declining agricultural prices and growing expectations brought pressure for out-migration. The willingness of farmers to allow relatives to remain on their land was sharply reduced as more extensive modes of production became more profitable, thus reducing the need for labour. At this stage, too, the children of the original farmers had reached an age when emigration was a possible option for them.

In contrast, during the Famine decade, the already fully occupied lowlands immediately showed a decline in population, the result of a fall in the number and average size of households. Dominating change was the reduction in the number of those households which did not directly control a farm, which were considerably more important to start with in the lowlands. The amount of tillage and the demand for agricultural labour fell, and the population which emigrated consisted either of former labourers who lived in separate households or those members of the farmers' families who were no longer required for farm work. The timing was different in the two regions, but in both the loss of population was dominated by the removal of that section of the population which did not directly possess a farm.

This local study brings out in microcosm what was happening more generally. The West reacted later to changes which took place earlier in the East, but then caught up with the situation found elsewhere in rural Ireland. In the early 1870s there were still considerable contrasts, with population totals in the poorer regions being relatively stable or declining quite slowly. At this stage, in many ways the critical turning point for many parts of western Ireland, various demographic changes became more obvious, associated with parallel social changes. The age of marriage became later in all parts of the countryside, the amount of celibacy grew, rates of natural increase fell, the amount of emigration expanded, and rural population decline became general (Walsh, 1970a).

Pre-Famine conditions most strongly reasserted themselves in those areas where hardship had been greatest, but longer-term population decline was largely independent of the Famine. By the end of the nineteenth century the internal contrasts which had grown in importance earlier in the century were largely removed, as change spread across the country; but in the hardcore areas of traditional life the outcome of this process became clearly visible in the decades after 1870 rather than being permanently stimulated by the potato failure.

Emigration, marriage and the rural economy

The longer-term decline in the Irish population was not the result of excess deaths but of two other demographic processes: emigration and declining levels of fertility. These were not independent of one another. Declining fertility was produced by later marriage, higher levels of celibacy, and the selective removal of young adults, all of which were influenced in some degree by the process of emigration. In turn, the social environment associated with lower fertility was a stimulus to emigration.

Later marriage and emigration were both part of the same social and economic pattern of behaviour. Increasingly rural society was dominated by a tradition in which only one son (usually, but not invariably, the eldest) would stay at home and continue to work the family farm. As a result there would be a restricted number of eligible marriage partners for daughters, so that, given any tempting opportunity, many of them would also be inclined to leave rural Ireland. Some adult children moved to nearby towns, perhaps setting up small businesses if their parents could raise the capital to get them started, or finding openings as servants and junior employees; others became skilled and unskilled workers in the two dominant cities of Ireland; but the majority sought their fortunes as longer-distance emigrants.

A continuing push to emigration during the second half of the nineteenth century was provided by the evolving nature of the rural economy. The emphasis on many farms swung towards the rearing of beef cattle and sheep by quite extensive methods and away from labour-demanding tillage. The impact of the Famine was a stimulus to this process with a sharp decrease in dependence on the potato, but the change in emphasis was already visible before the Famine and was more clearly confirmed by the decline in cereal production in the late 1850s and a parallel increase in the output of animals and animal products which continued throughout the remainder of the century.

Yet as the century proceeded there is some evidence that in some areas at least these agricultural changes themselves owed something to population decline. Increasingly people were not so much being forced to leave the land as were choosing to do so. In fact with each decade the general prosperity of rural Ireland was increasing. For example, the unrest which manifested itself in the so-called land wars of the 1880s was not so much the result of an intolerable land system, but was a reflection of rising expectations, as tenant farmers struggled in a period of economic difficulty to preserve the substantial material gains they had made since 1850, with most landlords being unwilling, perhaps unable, to make meaningful concessions (Donnelly, 1975, especially pp. 251–376). This situation makes more sense of the fact that fluctuations in the levels of Irish emigration to North America as the second half of the nineteenth century proceeded correlated more closely with 'pulls' from the American economy than with economic 'pushes' being experienced in Ireland.

The impact of emigration was heightened by the decline in the fertility rates of the Irish rural population, because of a number of related factors. One was a rise in the average age of marriage of both men and women. Another was a rise in the proportion of the population which never married. Finally, there was a reduction in the proportion of the population that was in the fertile age groups. In the social context of nineteenth-century Ireland, these various influences can be brought together by considering the decline in the proportion of the population made up of married women of fertile age (Figure 5.4). There was also a parallel decline in the number of men who were married.

Emigration was associated with these changes in a variety of ways. The smaller proportion of the number of people of fertile age was a direct result of emigration, which selectively removed young adults. Young adult women formed an important part of the migration, even in the earlier decades of the century; and they were more important than men towards the end of the century when migration to Britain as well as to North America is considered. In the end a rural population was produced with considerably more men than women, hence tending to increase the rate of celibacy among men. Emigration also operated indirectly in that some people who delayed marriage did so because they were still considering emigration as a possibility. Some women saw emigration as a possible escape from their subordinate role in rural society, a route to greater emancipation not to be lightly surrendered for the drudgery often associated with marriage and a large family.

There were also other relevant changes taking place within rural society and

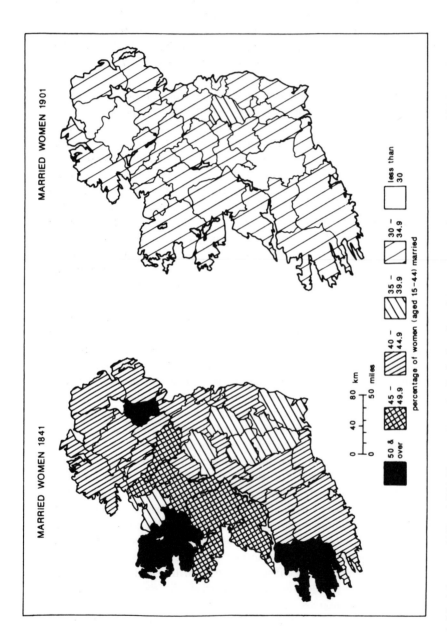

Figure 5.4 Married women, 1841 and 1901. The map shows the distribution of married women aged 15 to 44 at the censuses of 1841 and 1901, and is therefore an indication of the changing proportions of the population which (in the social context of Ireland) was available to produce children.

these have been elegantly described by K.H. Connell (1962). In his view, in the social and economic context of pre-Famine Ireland there was no benefit in delaying marriage, but in post-Famine Ireland, marriage took on a new role, increasingly concerned with monetary rather than emotional values and reflecting the increased commercialism of rural life. Connell argued that, in this economic context, a dowry which brought extra fields, cattle, or the cash to purchase them became an essential part of marriage customs. In addition, subdivision was no longer an acceptable strategy, if income rather than subsistence was the principal goal of farming. Hence a dowry was also important in providing funds to support the necessary emigration of the groom's siblings (or to provide a dowry for some of his sisters) (Kennedy, 1991).

In these circumstances the attractiveness of a bride was increasingly measured by what she brought to enhance the economic effectiveness of her prospective husband's farm, rather than her youthful beauty. At the same time a man could not take control of an undivided family farm until his father was willing to retire. In any case, landlords were also unwilling to see new small holdings created. Hence later marriage became established for men and the changing evaluation of the desirable attributes of marriage partners also produced later marriage for women.

In spite of Connell's persuasive argument it seems highly unlikely that the giving of a dowry suddenly sprang into existence in the closing decades of the nineteenth century. What appears to have happened is that the practice gained greater prominence because of the changing structure of the rural population. A dowry was largely irrelevant for the poorest farmers and labourers, but population change had greatly reduced their numbers. Therefore, a practice that was already well established earlier among substantial farmers became much more general, particularly as a more acquisitive society came to dominate the countryside.

As a result it is not surprising that later marriage spread from the south-east of Ireland, where it was found before the Famine, to be diffused throughout the whole of the island by the end of the nineteenth century. Celibacy also rose: the number of spinsters aged 46–55 increased from 12.5 per cent of their age group in 1841 to 21.9 per cent in 1901, and men also showed the same tendency. The reasons for this change are far from clear. Possibly intensive emigration had removed tolerable marriage partners in local rural areas; possibly (and controversially) those with the strongest sexual drive were not prepared to tolerate the social pattern of delayed marriage and had already followed the path of emigration; and possibly the disruption to single life which marriage implied was more unwelcome to those who had already become settled in their ways.

Emigration reduced the proportion of women of fertile age in the total population. At the same time later marriage and increased celibacy among women also reduced the number of married women of fertile age in the population which remained. In a society where illegitimacy was relatively rare this fall in the number of fertile married women must have produced a reduction in the crude birth rate. One rough estimate is that the effect of the fall in the number of fertile married women between 1841 and 1901 was to reduce the overall fertility of a number of Irish counties by more than 70 per cent (Johnson, 1957–58, p. 115). The immediate result was that, although no Irish county approached a situation of having natural decrease, nevertheless the effectiveness of emigration in reducing population numbers was enhanced.

Various features of the population geography of nineteenth-century Ireland were certainly different from those found elsewhere, but they were not peculiar in that they fitted logically with the economic and social context of Ireland. Rural depopulation, the growth of a more acquistive society, the spread of commercial farming, the development of a system which maintained the continuity of the family farm, the search for a better life away from home – such factors were in no way unique in nineteenth-century western Europe, although their combination and end-product in Ireland was certainly distinctive.

Further reading

Geographical contrasts in Ireland at the beginning of the nineteenth century are discussed in J.H. Johnson, 'The two "Irelands" at the beginning of the nineteenth century', in N. Stephens and R.E. Glasscock (eds), *Irish Geographical Studies in Honour of E. Estyn Evans* (Queen's University, Belfast, 1970), 224–44.

A classic account of population change in pre-Famine Ireland is K.H. Connell, *The Population of Ireland, 1750–1845* (Clarendon Press, Oxford, 1950), although some of his conclusions are in need of qualification. An important revisionist study of this period (and of developments later as well) is C. O'Grada, *Ireland before and after the Famine, Explorations, 1800–1925* (Manchester University Press, Manchester, 1988). See also C. O'Grada, *The Great Irish Famine* (Macmillan, Basingstoke, 1989). A rigorous statistical study which wrings out all that can be extracted from contemporary census material (and perhaps a bit more) is provided by J. Mokyr, *Why Ireland Starved: a Quantitative and Analytical History of the Irish Economy, 1846–1851* (Allen and Unwin, London, 1980).

A geographical interpretation of nineteenth century emigration is J.H. Johnson, 'The context of migration: the example of Ireland in the nineteenth century', *Transactions of the Institute of British Geographers* 15 (1990), 259–76. An important analysis of change in the last decades of the nineteenth century, supported by map evidence, is B.M. Walsh, 'Marriage rates and population pressure in Ireland, 1871 and 1911', *Economic History Review* 23 (1970), 148–62.

Studies of various aspects of Irish rural life in the nineteenth century, including speculation about the relationship between catholicism and marriage in the second half of the century, are found in K.H. Connell, *Irish Peasant Society: Four Historical Essays* (Clarendon Press, Oxford, 1968). A wide-ranging survey, which continues into the twentieth century and emphasizes the importance of family structure in encouraging emigration is R.E. Kennedy, *The Irish: Emigration, Marriage and Fertility* (University of California Press, Berkeley, 1973).

Chapter 6

Population in the twentieth century

In the twentieth century Ireland appeared to enter a new population regime. The rate of overall decline slackened and in the 1920s a period of relative stability in total population commenced. This change hides the fact that there was considerable continuity with what had been happening earlier. Emigration continued, the redistribution of population from rural to urban areas still occurred, and similar areas experienced the highest levels of rural depopulation. In the twentieth century, too, in spite of obvious differences, there were important underlying similarities between population changes in Northern Ireland and the Republic.

Republic of Ireland, 1926–1961

In the Republic of Ireland the stability in total population became clear after 1926, the year of the first census of the new state (Table 6.1). It was tempting for politicians to explain this new situation as a successful result of their activities following independence. After the establishment of the Irish Free State (as it was then called) new policies were evolved which were partly designed to promote economic independence from Britain, to parallel the political independence that had been achieved. They were also intended to create local employment and thus reverse the endemic population decline which, not surprisingly in the light of what had been happening during the previous 80 years, had become a major preoccupation with policy makers.

This new economic environment was firmly in place by the 1930s, by which time a substantial tariff wall had been erected, designed to provide an economic seedbed where new manufacturing industries could take root, with their production replacing imports on the home market. Economic protection was also seen as a mechanism which would encourage the growth of employment in the smaller towns, particularly in the West. Self-sufficiency was also encouraged by state intervention in such areas as electricity generation, in sugar production (using home grown beet) and in forestry.

Total population remained virtually unchanged until the census of 1951:

Table 6.1 Population of the Republic of Ireland, 1926–1991

Date of census	Total population	Natural increase	Net inter-censal migration*
1926	2,971,992		
1936	2,968,420	163,179	166,751
1946	2,955,107	173,798	187,111
1951	2,960,593	125,954	119,568
1956	2,898,264	134,434	196,763
1961	2,818,341	132,080	212,003
1966	2,884,002	146,266	80,605
1971	2,978,248	148,152	53,906
1979	3,378,217	281,032	+108,936
1981	3.443,405	80,234	5,046
1986	3,540,643	169,120	71,885
1991	3,523,401	119,200	136,442

* All out-migration except 1971–79

during this 25-year period the population of the Republic fell by only 11,000 and at first sight this would seem to suggest that the new policies had been dramatically successful. Non-agricultural employment expanded, with jobs in manufacturing rising by over 63 per cent from 164,000 in the 1920s to 268,000 in the early 1950s. The tertiary sector of the economy expanded as well, if somewhat less rapidly. The limited supply of local raw materials was also exploited: in particular, the electricity industry eventually managed to produce over 80 per cent of its total output from indigenous sources of peat and water power.

Yet there was an element of illusion in this apparent success. Even in the first decade of the twentieth century, before independence, the rate of population decline had already fallen sharply below that found towards the end of the nineteenth century. Certainly there was a more rapid decline between the censuses of 1911 and 1926, but the upheaval associated with the winning of independence was a special factor encouraging increased out-migration during this period. It is also clear that economic conditions in Britain and North America in the 1920s and 1930s would have checked out-migration from Ireland, whatever internal policies had been adopted.

Although the crude birth rate had fallen in the last decades of the nineteenth century to relatively low levels by the standards of the time, in the first half of the twentieth century the Irish Republic largely escaped most of the decline in the birth rate found elsewhere. The end result was that relative positions were reversed, with comparative levels of fertility in the Republic now appearing high by west European standards. Any slight reduction in the first half of the twentieth century was much more than offset by a sharp fall in infant mortality, which dropped from over 105 per 1000 live births in 1901 to 45 per 1000 in 1950. As a result the Republic showed a rise in natural increase during this period: natural increase between 1926 and 1936 was 163,179 but between 1951 and 1961 it had risen to 266,514. Although new jobs were being created in manufacturing, the parallel decline in agricultural employment meant that there was no rise in the total number of jobs to absorb the young people eventually coming on to the workforce. The stable total population merely indicated that emigration was continuing as a delayed response to natural increase.

Also hidden behind the population totals were important contrasts in population trends in different parts of the country. The population of rural areas was decreasing everywhere, but decline was particularly severe in the north and west, and less so in the south-east. In those areas where depopulation was most severe the reduction in numbers between censuses was relatively constant, since local opportunities always compared unfavourably with those available elsewhere, in particular the Dublin region and Great Britain. In more prosperous rural areas the rate of decline was more variable from census to census, presumably because the advantages of moving were less clear-cut from time to time.

Urban population growth in the Republic during the first 40 years of independence was highly concentrated in Dublin and its environs. The urban population of the county of Dublin – essentially the city of Dublin and its satellites – was 438,743 in 1926. By 1961 this figure had increased to 683,744. Dublin dominated population growth partly because it enjoyed higher rates of natural increase than most other parts of the Republic, but also because this area was the principal target of the longer-distance migration of population within the Republic of Ireland.

In contrast, the smaller towns often had declining populations, particularly those in the most remote locations. For example, a town like Westport, in county Galway, had a population of 3488 in 1926 which fell steadily to 2882 in 1961. Whatever the intentions, economic self-sufficiency did not bring economic growth to the West. Rural depopulation may have been inevitable everywhere, but its regional effects were not counteracted significantly in the west of Ireland, since alternative urban employment generally did not flourish there.

The absence of the emperor's new clothes became only too obvious when the illusion was shattered by the publication of the results of the 1961 census, although there had been earlier concern about these matters among the more alert politicians and commentators. The 1961 census revealed a dismal pattern of population change during the 1950s, with emigration at the highest levels that had been recorded in the twentieth century. The total population of the Republic was shown to have declined sharply between 1951 and 1961; and those areas where population had been decreasing in the 1920s and 1930s experienced a remarkable reduction in population, particularly when it is recalled that rural depopulation had been underway in these districts for over a century (Figure 6.1). With the exception of Dublin, which still experienced growth during this critical decade, the population of most urban areas was relatively static, and small urban areas often showed an absolute decline (Johnson, 1963c). The key to this change was the recovery of the British economy in the 1950s from the upheaval of the Second World War and its aftermath, coupled with a lack of economic growth within the Republic.

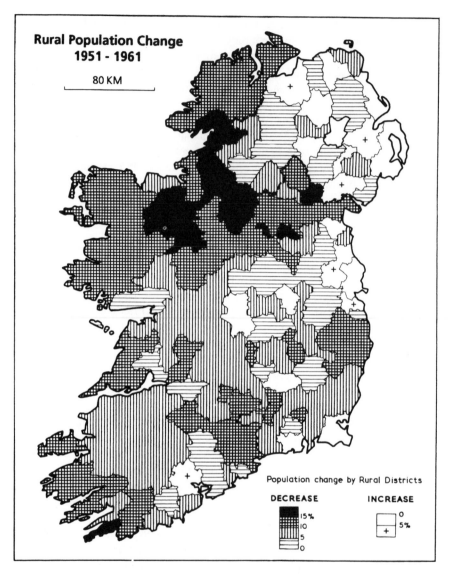

Figure 6.1 Population change, by rural districts, 1951–61. The decade between 1951 and 1961 saw the re-establishment of population decline in rural Ireland, at levels which rivalled those found during the second half of the nineteenth century.

Northern Ireland, 1926–1961

In apparent contrast, Northern Ireland was characterized by slow but steady increases in total population during this period (Table 6.2). The various censuses show a rise in total population from 1.26 million in 1926 to 1.42 million in 1961, a growth of 11 per cent over 35 years. The increase was in urban areas: in 1921

51 per cent of the population was classified as urban, and by 1961 this had risen to 54 per cent. Until 1951 most of this urban growth was concentrated in Belfast. The city then appeared to lose population over the next decade to 1961, but this was a false impression: what was involved was the outward spread of suburbs over the legal boundaries of the city at the same time as inner city population began to decline.

Table 6.2 Population of Northern Ireland, 1926–1991

Date of census	Total population	Natural increase	Net inter-censal emigration
1926	1,256,561		
1937	1,279,745	80,835	57,651
1951	1,370,921	158,443	67,267
1961	1,425,042	146,349	92,228
1966	1,484,775	97,434	37,701
1971	1,536,065	51,250	24,324
1981	1,532,619	107,554	136,554
1991	1,577,836	115,060	69,420

During the same period rural depopulation also occurred in Northern Ireland, particularly in its western rural areas. In comparison with the Republic, rural population decline was checked (but not completely halted) during the Second World War and the years which followed by the wartime stimulus to the rural economy and by the generous level of agricultural subsidies in the post-war years, which reflected the general need in the United Kingdom to replace food imports by increased home production during this period. Again, as in the Republic, east–west contrasts in rural population decline were noticeable, since in the east the restoration of prosperity to Belfast and its hinterland during and after the war brought new sources of employment to commuters from the countryside as well as to urban residents.

Emigration was also a repetitive feature of life, although the published emigration statistics are virtually useless in that they do not include migration to Britain. However, a comparison of natural increase with actual population change shows a net average loss by emigration of about 5000 per year between 1926 and 1951, less marked than in the Republic, but nevertheless a significant feature of life. Rates of natural increase were somewhat higher than in the Republic during this period, supported by a higher overall birth rate and a slightly lower death rate. Given the religious contrasts it is not surprising that fertility was lower in Northern Ireland (in 1951 an average of 186 births per 1000 married women aged under 45, compared with 270 in the Republic), but this was more than off-set by a higher frequency of marriage, which made an important contribution to a higher overall birth rate.

Population change in the Irish Republic after 1961

In the Republic of Ireland the next decade brought a check to the sharp population decline of the 1950s, partly a response to changes in government economic policy, a matter which must be returned to in a later chapter. Yet internal contrasts remained, with rural districts in the north-west still experiencing substantial population decline. Industrial policies evolved which were concerned with spreading new jobs to all major regions of the Republic, if not to every local district. In the 1970s growth was recorded in every planning region: just over 5 per cent in the North-West region, centred on Sligo, but at least 10 per cent in all other regions, and indeed over 21 per cent in the East region, centred on Dublin. (For a map of regions see Figure 10.3 on page 153.) This remarkable increase was fuelled by the return of earlier emigrants, and produced a gain of population by net immigration, an unprecedented event in Ireland. Natural increase was also noticeably higher, largely because reduced out-migration meant that more potential parents were retained in the population as a whole. There were still rural districts which were experiencing population decline, for example in the south-western peninsulas and in parts of Connacht, but in many areas elsewhere even rural depopulation appeared to have been reversed (Horner and Daultry, 1980).

This altered pattern of population change was remarkable because of the previous history of the Irish population, but it also proved to be short-lived. In the 1980s the previous condition of population decline reasserted itself, based on renewed levels of net emigration and lower levels of natural increase (Cawley, 1991). From 1981 to 1986 population increase continued (a growth of 2.8 per cent), but between 1986 and 1991 decline re-established itself and probably still continues, so that for the full decade the increase was only 2.3 per cent (80,000 people), giving a total population of 3.52 millions in 1991 (Figure 6.2). In the late 1980s, in contrast with the 1970s, the pattern was again one of widespread population decline, except in the immediate hinterlands of the largest urban areas (Walsh, 1991). In relation to what occurred earlier this recent fall in the total population has been relatively small, although a recovery of the British economy from recession would be likely to sharpen the rate of decline in Ireland.

A number of factors are involved in the changed situation of the late 1980s. As in the past, renewed emigration had made a contribution by the selective removal of more young adults from the population, but an emerging feature in the 1980s has been the first real signs of a decline in fertility as a result of social changes, rather than being caused by population structure. To start with, the number of marriages in the Republic of Ireland has been dropping over the last two decades, from 21,000 in the 1970s to under 16,859 in 1991 – giving a rate of 4.8 per 1000, one of the lowest in Europe – and, in turn, pushing the birth rate down, in spite of the fact that the number of births taking place outside marriage more than doubled between 1981 and 1991 and has now reached a level of over 16 per cent. But the decline in fertility is also taking place as a result of a reduction in family size, a belated response to social and economic pressures

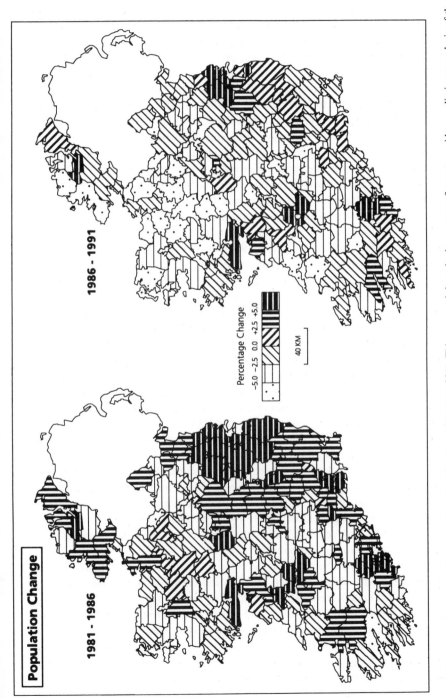

Figure 6.2 Population change, Irish Republic, 1981–91 (Source: Walsh, 1991). This map, and those in the next two figures, provide a preliminary analysis of the findings of the 1991 census of the Republic of Ireland by James Walsh.

which have been operating much earlier in other countries. In particular these underlying forces involve the gradual adoption of new mores concerning birth control and the appropriateness of married women taking paid employment.

The first hints of this change could be observed in the late 1960s but its impact as a significant demographic force has been very recent. Starting about 1980 the fertility of the population has declined by nearly one-third, from 21 births per 1000 of the total population in 1980 to 15 in 1991. Converted into actual births this has involved a reduction from 74,400 in 1980 to 52,690 in 1991. Although suburban areas still show relatively high birth rates because of the greater number of young couples in their populations, the greatest reductions in birth rate have been in the most urbanized counties of the Republic, no doubt reflecting the manner in which the underlying social changes are being diffused. The reduction in the birth rate has been much sharper than that of the death rate, which has fallen from about 9.4 per 1000 in 1980 to 8.9 in 1990.

As a result the annual average rates of natural increase per 1000 have dropped sharply, from 11.3 between 1971 and 1981 to 6.8 between 1986 and 1991. In the 1980s the contrasts between regions have been greatly reduced (Figure 6.3). Previously, urban birth rates had been higher than in the countryside because of more youthful age structures and a higher frequency of marriage, but now the contrast is becoming less marked because fertility in the larger urban areas has been reduced by falling marriage rates and smaller family sizes. When measured by the crude birth rate these potentially important changes are hidden by regional contrasts produced by the structure of the population. The highest figures were in the expanding suburbs of Dublin, although county Dublin as a whole merely had a rate of 15.7 per 1000 (the national average). The lowest rates, as in the past, were in western counties, the result of an elderly population because of continued out-migration and with rates of about 14 per 1000.

In spite of this drop in fertility, at the broad regional scale nowhere in Ireland has yet experienced natural decrease; and at the county level such a decline has been recorded only in Leitrim, where for the first time between 1985 and 1991 a very slight fall in population was caused by this mechanism. As a result the population decline of the late 1980s was ultimately a product of a renewal of higher levels of net emigration (Figure 6.4). Unemployment grew sharply from 88,000 in 1979 to over 280,000 in the summer of 1992, providing a clear outward stimulus for population movement.

Traditional ideas of the nature of the emigrants must be revised. Some are still unskilled and semi-skilled workers from a rural background, which is the never completely accurate stereotype which has been freely applied to Irish emigrants; many now come from urban areas and often obtain informal employment, for example in the construction industry, not just in Britain but as far afield as New York. To these must now be added a considerable number of emigrants who are skilled workers; and a notable feature of recent out-migration has been the large number of graduates involved. It remains to be seen whether these valuable workers will eventually return to Ireland or whether, more likely, they will be lost for ever from the Irish labour market.

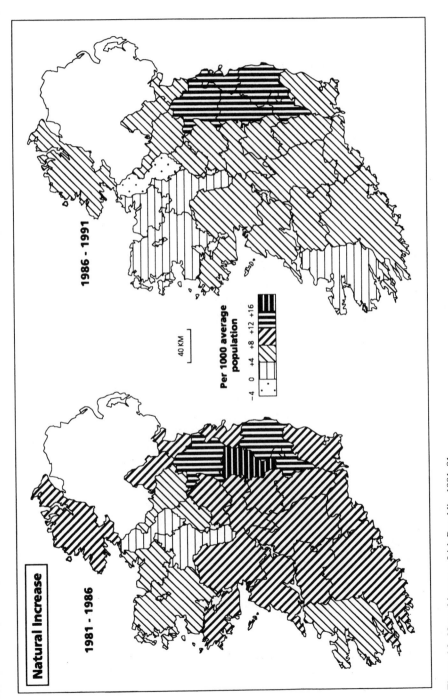

Figure 6.3 Natural increase, Irish Republic, 1981—91.

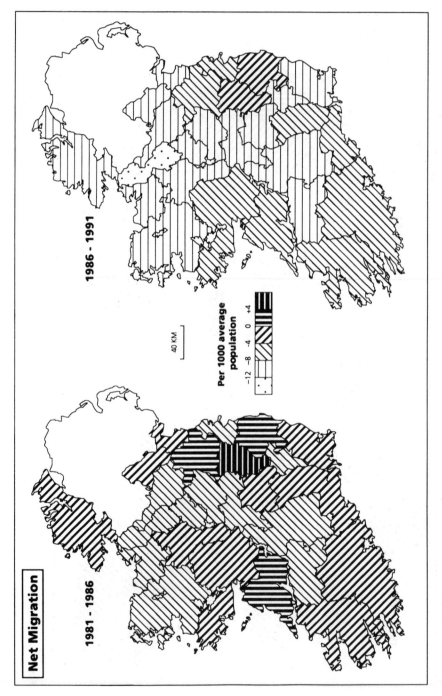

Figure 6.4 Net migration, Irish Republic, 1981–91.

At a time when confusing signals about the future population of the Republic have been given by changes in the last few decades it is difficult to assess the broader implications of total population numbers. The small domestic market has often been seen as a disadvantage to the Irish economy, but it is difficult to postulate a population increase of a size which would make any real difference to the strength of the domestic market for goods and services. In any case, such concerns may be much less relevant now that the European Community can increasingly be viewed as a potential 'home' market. Indeed, if return migration is simply a response to economic adversity elsewhere, the resulting population growth would prove a grave embarrassment, unless sustainable economic expansion could also be created to provide an acceptable standard of living and to support appropriate levels of public services for the enlarged population – a somewhat unlikely development at times when overseas economies are in recession.

Population in Northern Ireland after 1961

The increase in the population of Northern Ireland continued for another decade after 1961, but then levelled out at just over 1.5 million. Previously high natural increase had generally exceeded losses through emigration, but between 1971 and 1981 net outward movement increased sharply from 4.2 per 1000 in the previous decade to 7.1, stimulated by civil disturbances, particularly in the early 1970s, and by a stagnant local economy. At the same time natural increase dropped from 10.1 per 1000 in 1971 to 6.9 in 1981, thus producing a slight fall in total population. In the early 1980s net migration returned to earlier levels, no doubt checked by rising unemployment in Britain, and although natural increase remained stable at the new lower level it produced a slight increase in total population. As a result in the past two decades it can be said that the total population of Northern Ireland has been virtually stable, although contrasts exist in levels of local population change (Figure 6.5).

Net migration produced a loss of population in most districts of Northern Ireland, particularly, but not exclusively, in those which lay to the west of Lough Neagh. The only districts to experience substantial in-migration during this decade were those located around the outer fringe of Belfast, although the city itself had the largest absolute loss of population because of migration. In large measure what was involved here was essentially local urban redistribution of population, to be discussed elsewhere, although the process was exaggerated by the special public safety problems which Belfast was experiencing.

At the same time other processes were going on, superimposed on the loss of population by out-migration. Looking at population at a more detailed scale, quite a number of non-urban electoral wards experienced population growth during this decade; and also the population of smaller urban areas outside the immediate zones of influence of Belfast and Derry City showed population growth. It has been suggested by Aileen Stockdale (1991) that this may have

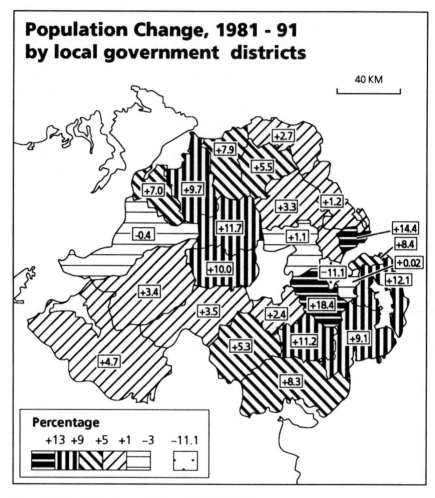

Figure 6.5 Population change, Northern Ireland, 1981–91

been an expression of the process of counterurbanization, which was rather generally found in western Europe and north America during the 1970s and 1980s, by which former rural depopulation was replaced by population increase. There are two qualifications to make. These local increases were set in a context of net loss by migration, so that natural increase was the underlying factor in producing this result. It should also be observed that the numbers of people involved were relatively small: in 47 per cent of the wards showing an increase the actual number involved was less than 50. As a result it is much too early to see these local expressions of population increase at some distance from the two major urban areas of Northern Ireland as anything more than a temporary blip.

A further, and potentially important process is the continued fall in the birth rate in Northern Ireland, which was reduced from 22.4 births per 1000 people in

1961, to 20.7 in 1971, 17.8 in 1981 and 16.7 in 1990. These statistics mask fertility differences between the Catholic and Protestant population of the province, which remain sharp. As in the Republic of Ireland there has been a reduction in Catholic family sizes, but this has been offset by quite a sharp rise in marriage rates over the last couple of decades. As a result Paul Compton's estimates show a noticeable decline in Protestant fertility during the 1970s but little overall decline in the Catholic birth rate. His estimate for 1980 (which, as he points out, must be treated with caution) was a birth rate for Roman Catholics of 24.1 per 1000 and 15.4 per 1000 for non-Catholics (Compton, 1986, table 2.8). The net result of this, converted into actual births, was that the number of 'Catholic' births roughly equalled the number of 'Protestant' births. This hides the fact that Catholic family sizes have been declining gradually since 1950 and much more sharply in recent decades; what has been happening is that rising marriage rates among Catholics have offset falls in family size. Since 1980 overall fertility in Northern Ireland has declined somewhat further and it may be guessed that the Catholic birth rate has been drifting downwards in the last decade, although further research when the full details of the 1991 census are published will be needed to resolve that issue.

Convergence between Northern Ireland and the Republic

The overall effect in the twentieth century of the factors producing population change in Northern Ireland was a rise rather than a fall in total population; but the contrast with the Irish Republic should not be overstressed. The growth of a dominant city, uneven rural depopulation, continued emigration and relatively high levels of natural increase by west European standards are now long-standing features common to both Northern Ireland and the Republic of Ireland.

Indeed, as the years have gone by, greater similarities in the population geography of the Northern Ireland and the Republic have emerged. For example, in 1926, shortly after the beginning of its independent existence, the Irish Republic could still be described as a predominantly rural state by European standards, with only 32 per cent of its population living in settlements of 1500 people and over. Dublin had certainly grown briskly from 1901 to 1926, but even then only represented just over 13 per cent of the Irish population in 1926. The census statistics do not allow a precise comparison, but in 1926 nearly 51 per cent of the total population of Northern Ireland was classified as urban and 33 per cent of the population lived in Belfast and thus participated in the life of a major city.

During the twentieth century the Republic and Northern Ireland have gone through contrasting economic experiences, but recent employment growth in the Republic has been urban-centred. At the same time in Northern Ireland a check to urban growth has been provided by the now quite long-standing decline in its industrial base. As as result, by 1971 over 52 per cent of the population of the Republic was classified as urban, not far removed from the 55 per cent by then recorded in Northern Ireland. By 1981 the urban population of the Republic had risen further to 55.6 per cent of the population; and although alterations in the method of handling urban populations in the Northern Ireland census makes a direct comparison impossible, it is likely that by this date the level of urbanization was very similar in the two areas. That increased level of urbanization is also reflected in the increased dominance of the Dublin region, giving another example of convergence. Unlike the situation in the 1920s, by 1981 Greater Dublin contained 29.1 per cent of the population of the Republic and at the same date Belfast's built-up area contained 34 per cent of the population of Northern Ireland. When the detailed results of the 1991 census are available it is likely that these two figures will be even closer.

Fertility also shows some parallels, although interpretation is difficult because of religious differences. The signs of a recent reduction both North and South have already been observed. There is little doubt that this change will be of great potential social and political importance, but at present the reductions in fertility which have so far occurred in Northern Ireland and the Irish Republic are still low by international standards and represent an early stage in the process. As a result of high fertility in the past, both countries have a relatively large number of young people in their populations. This is the major factor producing a high dependency ratio – that is, the proportion of the population too young or too old to form part of the workforce – which reaches 72 per cent in the Republic and 61 per cent in Northern Ireland (in comparison with the 54 per cent found in France and in Great Britain). They also face the common problem of accommodating (or, to be more accurate, failing to accommodate) relatively large flows of young people into the labour force.

Clearly connected with this are the high levels of emigration which the two parts of Ireland have experienced. In the 1970s the net loss in the Republic was much less than in Northern Ireland (reversing the usual situation and reflecting high government spending on employment generation in the Republic and civil unrest in Northern Ireland). In the 1980s, however, emigration levels were remarkably similar. Northern Ireland, as well as the Republic, lost two types of emigrants: unskilled manual workers, but also more highly educated workers. From the point of view of politicians and civil servants, high levels of net emigration may be taken to signify a failure in their job creation policies, although in the longer run the process does at least serve to hold down unemployment levels.

From the individual point of view the position is less clear-cut. There are unquantifiable social costs involved as a result of the selective removal of young adults from the home population. This has produced problems which are particularly visible in the social life of rural areas, although it is not clear what feasible policies in the modern world could reverse the flow of surplus population from the more purely agricultural areas, as those who are not going to inherit a farm seek an acceptable standard of living elsewhere. However, with Britain being the principal destination for emigrants and with the emergence of rapid and cheaper air transport, the separation of emigrants from their original homes and their kith and kin is far from being as complete (and not necessarily as permanent) as in the past. Individual emigrants are following a long-established tradition and almost certainly achieve a higher material standard of living than they could hope for at home. The loss to Ireland of those who have received higher education represents a probable waste of national investment in advanced training, although at least in the case of Northern Ireland young people educated by United Kingdom expenditure largely end up elsewhere in Britain.

More generally, it is impossible to establish whether those who are left behind are on average less enterprising, less skillful, less intelligent, less radical and less innovative than those who have gone. Such views have been asserted, although a cynic might observe that they represent an interpretation more favoured by commentators who have themselves emigrated than by those who have stayed in Ireland.

Distribution of rural deprivation

Studies of population change often fail to convey a real feeling of life as it is lived, but underlying differential population movements is the existence of variable opportunities for living a good life. Almost inevitably modern studies of levels of living are circumscribed by a necessary reliance on quantitative data about various aspects of the human condition, which are then compressed by sophisticated statistical techniques to give an overall summary of the quality of life. It is certainly possible to summarize such features as the availability of piped water and electricity, of accessibility to schools and doctors, of the existence of unemployment and low pay, and of the proportion of elderly people in the population. Such information gives one important materialistic dimension of life, but it suffers from disadvantages as well. For one thing these studies must use administrative units of some kind as their basis, a process which masks local variations and, in particular, implies wrongly that average conditions apply to everyone who lives in a particular area. More fundamentally, they cannot hope to capture the qualities associated with a rich or impoverished social life, a magnificent or a degraded landscape, the presence of seclusion or an absence of privacy, pressure to meet deadlines or a lack of urgency in daily matters. The evaluation of these intangibles is more a matter of individual psychology, although certainly shaped by more general characteristics like age, class and education. The result is that far from everyone in areas defined as offering bad conditions view their daily lives as being deprived.

Given these reservations it is also true that the human problems of the more rural areas in Ireland, North and South, have exercised the minds of politicians and planners over the years and that there has been a concern with studying the distribution of deprivation. The results of these studies reflect the regional pattern of population decline (Figure 6.6). In Northern Ireland a broad east–west division has been revealed, with the most favourable living conditions being found within 20 miles of Belfast, with the worst being found west of Lough

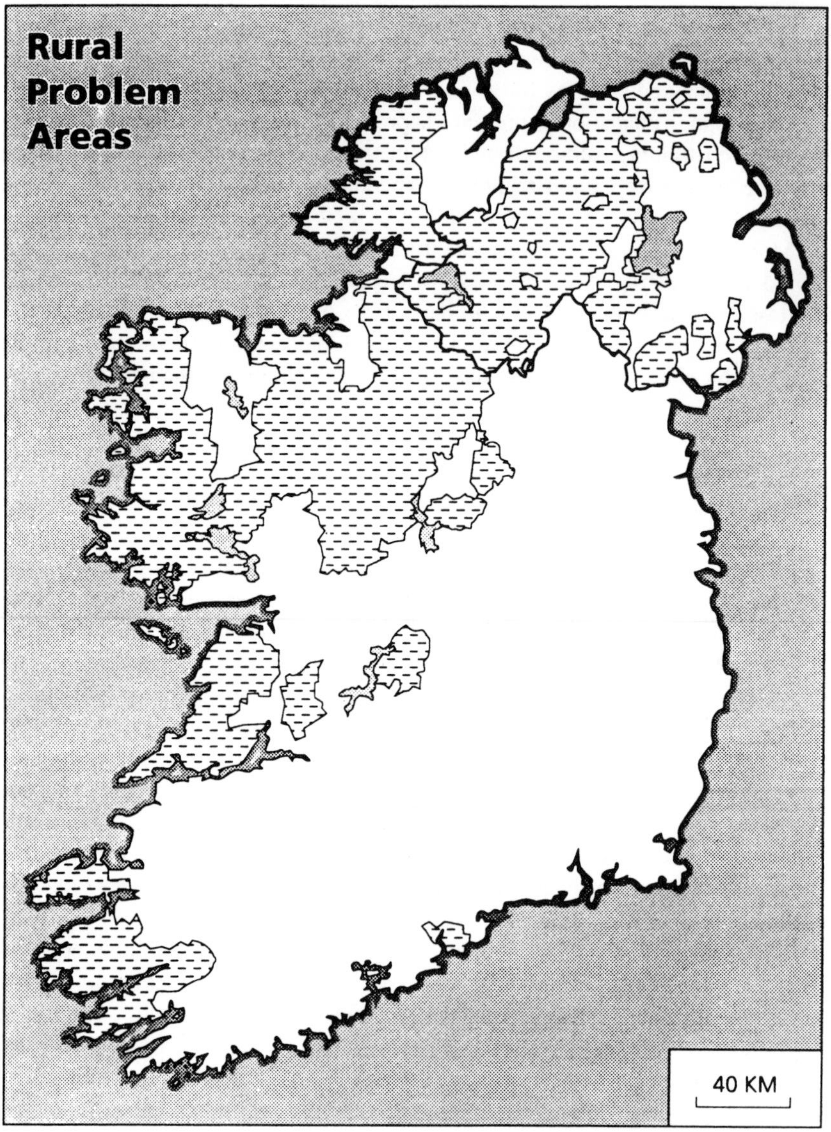

Figure 6.6 Rural problem areas. This map, compiled by Mary Cawley, is based on a statistical analysis of census information. In the Irish Republic areas of greatest rural deprivation combined contemporary population decline, low densities, above average numbers of elderly people, and a long history of out-migration. They also had poorer than average housing and below average levels of car ownership (Cawley, 1986). Similar characteristics were found in Northern Ireland (Armstrong *et al.*, 1980).

Neagh, in south Down and in parts of north Antrim. In the areas of worst conditions urban areas emerge as islands of superior conditions, but within Belfast the inner city and parts of west Belfast exhibited low living conditions (Goodyear and Eastwood, 1978). The Republic of Ireland shows a similar pattern, with areas in the west and north-west constituting rural problem areas, when assessed by their social and economic characteristics. Areas on the west coast stretching from Donegal to west Cork, and an inland belt stretching east from Mayo along the zone of small farms into Roscommon, Leitrim and Longford, emerge as regions of difficulty (Cawley, 1986). This is not surprising because these areas lack alternative urban centres for the employment of a surplus rural population and also because of their degraded social structures, produced by generation after generation of out-migration. This pattern also reflects the problems that undercapitalized small farmers increasingly find in achieving an acceptable standard of living, particularly in areas of environmental difficulty.

Further reading

P. Compton presents the 1971 information for Northern Ireland in *Northern Ireland: a Census Atlas* (Gill and Macmillan, Dublin, 1978). A. Horner, J.A. Walsh and V.P. Harrington, *Population in Ireland: a Census Atlas* (University College, Dublin, 1987) provides a similar, but more recent perspective for the Irish Republic. Maps of population change and further details of the processes involved during this critical period are in J.H. Johnson, 'Population changes in Ireland, 1951–1961', *Geographical Journal* 129 (1963), 167–74. P. Compton provides a summary of the demographic situation in Northern Ireland in *Demographic Trends in Northern Ireland* (Northern Ireland Economic Development Office, Report no. 57, Belfast, 1986). Rural population change as shown in the 1981 censuses is summarized in A. Horner, 'Rural population change in Ireland', in P. Breathnach and M. Cawley (eds), *Change and Development in Rural Ireland* (Geographical Society of Ireland, Special Publication 1, Maynooth, 1986), 34–47. A recent survey of various aspects of contemporary migration in Ireland is R. King (ed.), *Geographical Perspectives on Contemporary Irish Migration* (Geographical Society of Ireland, Special Publication 6, Dublin, 1991). Areas of rural disadvantage are described in M. Cawley, 'Problems of rural Ireland', in R. Carter and A.L. Parker (eds), *Ireland: a Contemporary Geographical Perspective* (Routledge, London, 1989), 145–70.

Chapter 7

The urban pattern

The origin of Irish towns

It has been suggested that the first stirrings of urban life in Ireland were associated with Celtic monastic sites (Butlin, 1977), although there are a number of
difficulties with this idea. One is a problem in classification: was the range
of non-agricultural activities associated with Celtic monasteries sufficient to
allow the term 'urban' to be applies to these settlements? Certainly these monasteries provided a focus for the social and economic organization of the countryside immediately about them – one index of an urban settlement. Their size and
range, however, were small and their functions restricted, so that it would be
more sensible to classify these settlements as being, at best, proto-urban, rather
than fully-fledged towns. A second difficulty is that when one looks at the
scatter of small towns which are spread over the modern Irish landscape only a
very small number can firmly trace their roots back to Gaelic-ecclesiastical sites.
Tuam in county Galway may be one and Kells in Meath another, but there the
list essentially ends. Finally, even in these cases there must be doubt about
whether there was continuity between these ecclesiastical settlements and the
unambiguous towns which eventually followed them: their sites may have
continued to have significance, but the establishment of continuous urban life in
these locations may well have been an independent development.

Continuous urban settlement is more likely in the case of Norse seaports like
Dublin, Wexford, Waterford, Limerick and Cork, although again the term 'proto-
urban' may be the appropriate label to place on these harbour settlements. It was
the coming of the Anglo-Normans in 1169 which unequivocally introduced
urban life into Ireland, as an integral part of the process of colonization (Figure
7.1). The Anglo-Normans formed alliances and intermarried with the Gaelic
population, so that some of that urbanizing influence spread more widely into settlements with Gaelic origins. A further wave of urban foundations accompanied
the process of colonization in the Tudor and Stuart times during the sixteenth and
seventeenth centuries, often associated with various so-called plantations. Such
towns were widespread, but the best known group was that associated with the

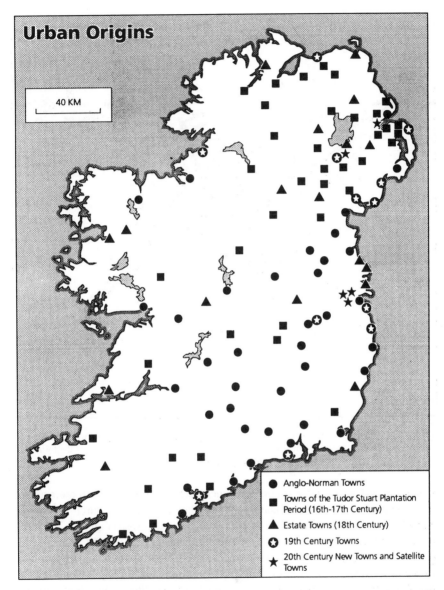

Urban Origins

40 KM

● Anglo-Norman Towns

■ Towns of the Tudor Stuart Plantation
Period (16th-17th Century)

▲ Estate Towns (18th Century)

✪ 19th Century Towns

★ 20th Century New Towns and Satellite
Towns

Figure 7.1 Periods of urban foundation. Some of the towns shown on this map were preceded by what might be called proto-towns, like Viking ports or Celtic ecclesiatical settlements. Establishing continuity poses difficulties and this map, simplified from a much more complex original by Anngrit Simms (1979), merely picks out the periods from which continuous urban settlement indisputably took place.

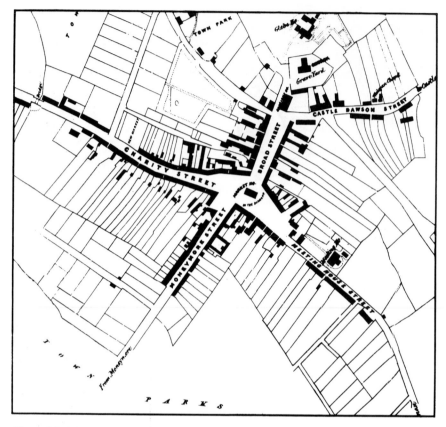

Figure 7.2 Magherafelt, Londonderry, 1837. The map is an extract from a map printed for the Salters' Company of London, which was the local landlord of the time, and illustrates the form of a typical plantation town before being modified by modern developments.

Plantation of Ulster whose origin and functions are still reflected in their urban plans, centred on the market square, with the Church of Ireland church at one end and a Presbyterian meeting house usually incorporated as well (Figure 7.2). Later, in the eighteenth century, when landlords had the prosperity and incentive to develop their estates, that process also involved them in founding towns, like Listowel in Kerry or Michelstown in Cork, and in redeveloping existing towns, like Cookstown in Tyrone. During the nineteenth century some coastal towns were founded: for example, Portstewart in county Londonderry was developed as a seaside resort and Donaghadee in county Down grew around a new harbour which offered a short sea-crossing by steamship to Port Patrick in Scotland and was seen as a potential outport for Belfast, although it did not succeed in retaining that role. The substantial reshaping of the urban map of Ireland in the nineteenth century, however, was not produced by the foundation of new towns but by the considerable industrial expansion of a group of small towns in the north-east, the extremely rapid growth of Belfast and the more ponderous expansion of Dublin.

The dates of foundation varied, but the different periods of urban building implied by these various urban origins were usually combined in the plans of most towns. Kells, for example, still bears the marks of various periods of urban growth (Simms and Simms, 1990). It was the site of a major monastery in early medieval times; and the Anglo-Normans developed the town in the late twelfth century when it became an expression of the western expansion of feudal power with the pattern of landholding by burgesses found elsewhere in western Europe. In the eighteenth century Kells flourished as a landlord town with pleasant eighteenth-century houses being added to its townscape. In the second half of the nineteenth century its role as a service centre suffered as the surrounding rural population declined in numbers and as local traditional industries like brewing and tanning found it difficult to compete with larger units of production elsewhere. However growth was re-established in the second half of the twentieth century, with new residential building reflecting its location within 30 miles of Dublin. At least some parts of this sequence of development are repeated in the form of most Irish towns.

The urban hierarchy

Outside the realms of speculation, there is an inevitable problem in recognizing the existence of a genuine urban hierarchy, in which towns and cities fall into clearly defined size groups. This is because, even in a relatively simple example like Ireland, there are frequently other urban-sustaining functions which are less logically distributed than the provision of services (which might in theory be expected to produce a hierarchical arrangement of urban sizes). In any case the uneven distribution of population for environmental and historical reasons complicates the recognition of an urban hierarchy in the real world.

Yet, provided it is not taken too literally, it is convenient to examine the spatial scatter of Irish towns as a hierarchy of settlements of different sizes (Figure 7.3). Although modern industrial development has encouraged the population growth of the larger settlements, the main determinant of the essential differences between most towns has been the range of services which they offer. Dublin and Belfast are, of course, completely pre-eminent and they must be returned to in the next chapter. Below them in the urban hierarchy it is more difficult to distinguish between the services provided by Irish towns, but the next four most important towns, much smaller than the two primate cities but clearly differentiated from other urban settlements in Ireland, are Derry in Northern Ireland and three county boroughs in the Republic of Ireland: Cork, Limerick, and Galway.

These urban settlements have a number of things in common. The first and most obvious is the very clear break in size between them and Dublin and Belfast. Second, they are all located relatively far away from the two largest cities. As a result they draw advantage from not being in immediate competition with them and as a result they are able to support some regional functions which

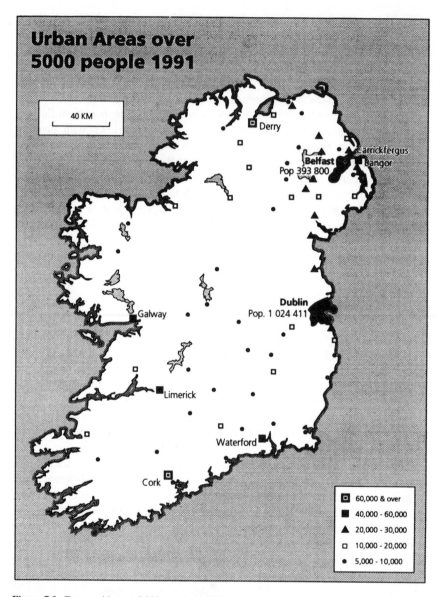

Figure 7.3 Towns with over 5,000 people in 1991

would not be viable closer to such dominant competitors. Finally, these cities are all ports, a role which may have been more important in the later nineteenth century, but which still gives them an additional urban-building function over other settlements.

In 1991 Cork, the second largest city in the Republic, had only about 127,000 people according to the census of that year. This shows a slight reduction from

Photo 12 St Patrick's Hill, Cork City. Cork is the third largest city in Ireland, although the gap in size between it and Dublin and Belfast is considerable. Although a medieval city, nothing of note has survived. A few elegant private houses date from the eighteenth century, but most notable buildings are of nineteenth-century origin. The picture captures some of the traffic problem of central Cork and looks across part of the central shopping area. (Courtesy of Bord Failte)

the 133,000 recorded in 1986, but almost certainly reflects redistribution of population to the commuting zone outside the city, rather than an actual fall, and does not include the population living outside the formal city boundaries, a figure which was not available at the time of writing. In spite of these qualifications it remains a small city by standards elsewhere, but large enough to make it quite clearly the third largest urban area in all Ireland and to have given its citizens an independent turn of mind and a reputation for commercial acumen. With its University College, established in 1845, and other advanced educational facilities, with the best shopping centre in the Republic outside Dublin, with its long-standing port activities with trade connections with south-west England and France, and its regional airport with services to Britain and elsewhere in Europe as well as to Dublin and Shannon, Cork should enjoy considerable potential advantages for economic growth, reflected in its expansion from a city of about 78,000 people in 1926. This economic success is not a new feature: nineteenth-century prosperity was associated with its famous passenger services by steamship to North America, its role for the dairying industry dating from the eighteenth century and earlier, its supply services for ships, and its local agri-culturally based industries (for example, in brewing and distilling) which, unlike those found in many small towns in Ireland, managed to survive throughout the nineteenth century. During the regime of economic protection in the 1930s and 1940s the availability of industrial land close to deep water was attractive for port-related industrial development including a heavy steel mill, which still survives, a motor car assembly plant and a tyre factory, both now defunct.

New industries supplemented these protected activities in the 1960s, and in the late 1970s Cork still possessed the largest concentration of heavy industry in the Republic, in particular chemical industries which exploited its deep-water port. Unfortunately, in the economic upheavals of the past 15 years many of the manufacturing industries of Cork have declined: some non-central industries were extinguished, like the Dunlop tyre factory and the Ford car assembly plant; but the most dramatic decline was in central Cork, where from 1977 to 1986 almost half of the manufacturing industries have been lost. Eighty per cent of this loss was the result of complete closures rather than relocation in new suburban plants (Hourihan and Spillane, 1989); but this decline should not be allowed to mask the fact that new activities have colonized 69 per cent of the better vacant industrial premises. Part of the change has involved replacement by new indus-trial activities, although most of the replacement has come in the form of tertiary activities, with retailing occupying 27 per cent of the vacant premises and offices 14 per cent. Unfortunately, it seems likely that Cork, in competition with Dublin, is simply not large enough or possesses insufficient national accessibility to attract substantial amounts of new office employment, the growing sector in so many national economies. It has to be said that local pessimism has replaced the considerable optimism which abounded in the 1960s, partly as a result of a phase of government policy which made an explicit attempt to spread economic devel-opment away from the locations where it might be expected to take root most easily. There are signs that high levels of unemployment everywhere in Ireland are leading to the demise of that policy and, in the longer term, Cork has inherent advantages which will surely support its economic position as the second city in the Republic.

Derry, the second urban settlement in Northern Ireland and the fourth largest in Ireland, had 72,334 people in 1991. Like Cork, Derry's nineteenth-century commodity and passenger trade (in this case with North America and with Scotland) produced growth when the population of many other small Irish urban areas was static. Derry was a settlement of just over 15,000 people in 1841 and had passed 39,000 in 1901. At the same time it succeeded in developing a shirt industry, which tapped the British market, acting first as an organizing centre for a domestic industry, and later providing the location for shirt factories. This industry provided work for women in particular – although traditionally it was a poorly paid occupation and is now suffering from overseas competition.

The development of the city has been restricted in the twentieth century by the partial loss of part of its zone of influence in Donegal by the creation of the Irish border, although the responsibilities of EC membership, which involve the removal of trade barriers at national frontiers of member states, have been lessening that handicap and are likely to remove it completely in the future. More of a problem has been the strong sectarian split in the city, which may well have reduced its appeal for new industrial employers, although the location of Derry away from eastern Ulster, where there is a greater concentration of the factors which are likely to attract modern industries, is probably of even greater significance, particularly in the context of the various economic recessions since the mid-1970s which have had a particularly adverse affect on employment in the city.

Limerick (with a population of 52,040 in 1991) has long dominated its local region. It still operates as a port – a role which it has had since its original Norse foundation – although its port activities are now relatively less important than they were in the nineteenth century. Its industrial activities are often associated with agriculture including bacon curing, grain milling and the manufacture of milk products and leather. Other activities were stimulated by economic protection in the 1930s and 1940s, like the manufacture of clothing and cement. Limerick's significance as a market centre was ensured by the bridging of the Shannon here in Norman times, widening its sphere of influence. Around its medieval core considerable elegant residential growth took place in the later eighteenth century, when agriculture in its hinterland prospered. In recent years Limerick has grown because of its close association with developments at Shannon Airport. Far enough away from Dublin to prosper, it is an active commercial town, its cathedral indicates its organizational role in a non-commercial sphere and its growing importance as an educational centre has been indicated by the creation of the National Institute for Higher Education in 1970, which was designated the University of Limerick in 1989. Limerick has been one of the most rapidly growing of the urban settlements in the Republic outside Dublin – its population was less than 40,000 in 1926 – but in spite of its advantages it appears that, like Cork, it cannot rival Dublin in attracting the highest levels of business management and the most specialized service activities, since its lacks the critical mass that would make developments of this kind possible.

Galway (with a population of 50,842 in 1991) is smaller still, but it also is a regional capital – 'the key to West Connacht' in T.W. Freeman's (1957) phrase – although in fact it probably does more business with the more prosperous agricultural area to the east. A Norman foundation and a port since medieval times, but with a relatively impoverished hinterland, Galway ended the nineteenth century with a population of only just over 13,000, in comparison with 20,000 in 1851, reflecting its role as a centre for a sharply declining rural population, without any other important secondary activities. Since Irish independence its population has steadily expanded, from just over 14,000 in 1926 to over 29,000 in 1971; and even more remarkable is its growth by 73 per cent over two decades to reach its present population. Partly this is an expression of the widening range of government and other services operated from this urban centre, a role which is enhanced by the fact that it has little or no competition from nearby urban areas. Its new cathedral, dedicated in 1962, and its University College – founded in 1849, but growing substantially in recent years (and now with over 5600 students) – and its regional hospital reflect the most specialized of these non-commercial activities. Its shopping centre seems large for the size of the settlement and indicates the continuing importance of its commercial role for the region and the impact of tourist shopping in the summer months. In recent years the establishment of a successful industrial estate is the local expression of the substantial growth of the manufacturing sector in Ireland since the 1950s and of government encouragement for the dispersal of a proper share of that growth to the west of Ireland.

Waterford (with a population of 40,345 in 1991) is only slightly smaller than Galway. It has been successful in attracting industrial development, and its current activity as a port is more important because of its location in eastern Ireland, giving more direct access to Britain. Again it has benefited because of the range of regional government services, like the regional technical college which has been located there, but to the visitor it appears to have more in common with a group of port towns, which form most of the next level in the urban hierarchy of the Irish Republic.

These port towns include Dundalk (with a population of 30,160 in 1991, including the population living outside its legal boundaries) and Drogheda (23,914), both also with nineteenth century industrial development (partly an expression of general industrial growth in the north-east) and with a disproportionate share of the increase in manufacturing employment associated with economic protection in the first half of the twentieth century. Smaller still, but with an impressive range of functions in comparison with many towns of a similar size elsewhere in western Europe are Tralee (17,206), Sligo (17,297) and Wexford (9537). In Northern Ireland Newry (21,633 people in 1991) might be thought of as a similar type of town, with formerly quite important port and industrial functions in the nineteenth century, now largely defunct. It now acts as

Photo 13 River frontage of Waterford City. All the large urban settlements of Ireland are ports. Waterford is on the tideway of the Suir. In addition to its function as a port and as an urban market centre Waterford has added the production of pharmaceuticals, optical goods and electronics to longer-established manufacturing industries like glass-making, meat processing and brewing. (Courtesy of Bord Failte)

a regional centre for south Down and Armagh and, even more than Enniskillen, Omagh and Derry, it is at present attracting considerable retail trade across the Irish border because of cheaper prices in Northern Ireland (although this may probably be a temporary advantage).

Also in this order of size are a group of towns in Northern Ireland, associated in particular with the lower Lagan valley and the area to the south of Lough Neagh. This concentration reflects the growth of industrial population in north-east Ireland in the nineteenth century; but manufacturing industry is now less important, although Portadown (21,299) and Lurgan (21,905), linked with the new town of Craigavon (9201), have gained population as a result of planning initiatives (though much less than was hoped for). Some towns, like Newtownabbey (56,811), Lisburn (42,110), Carrickfergus (22,786), Bangor (52,437), Newtownards (56,811) and Larne (17,575), largely function as part of the Belfast city region, broadly conceived. Ballymena (28,112) lies on the northern fringe of the journey-to-work area based on Belfast. With a sturdy independence born of industrial success in the nineteenth century and a reputation for business acumen, which is reflected in commercial and retailing

Photo 14 Part of the Town of Kilkenny. Although it is one of the largest inland towns of the Irish Republic, Kilkenny has only a population of just over 8,500 people. An urban settlement of long-standing, it was one of the principal meeting places of Anglo-Irish parliaments in the Middle Ages. Now its principal function is that of a market town, located about 73 miles from Dublin. (Courtesy of Bord Failte)

activities which seem extensive for the size of the town, it has become the largest settlement in the lower Bann valley. Others like Omagh (17,280), Coleraine (now with a new university and a total population of 20,721 people) and Armagh (14,265) function as market towns and local regional centres. The end result is that by one calculation ten of the top ranking fifteen towns in Ireland, measured by their range of functions, are located in Northern Ireland (Forbes, 1970).

Lower level towns are more evenly spread, although they are larger and more frequent in the agriculturally more prosperous south-east and generally smaller and further apart in the West. It is only in the agriculturally more prosperous south-east, for example, that Kilkenny (8513) could become the largest inland town in the Republic, without navigable access by water but on the main road from Dublin to Cork. Towns in the north-west with similar functions are characteristically much smaller: for example, Castlebar in Mayo could only attain a population of 6071.

The smaller inland towns have traditionally provided the day-to-day services which in some other parts of Europe might be provided by villages, but they also offer more clearly defined urban services like banks and larger shops which would be visited rather less frequently. Generally speaking the smaller towns (except in the ambit of Dublin) have had stable or even declining populations; and larger towns exhibited slow but unspectacular growth, generally because they had some industrial enterprises to add to their service function. It has been suggested that the Irish pattern of a primate city, a number of larger port towns, and small service centres (which provide a path for the export of agricultural products and whose size and density reflect local agricultural productivity) is an arrangement which has been produced by the colonial status of Ireland (Huff and Lutz, 1979), although Belfast and the urban cluster in north-east Ireland obviously do not fit very neatly into that interpretation.

Some changes to the urban pattern

The influence of the pre-existing pattern continued after political independence. Even in the period of economic protection in the 1930s and 1940s the urban settlements which benefited most were the larger port towns. As there was no effective government policy steering industrial location to the smaller towns, these ports had substantial advantages because of the larger pool of labour which they had available and because of their accessibility, even in a situation in which manufacturing was largely catering for a protected home market.

Since the 1960s, with the development of a much more wholehearted government policy of encouraging economic growth, a parallel policy has evolved of distributing the benefits of economic growth as widely around the country as possible. Yet even with a clear perception of a need to steer development to a wider variety of locations, in practice this revised policy has still meant that those towns with good transport connections have tended to grow more than others, not just by attracting additional manufacturing employment, but also (and more importantly) by enhancing the range of governmental and other services that they provide. In turn such changes have increased the attractiveness of these more fortunate towns as residential locations, for example for commuters in the broad hinterland of Dublin or simply for those seeking pleasant, well-served places for retirement.

In the Irish Republic the reduction in total population decline in the 1960s and the actual increase of the 1970s resulted in urban, rather than genuinely rural population growth. Between 1971 and 1981, for example, most towns expanded and some showed very high rates of growth. During the 1980s the overall rate of urban population growth declined; and although the total urban population increased, the total number of towns experiencing growth fell. Given the uneven distribution of urban population this suggests that the concentration of the benefits of economic growth will, in absolute terms, be more effectively concentrated in the south and east, simply because of the pre-existing urban pattern; and it is significant that the larger provincial cities and towns were particularly influenced by the expansion of educational and health services during the 1970s, which added to their employment bases. During this most recent period of urban growth, the medium-sized and large towns made the greatest gains in terms of their share of the total population. To redress the imbalance somewhat, the decentralization from Dublin of employees in various sections of government departments has taken place between 1989 and 1991 and has been targeted at six towns in the west and north-west (Galway, Sligo, Ballina, Cavan, Letterkenny and Killarney), although it is not yet clear what effect this will have on their longer-term growth.

Urban change is, of course, a normal event, as a direct reflection of general social and economic developments which, almost automatically, have their earliest and clearest expression in urban centres. Such elements of change are found, even if the total population shows no great alteration. For example, the decline of cinema-going, the amalgamation of banking chains and the rise of supermarkets provide three areas which have changed the character of many small towns, not only in Ireland. In a more specific Irish context one of the great changes has been in the role of the Irish country fair.

The fair was a great staple activity of life in the small Irish town; and the primary function of the fair was the exchange of livestock, particularly cattle, which was one of the important processes in the functioning of the various farming regions of Ireland. For example, in the early nineteenth century the great fair of Ballinasloe in county Galway involved the transfer of ownership of as many as 20,000 cattle and 90,000 sheep. Such large livestock fairs tended to occur at changes in the seasons, with May and November being favoured times, and were also linked with hiring fairs when agricultural labourers were taken on by farmers. These seasonal events were almost certainly of pre-urban origin. The much more mundane weekly market at which animals and other agricultural products were sold was probably more important for the survival of most modern towns. Such markets still remain, but their role has been greatly curtailed by the rise of cattle auctions, rural cooperatives and marketing boards. The need for a mechanism for the sale of agricultural products obviously remains, but road transport (and hence the removal of the need to drive cattle to the nearest point of sale) and the wider market provided by the successful auction mart have produced a concentration of these activities in a smaller number of urban centres and produced a more efficient economic transaction if, arguably, a more impoverished social event.

The larger towns also reveal another example of change in the process of redistribution of population from inner urban areas to suburbs, both a product and cause of accompanying inner city dereliction. Although the problem is far from as serious as in Belfast and Dublin, in order to deal with inner area dereliction in other towns in the Republic the government has found it necessary to extend its Urban Renewal Act of 1986, which originally applied to Dublin, Cork, Limerick and Waterford, to nine other settlements in 1988 (Cawley, 1991, p. 114). In 1990 eight more towns came under the terms of the Act. The end result is that most towns of any size are in receipt of financial incentives to encourage commercial and residential property development in designated areas within them. Compared to large cities the natural pressures for redevelopment are naturally much more limited, although the possibility of an insensitive destruction of the existing townscape is just as great.

Conclusion

The lack of pressure for extensive redevelopment and their relatively modest growth has been an important factor in preserving the unpresumptuous charm of many Irish small towns. Yet the pressures of the motor car and the growth of smaller towns as a result of investment in new employment have already produced important stimuli for change, which require careful planning. It is probably fair to say that there is no longstanding, deeply rooted respect for the process of town planning among many local Irish politicians. In the Republic of Ireland, in the early days of its independence, a number of important opinion formers presented urban life as an alien imposition which had hastened the process of anglicization in Ireland. Such aims as the restoration of traditional values, the rebuilding of a Gaelic heritage, and the reversal of rural depopulation were promoted as vital goals for the new state; and in this context the development of a system to allow for the civilized planning of towns was low on the political agenda. But affirmations of intent (and even actual government policies) turned out to be powerless in the face of inescapable trends. Almost by stealth Ireland has emerged as a predominantly urban country, South as well as North, and although much of that growth has been concentrated in and around the two major cities, there are now growing pressures on other urban areas as well. *Laissez-faire* attitudes are no longer appropriate, since the gradual accretion of change which was characteristic of the past is being replaced by much more radical forces for transformation, in small towns as well as large.

Further reading

The most recent examination of urban origins in Ireland, set firmly in a comparative European context, is H.B. Clarke and A. Simms (eds), *The Comparative History of Urban Origins in Non-Roman Europe: Ireland, Wales, Denmark, Germany, Poland and Russia from the 9th to the 13th Century* (British Archaeological Reports, International Series, Oxford, 1985). The evolution of Irish towns is being documented by the various folios of the *Irish Historic Towns Atlas*, edited by J. Andrews and A. Simms (Royal Irish Academy, Dublin, 1986–). So far folios on Kildare, Carrickfergus, Bandon and Kells have been published. B. Brunt, in *The Republic of Ireland* (Chapman, London, 1988), 133–68, gives an effective presentation of the recent evolution of the urban system in the Irish Republic, including material on the smaller urban settlements.

A definitive survey of the changing planning context is provided by M.J. Bannon (ed.), *Planning: the Irish Experience, 1921–1988* (Wolfhound Press, Dublin, 1989). A rigorous and pioneering attempt to reveal a settlement hierarchy in one Irish region is P.N. O'Farrell, 'Continuous regularities and discontinuities in the central place system', *Geografiska Annaler* 52B (1969), 104–14. A recent overview of urban change and its economic context is provided by D. Pringle, 'Urban growth and economic change in the Republic of Ireland, 1971–1981', in M.J. Bannon, L.S. Bourne and R. Sinclair (eds), *Urbanization and Urban Development: Recent Trends in a Global Context* (Service Industries Research Centre, University College, Dublin, 1991), 151–62.

Chapter 8

Belfast: a catalyst of geographical change

Dublin and Belfast dominate the human geography of Ireland. Partly this is because they are so clearly differentiated from other towns and cities by the range and the importance of their functions. They are also distinctive simply because of the high proportion of the population of both Northern Ireland and the Republic of Ireland which lives in them. Finally, their considerable social and economic problems pose special difficulties for the State and the Province in which they are located. To a casual visitor they may appear very contrasting cities, clearly different in their appearance and in the temperament and attitudes of their inhabitants. In fact, the basic similarities between them are much greater than first impressions would suggest.

The site of Belfast

Using the wisdom of hindsight and the guidance of a school atlas, the presence of Belfast might seem to be almost pre-ordained by the physical geography of north-east Ireland, as the banks of the river Lagan at the head of Belfast Lough appear to offer a naturally favoured position for the growth of a port city. In fact, its site and location are somewhat more complex than they seem and have operated in a variety of ways at different stages in the city's history (Evans, 1944) (Figure 8.1).

Certainly Belfast Lough faces Great Britain and marks the main point of entry into the Ulster Basin; but the site of Belfast was not occupied until 1613, when a castle was built there to consolidate the settlement of the local region by Scottish and English settlers, which was taking place at the time. The original site lay at a crossing point of the Lagan, where a tributary joined the tidal stretch at the river mouth and formed a creek where small ships could dock. To the south-west the lower Lagan valley consisted of generally good agricultural land, with quick-draining soils derived from glacial drift and Triassic sandstones and marls. Not surprisingly the castle near the mouth of the Lagan attracted around it a relatively prosperous if not outstanding market centre, serving the local agricultural community.

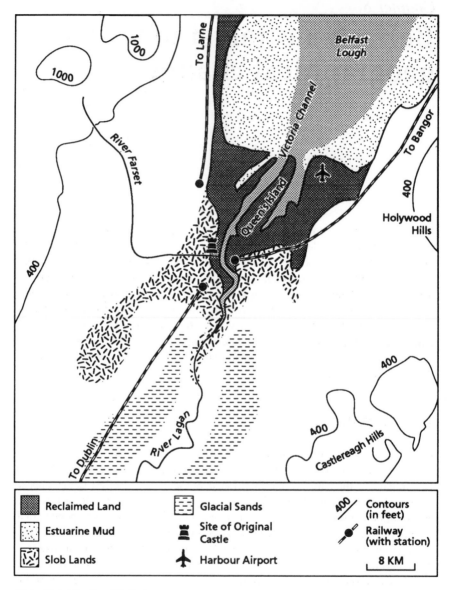

Figure 8.1 The site of Belfast

The development of the domestic linen industry in the eighteenth century gave further importance to the place, which was in a strategic location for the collection of brown linen from many parts of the Ulster Basin and formed a centre for the export of bleached linen. Its role as the largest centre in north-east Ireland made it a magnet for Scottish immigrants who developed it as a manufacturing centre. As Belfast grew the Lagan valley gave direct access to the area south and west of Lough Neagh and the locational advantage provided by this apparently

Photo 15 Belfast, looking towards Belfast Lough. The twin bridges in the left foreground are close to the original crossing point of the river Lagan. In the right centre is the Harland and Woolf shipyard, located on the Queen's Island, with its output now sadly reduced. To its left is the Victoria Channel, with other port installations at its side. At the top right is the edge of reclaimed land on which Belfast Harbour Airport and Short's aircraft factory are located. (Courtesy of the Industrial Development Board)

natural line of access was converted into functioning reality, first by a canal and a turnpike road, later by railway building. The basalt scarp to the north-west provides a scenically attractive backdrop to the city, but also seems to check accessibility in that direction. Yet in fact there are gaps in the scarp which allowed access to the lower Bann valley by both road and railway.

Local conditions also influenced the internal geography of the growing city. The possibility of draining land – the so-called 'slob' lands at the head of Belfast Lough – provided space for the expansion of central Belfast and the growth of the nineteenth-century commercial city. The same possibility also offered potential sites for industrial developments, in particular the shipyards and, in the twentieth century, for the creation of an airport and an associated aircraft factory. The winding navigable channel concealed in the apparently wide Belfast Lough and the tidal river banks of the Lagan in fact did not constitute a suitable natural harbour for larger ships, but the Lough could be dredged; and the creation of the Victoria Channel and other extensive harbour installations not only became a necessary requirement for the shipbuilding industry but also allowed Belfast to emerge as one of the larger ports in the British Isles.

Industrial growth in the Belfast region

The conversion of Belfast from a small eighteenth-century town to a large modern city was intimately connected with the impact of the industrial revolution in north-east Ireland. In a sense the very presence of this industrial region poses a problem in explanation, since Ireland was largely devoid of easily worked coal and iron, the 'natural resources' normally considered necessary for such a development in the nineteenth-century British Isles. In seeking an explanation the possibility of capital accumulation, the availability of credit, the existence of a proto-industrial base and the proximity of Scotland are all relevant.

One possibility is that the less onerous demands made by landlords in the north of Ireland as a result of the so-called Ulster Custom of Tenant Right contributed to the process. The Ulster Custom, among other things, guaranteed a tenant farmer fixity of tenure if his rent was paid at the appropriate time and allowed a cash payment to be made to a tenant if he was evicted or if he sold his tenancy, notionally at least as compensation for improvements he had made to his farm. In some cases this compensation was simply a payment of 'key money' by an incoming tenant, anxious to obtain access to a farm; but, however Tenant Right worked in practice, the net result was that a number of successful farmers, secure in their tenure, were able to become more prosperous by accumulating capital in their farms, sometimes by investing in equipment associated with the domestic linen industry like bleach greens and mills for scutching flax.

It was from this class of more prosperous farmers that the small entrepreneurs of the domestic linen industry – the bleachers and the merchants – emerged. The organization of the domestic industry became more elaborate in the late eighteenth century and in the early decades of the nineteenth, with 'manufacturers' importing linen thread spun by machinery in Britain and issuing it to farmer-weavers, who increasingly produced cloth under contract. Using their own plant or again subcontracting the work, these entrepreneurs undertook the bleaching of the brown linen produced by handloom weavers, a growing number of whom devoted all their time to linen production. The finished product, originally sold through Dublin, was increasingly routed through Belfast, where merchants of the Lagan valley had built a White Linen Hall as early as 1783 in an eventually successful effort to break the monopoly of Dublin in the bleached-linen trade. This more sophisticated organization steadily replaced what was formerly a purely domestic industry, with linen as a by-product of farming, just like butter or cattle. In this process the location of profitable linen weaving was increasingly concentrated in the hinterland of Belfast, particularly in the Lagan valley.

The development of the domestic linen industry also led to the availability of credit in north-east Ireland, provided by institutions which were willing to invest money in the industry. This influence was particularly marked after 1825 when joint-stock banking became possible in Ireland. The first provincial joint-stock bank was founded in Belfast and by the middle of the 1830s, although such banks had been diffused throughout Ireland by this time, the numerical concentration in the north-east was still clearly marked. These banks had knowledge of the textile industry and were prepared to invest in it and in other industrial activities.

In fact cotton and not linen pioneered the introduction of genuine factory industry. In this development the close connections between north-east Ireland and Scotland were influential, since at least some of the early pioneers knew of conditions in Scotland. For example, the first steam engine used in Ireland was imported from Glasgow in 1790 and installed in a Lisburn cotton mill; by 1811 there were 15 steam-driven cotton spinning mills in Belfast. The Irish cotton industry was highly concentrated in the growing town of Belfast and in its immediate environs because it depended on imported raw materials. Before changing to steam the spinning mills were driven by water power, particularly where fast streams flowed down from the basalt escarpment which lay to the north-west of Belfast. The adoption of steam-power encouraged further concentration in Belfast, close to the port facilities where coal, as well as raw cotton, was imported.

The cotton industry had grown behind protective tariffs originally introduced by the Irish parliament before the Union of Great Britain and Ireland was imposed in 1801. When these tariffs were removed in the 1820s it turned out that the Irish cotton industry was on too small a scale to compete with Lancashire, although remnants of the industry survived until the American Civil War, when the resulting cotton famine administered its *coup de grâce*. Yet before it died the cotton industry served as a model for the further reorganization of the production of linen.

The evolving linen industry had a number of advantages. It was able to use workers, techniques and industrial premises taken over from the cotton industry. It could also recruit workers from the decaying domestic linen industry. As it produced a more expensive fabric the linen industry could bear the cost of importing fuel and exporting much of its finished product and still be internationally competitive. Finally, it had in flax a locally produced raw material, until the expansion of the industry eventually resulted in local demand far exceeding indigenous supplies. The result was that existing cotton mills were rapidly converted to spinning linen thread and new factories were specially built. The final step in the emergence of a factory-based industry was taken in the 1850s, when new power-weaving machinery for producing linen cloth was perfected and generally adopted. Linen weaving was less tied to Belfast and had a fairly wide distribution in the smaller towns of north-east Ireland, possibly reflecting its development from the domestic weaving industry. Spinning, the first manufacturing stage in the production of linen, was much more strictly confined to Belfast.

Shipbuilding provided a second foundation stone in the industrial base of Belfast. After a number of tentative beginnings shipbuilding was firmly added to its industrial structure in 1853, but the assured growth of the shipyards came after 1859, when the business was taken over by Edward Harland and eventually became the famous firm of Harland and Woolf. Without local coal or iron the initial expansion of shipbuilding was the result of the enterprise and inventiveness of this Scot – once again a Scottish influence had made its presence felt in the north of Ireland. In a very real sense the shipbuilding industry was a branch of an enterprise that had begun earlier on the Clyde with, to start with, hulls being towed to Scotland for their engines to be fitted. That connection continued for quite some time; until as late as the 1880s engines were not produced locally but were imported, mainly from Scotland. Shipbuilding was naturally concentrated alongside the port installations of Belfast Lough, with associated engineering suppliers not far away. No doubt benefiting from the resulting external economies, a second shipbuilding firm, Workman and Clark, was also established on the shores of Belfast Lough in 1880 and grew rapidly to achieve the greatest output of any single yard in the United Kingdom in 1902, before being battered into failure in 1934 by the collapse of orders during the Recession.

To an industrial structure dominated by ships and linen was added an associated engineering industry, eventually involving such activities as the production of textile machinery, ventilating plant and steam engines. Originally a direct outcome of the linen and shipbuilding industries these products also established an independent niche for themselves in the international market. Other industries grew to serve the local concentration of population and in time some of these, too, managed to penetrate wider markets, in particular for tobacco and cigarettes, mineral waters and food products. Manufacturers of ropes and clothing (both linked with the original economic base of the city) were also able to establish a broader market for their products.

The emerging city

At first sight it is tempting to interpret the city which grew in the nineteenth century as a drab collection of industrial necessities; certainly much of the Victorian townscape that has survived appears to confirm that view. Yet it is easy to overlook Belfast's growth as a financial, social and educational centre (Figure 8.2). Its university college became the most effective of the four institutions

Table 8.1 Population of Belfast, 1821–1911

Date	Population
1821	37,277
1831	53,287
1841	75,308
1851	97,784
1861	119,393
1871	174,412
1881	208,122
1891	255,950
1901	349,180
1911	386,947

Institutional Growth of Belfast

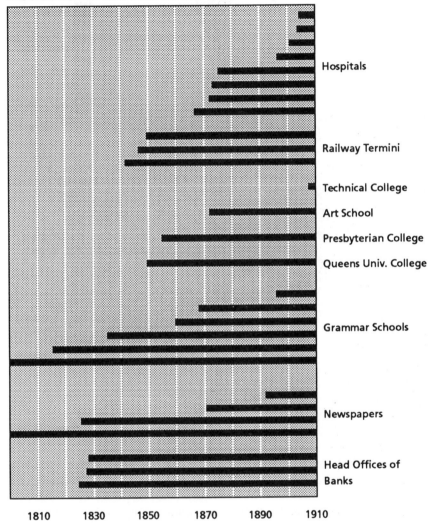

Figure 8.2 Institutional developments in nineteenth century Belfast

established in 1845 to form the Royal University of Ireland, so that by 1909 it had become an independent degree-awarding university in its own right, long before many provincial cities in England were near to achieving that status. Secondary schools and libraries were established and private investment was involved in other non-industrial dimensions of the growing city: for example, by the end of the nineteenth century an opera house and other theatres were built, four daily newspapers catered for different political tastes and eight hospitals were active. By this time, too, its shops and professional life rivalled those

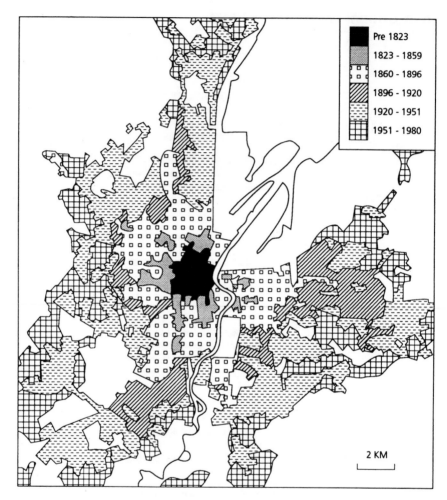

Figure 8.2 The growth of Belfast

of Dublin, not surprisingly as Belfast was nearly as large a city by 1901 (see Table 8.1).

Urban growth required institutional change – municipal activity was intense, although perhaps driven as much by necessity as by civic pride. From the 1840s a local board of commissioners was developing the town's water supply, culminating in the harnessing of the watersheds of the Mourne mountains to serve the city. A similar body was active throughout the century in successfully developing the harbour facilities, and private enterprise had produced a local railway network which focused on Belfast where there were three railway terminals. The municipal tram services were electrified in 1904, stimulating the further outward expansion of the city. In 1906 a grandiose city hall was completed, symbolizing Belfast's quest for enhanced status as well as industrial success. So too did the decision to build the Church of Ireland cathedral taken in 1896, and the Assembly Hall of the Presbyterian Church, opened in 1905 (Brett, 1967).

By 1901 the population of the city had reached 350,000, roughly the same size as Dublin. Belfast's population growth continued into the twentieth century and its areal expansion was even more rapid, reflecting lower residential densities, extended municipal transport services, and eventually the urban restructuring associated with the private car and road freight (Figure 8.2 and Table 8.2). The contribution of manufacturing industry to that growth has become much more uncertain, particularly in the 1930s and since the 1970s, but other sources of employment have played their part.

Table 8.2 Population of Belfast, 1926–1991

Date	Population	
1926	415,151*	
1937	438,086*	
1951	443,671*	503,000†
1961	415,856*	529,000†
1971	416,679**	612,600†
1981	314,000**	519,500†
1991	279,237**	518,700†

*   Belfast County Borough
** Belfast Local Government Area
†   Belfast built-up area (estimate)

Throughout the twentieth century Belfast's role as the chief port for the north of Ireland and as the major industrial centre has continued, although more recently air travel, industrial dispersal, the decline of shipbuilding and the development of roll-on/roll-off ferry services through Larne have made the Belfast docks less central in the functioning of the city. Its role as the capital of a semi-independent province of the United Kingdom has increased the number of government employees in the city. Because of its completely dominant position as the largest city in Northern Ireland it has enjoyed a disproportionate share of the growth of service employment. The shops and offices of central Belfast have expanded throughout the century and, against the odds perhaps, still continue to flourish. As a result, the population of greater Belfast reached over 503,000 by 1951 and peaked at 612,000 in 1971. In detail the census returns suggest that the growth of the administrative area of Belfast ceased in 1961; but in fact the population of the continuous built-up area spread into legally independent suburbs, while the decline of the older residential areas became sharper.

During the 1970s population change became more complex as terrorist activities and civil unrest disturbed a pattern that was already evolving. Inner city decline was further emphasized, although a sharp fall in the population density of these areas was inevitable as the by-law houses of the late nineteenth century, so characteristic of the townscape of the older parts of Belfast, increasingly exceeded their shelf-lives. Breaking away from the previous situation, the continuous built-up area of Belfast also suffered some population decline; the Belfast urban area – a new census unit created in the 1970s – fell very sharply from 417,000 to 314,000, thus producing a reduction in the population of the whole built-up area from 613,000 to 520,000. This fall continued in the following decade, although nearly 33 per cent of the population of Northern Ireland still lives in the Belfast area.

To off-set this decrease the highest level of population increase was concentrated in the ring of satellite towns around the city, where retailing, manufacturing and warehousing activities grew as well as residential land use. Here population was increased by in-migration and also its rate of natural increase was approximately twice that of Belfast. The net result was an increase of population in this so-called 'inner ring' of Northern Ireland from 469,000 in 1971 to 531,000 in 1981 and an estimated 555,000 in 1987 (Compton, 1990, Table 3). If, as is reasonable in these days of more flexible personal transport for car owners, the functional city is seen as operating beyond the limits of its built-up area, the population directly associated with the Belfast economic and social system has stabilized at approximately just over one million people.

One expression of urban restructuring is seen in the marked decentralization of retailing into superstores, discount warehouses and planned shopping centres. This process is, of course, international in its impact, but it was given particular emphasis in Belfast in the 1970s, when the city centre was an important target of the IRA bombing campaign, hence encouraging a more rapid decline than would otherwise have occurred. In the 1970s five major shopping complexes were established on the periphery of Belfast, the largest and most successful being the Ards centre, some 15 kilometres east of Belfast, with 100,000 shoppers per week. The 1980s have seen attempts to revitalize the centre of Belfast by enhancing the environment of the principal shopping streets, by developing more car parking and road connections, and by improving public transport (Brown, 1990). This activity has been successful in producing a renaissance in central shopping, partly because of a political initiative designed to re-establish normality, partly because of a reorientation of IRA strategy, but also because a large city centre location still offers attractions for the right kind of development. That last factor will inevitably demand further changes in the Belfast city centre, since only specialist, central-area activities will in the longer run be able to resist the new high levels of suburban competition.

It was in this context that the Belfast Urban Area Plan was published in 1988, with various ambitious proposals for further development through until 2001 (Department of the Environment, Northern Ireland, 1988). It suggested that derelict land around the centre should be used for commercial development, including comprehensive redevelopment schemes and private residential developments designed to attract some 5000 young professional people and young married couples to private housing on politically 'neutral' areas – an important consideration in Belfast. The river Lagan was seen as a potential asset and it was proposed that 'Laganside' would consist of high quality business and residential developments and also include leisure activities such as marinas. To balance this, in the suburbs there were to be 10,000 new dwellings on sites within the existing urban area and 6000 on the green belt around Belfast, thus breaking the stop-line proposals of the 1960s, which will be discussed later. It remains to be seen whether the implicit optimism about the economic future of Belfast (which has been losing rather than gaining population in recent years) will convert these ideas into reality. Certainly the idea of waterside development has been inspired by experiments in dockside developments in Britain; but transplants of this kind may not root very effectively in the leaner economic soils of Belfast.

Social areas in Belfast

In the real world of today a more pressing concern has been the social and religious dichotomy in the city. As in other western cities social areas within Belfast can be fitted into traditional spatial models, if suitable allowance is made for the quirks of the local site. Those census measures which highlight age and family structure reveal a concentric distribution, with elderly persons and young single people being particularly characteristic of the inner city. Unsurprisingly, on a traverse towards the suburbs the proportion of married people with children increases, with the highest percentage of married couples with young children being found in fairly recent peripheral housing estates. Those characteristics of the population which are more closely associated with people's socio-economic status reveal a sectoral arrangement. The details are complicated, as Paul Doherty's careful analysis of the 1971 and 1981 census reveals (Doherty, 1978; 1988), but low status areas form sectors along the shores of Belfast Lough and in both east and west Belfast. Between these sectors lie high status areas, like, for example the Malone area to the south-west and a section of the Antrim Road to the north.

Many western cities also show evidence of distinctive ethnic clusters, where communities with distinguishing racial or religious attributes group together, perhaps because of discrimination against them in the housing market, but also to derive mutual support in a potentially hostile environment. Belfast is often looked upon as being particularly notable in this characteristic, in that its social geography is so strongly marked by clustering based on two brands of the Christian religion rather than on seemingly more profound ethnic differences. It also may seem more unique in being stimulated by long-standing local social and political attitudes rather than as a reaction to recent in-migration.

The political implications of the division between Catholic and Protestant, which were not always as clear cut in the nineteenth century as they are today, will be returned to later, but the general locational pattern in Belfast may be described here. There are technical problems with recent census returns of religious affiliation because of a high level of non-response, but Doherty's map, based on his recalculation of information in the 1981 census by 1-kilometre squares, gives

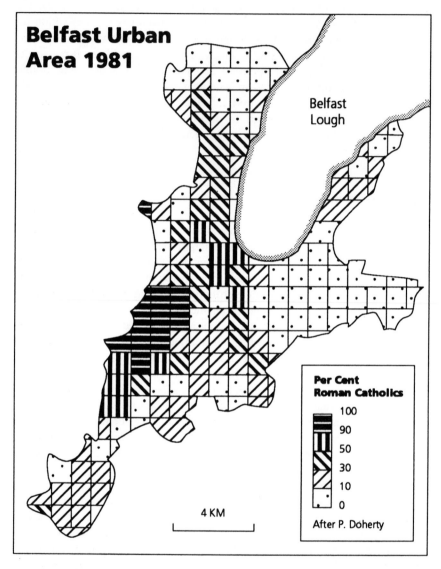

Figure 8.4 Distribution of Roman Catholics in Belfast, 1981. The map (Doherty, 1990) is based on an analysis of census data by kilometre squares. It shows greater detail than published statistics are able to do, but in spite of this some (but not all) of the areas that emerge as 'mixed' are much more segregated at the level of individual streets or small districts.

a useful overview of segregation in Belfast (Doherty, 1990b) (Figure 8.4). What the map shows is that, as well as extensive areas where there is a segregated Catholic population (with 90–100 per cent Catholic), there are also areas of segregated Protestant population (0–10 per cent Catholic on the map). What stands out at this scale is not only the large Catholic area in west Belfast, but also the extensive Protestant areas in east Belfast and in the Rathcool area in the extreme north of the city. In fact, of the 157 squares on Doherty's map only ten have more than 90 per cent Catholic, while a further nine are mixed with Catholic majorities (50 per cent and over). The remaining 138 squares are dominated numerically by Protestants; of these, 72 squares are strongly segregated (with more than 90 per cent Protestant) and form almost half of the city. What also stands out, contrary to many preconceptions outside Ireland, is the continued presence of mixed areas in the city.

There are a number of matters arising from this. The first is that it is difficult to specify at what level segregation may be said to be found. Some of the kilometre squares with similar numbers of Protestants and Catholics are not necessarily mixed areas at the level of individual streets, but simply reflect the broad scale of analysis. At the same time, uneven numbers of the two faiths do not necessarily indicate segregation: if there was no segregation in the city, although all the grid squares would be mixed, they would also all have a Protestant majority, reflecting the different total numbers in the two faiths in Belfast. Finally, class as well as religion is involved in the spatial pattern that the map reveals, since genuinely mixed areas are often in middle-class areas (although not exclusively so). This may seem surprising, but it has to be recalled that although Catholics more commonly occupy unskilled manual jobs (although, again, far from exclusively), there is also a Catholic middle class, and the *ethos* of life in the prosperous suburbs demands more tolerance than that commonly found in the grimmer surroundings of inner Belfast.

Yet Paul Doherty's suggested classification of Belfast into two 'cities' remains largely valid. One is the Protestant city, consisting of 72 grid squares with more than 90 per cent of their population claiming to be Protestant, and the second is the 10 grid squares which make up the Catholic city, each with more than 90 per cent Catholic. In 1981 just over 44 per cent of the total population of the Belfast Urban Area lived in the Protestant city and nearly 10 per cent lived in the Catholic city, so that in total 53.8 per cent of the population lived in highly segregated areas. When population is allocated to these areas by religious affiliation, the perhaps somewhat surprising result is that 60 per cent of Protestants and just less than 34 per cent of Catholics lived in the most segregated areas.

Religious segregation is long-standing in Belfast going back, it has been suggested, to the earliest days of the settlement, but reinforced during the period of growth in the last quarter of the nineteenth century by periodic outbreaks of civic disorder. During the 1950s and for much of the 1960s the amount of segregation in Belfast was decreasing, but the civil disturbances which began in 1968 strongly reversed that trend. Minorities of both religions, who had strayed into majority communities in those parts of the city where violence was high and tolerance low, found it necessary to retreat into their own bailiwicks in the face of intimidation from some of their more aggressive neighbours of a different faith. In 1971, when this kind of population redistribution was already underway, only seven of Doherty's grid squares had more than 90 per cent Catholics and only 61 squares were in the highly segregated Protestant group, revealing that the amount of intra-urban movement stimulated in this way over the inter-censal decade had been considerable, although it is probable that relative stability has now reasserted itself. Other calculations also confirm the rise of segregation since the early 1970s.

For the Belfast Urban Area as a whole an index of dissimilarity can be calculated for 1971, giving a result of 49.6. What this means in simple terms is that this percentage of the Catholic population would have to move if a totally desegregated population was to be created. By 1981 that figure had risen to an estimated 57.7 per cent (Doherty, 1989). Much of this change is the result of individual decision making, but it has been enhanced by the allocation procedures which have been adopted by those administering publicly owned housing. These procedures have arisen, not because of any formal policy of encouraging segregation, but as a pragmatic reaction to the locations which families on waiting lists were prepared to accept when they were offered accommodation, a process which in the difficult circumstances of the time almost inevitably developed into a dual allocation system (Brett, 1986, especially pp. 62–88). Although the recent population movements which have further enhanced the division between religious groups are completely understandable in the face of real threats and probable danger, these short-term adjustments do not offer the hope of any longer-term increase in mutual understanding.

Other social and economic contrasts can be fitted into this classification. Mixed areas with Protestant majorities were roughly the better suburbs of Belfast, with the highest living standards. The so-called Protestant city, although less prosperous, emerged on average as having better conditions than the Catholic city. The mixed areas with Catholic majorities (which in fact often are inner city areas with particular social problems and a high level of local segregation masked by the scale of analysis) revealed some of the worst conditions. What stood out, however, was the Catholic city, which combined the greatest proportion of people with the lowest social class and the highest levels of deprivation (although it should be noted that there was also substantial deprivation in some Protestant areas).

Further reading

A wide-ranging survey of the development of Belfast is J.C. Beckett and R.E. Glasscock (eds), *Belfast: the Origin and Growth of an Industrial City* (BBC, London, 1967). The concentration of the domestic linen industry is described in E.R.R. Green, *The Lagan Valley, 1800–1850: a Local History of the Industrial Revolution* (Faber, London, 1949). A classic study is E. Jones, *A Social Geography of Belfast* (Oxford University Press, London, 1960). A *mélange* of recent geographical contributions is P. Doherty (ed.), *Geographical Perspectives on the Belfast Region* (Geographical Society of Ireland, Special Publication 5, Jordanstown, 1990).

An interesting account of the city's twentieth-century growth is provided by F.W. Boal and S. Royle, 'Belfast: boom, blitz and bureaucracy', in G. Gordon (ed.), *Regional Cities in the United Kingdom, 1890–1980* (Harper and Row, London, 1986), 191–216. The most recent planning proposals for the Belfast Urban Area are summarized in E. Gaffikin *et al.*, 'Planning for a change in Belfast: the urban economy, urban regeneration and the Belfast Urban Area Plan 1988', *Town Planning Review* 62 (1991), 415–30.

Chapter 9

Dublin: a European capital

Every geographical location is unique; the detailed site, the evolving history and the modern appearance of Dublin certainly differs from that of Belfast. Yet, putting on one side superficial architectural differences, there are a remarkable number of basic similarities in the sites and locations of the two large cities and in their contemporary geographies.

The site of Dublin

Like Belfast the site of Dublin offers access to an extensive hinterland (Haughton, 1946). To the west, lines of glacial sands – the kames and eskers of central Ireland – constituted potential routeways across the bogland interior. Immediately to the south, entry to the interior from the sea was barred by the mountains of the Leinster Chain. To the east, directly across the Irish Sea, coastal north Wales juts out and provided a routeway and a shorter sea crossing for invaders from Britain. Like Belfast, Dublin is sited on a river mouth facing Britain. The immediate surroundings of the city provide good agricultural land supporting arable farming in an area of relatively low rainfall by Irish standards. Although the Liffey does not have the dramatic approach offered by Belfast Lough, the river mouth constituted a better potential harbour than other rival locations in the gap between the Leinster Chain and the Carlingford Mountains.

Human endeavour has made use of natural conditions to exploit these advantages. Like Belfast Lough, the mouth of the Liffey required considerable investment to reclaim its slob-lands, to produce harbour facilities which would accommodate modern ships, and to reduce the silting in its immediate sea approaches. Just as Larne Harbour provided a necessary outport for Belfast with rapid connections to Scotland, Kingstown (now Dun Laoghaire) provided an outport on a much grander scale for Dublin, with express connections to Wales. The building of the Royal and Grand canals in the 1790s pushed Dublin's effective sphere of influence westward to the Shannon; and the railway system, starting with a connection between Kingstown and Dublin in 1834, was inevitably focused on what was the largest city in Ireland for most of the nineteenth century. The terraces of the Liffey offered the possibility of residential expansion along roads to the west, and growth also took place to the south-east along the coastal fringe of the Leinster mountains and also north along the coast to Howth and beyond.

The evolving townscape

In spite of these similarities, the evolving history of the two cities differs greatly. Dublin goes back to the beginnings of urban settlement in Ireland: the earliest known port on the site of Dublin was a Viking base in the ninth century A.D., adjoining a pre-existing Celtic monastic settlement. Then, in 1170 the site was occupied by the Normans, who developed what was indisputably a genuine urban settlement, some relics of which are still just visible in the modern townscape (Simms, 1979). For example, the very much restored Christ Church and St Patrick's cathedrals remain, parts of the medieval street plan are still visible on the ground and a few street names survive. The function of the Norman city was as a centre of political and military power for invaders from Britain, although its effective and permanent influence did not extend far beyond the Pale – a zone of variable size where intensive control was exercised, originally surrounded by a rampart, which stretched north to Dundalk, some 25 miles to the west, and south to the foothills of the Wicklow mountains.

During the second half of the seventeenth century, when the English colonization of the previous century was being consolidated, a stimulus was given to the growth of Dublin, by then the dominant urban settlement in Ireland and the major point of entry to Ireland from England. It was only at this stage that Dublin became a capital city in any modern sense. Under the Duke of Ormonde, who became Viceroy in 1662, Dublin was converted from being essentially a garrison with a population of probably less than 9000 to a city with architectural pretensions and cultural as well as military functions. Phoenix Park (larger than all the royal parks of London put together) was enclosed, the 27 acres of St Stephen's Green was converted from being an ancient common into an elegant, publicly owned square, the growth of Trinity College Dublin commenced and substantial public buildings were constructed. The Jacobite defeat at the end of the seventeenth century introduced a period of relative calm in Irish history and stimulated what might be seen as a golden era of Dublin life – at least for those who were prosperous and exercised power. The Irish parliament developed its authority and, although only Anglicans could participate, its activities were not incompatible with the growth of prosperity in various parts of Ireland and, in particular, Dublin.

In the eighteenth century Dublin evolved as a centre of administrative, parliamentary, legal and commercial power. Great public buildings were constructed to fulfil these functions and many of these still grace the townscape of modern Dublin. Not least among them was the Parliament House, now the Bank of

Photo 16 St Stephen's Green, Dublin. St Stephen's Green is the largest of Dublin's great squares. It was enclosed in 1664–5 and surrounded by elegant houses, but the park which occupies the centre of the square owes its appearance to landscaping in 1880 using funds provided by Sir Arthur Guinness. What is remarkable is the manner in which the park introduces an island of calm into the heart of the modern busy city. (Courtesy of Bord Failte)

Ireland, which was commenced in 1729 and perhaps provides an index of the growth of parliamentary self-respect. James Gandon's superb Customs House, which was completed in 1792 on the slob-lands at the mouth of the Liffey, perhaps serves to illustrate the importance of commercial activity; and his King's Inn (now the Four Courts), begun in 1786, indicates the city's expanding legal function. During the century, too, the educational role of Dublin was expressed in the growth of Trinity College, which added many fine buildings to form the basis of what eventually emerged as arguably the most attractive group of university buildings in the British Isles.

Less commented upon perhaps, but geographically more significant, the built-up area of Dublin expanded, so that by the beginning of the nineteenth century its outer limits approached close to the two canals and the wide circular road which looped around the growing city (Figure 9.1). For example, starting in 1730, an estate of substantial residences was developed north of central Dublin by the banker Luke Gardiner and to the south the Fitzwilliam estate expanded over 5000 acres, stretching from St Stephen's Green to Blackrock. A framework for this kind of development was provided by the operation of the Wide Street Commissioners, appointed in 1758, with the right of compulsory purchase and with the duty of replacing narrow and crooked streets with 'wide and convenient' ones.

Photo 17 Trinity College, Dublin. Although a more ancient foundation, the college buildings were reconstructed in the eighteenth century and extended in the nineteenth century. On the left are modern buildings added to the college in the 1970s. Yet the impression of architectural coherence is strong and together they form what is arguably the most elegant assembly of university buildings in the British Isles. Beyond the College is the headquarters building of the Bank of Ireland, which was formerly the Irish Parliament Building before the union of Great Britain and Ireland in 1801. (Courtesy of Bord Failte)

Dublin in the nineteenth century

The demand for houses of a kind which allowed stately and sumptuous living reflected the role of Dublin as the centre of Irish politics and fashion. At the end of the eighteenth century Dublin had become the second largest city in the British Isles, but its golden era ended in 1801 when the Act of Union was implemented, bringing to an end its parliamentary function and inaugurating a sharp reduction in its social eminence. Some accounts of Dublin in the nineteenth century have presented it as a city in decline as a result of this change, but this was true only in a very limited sense. High society may have gone but Dublin remained the

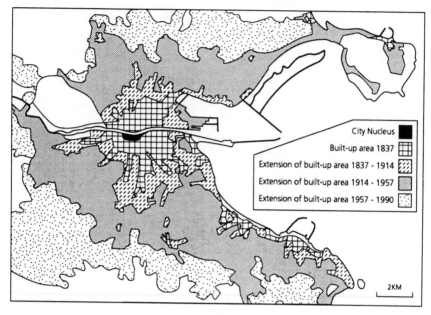

Figure 9.1 The expansion of Dublin

centre of Irish social life and commerce; the law courts continued as before; and the administrators remained and increased in number as government involvement in day-to-day life grew.

Dublin certainly did not experience the massive industrial growth of Belfast, but it became even more firmly tied into the English urban system: by the middle of the century the establishment of steamship services meant that London had been brought within a day's journey. It also lay at the centre of the growing Irish railway network. These connections brought penalties as well as advantages. The highest administrative decisions affecting Ireland were certainly taken away from Dublin, although an increasing range of routine matters were more effectively concentrated there. Its eighteenth-century textile trades shrank rapidly in the face of outside competition with the only survivor being the highly specialized manufacture of poplin, and the market for fine furniture and silver was decimated by the desertion of the city by the Irish aristocracy. Yet Dublin was not untouched by the industrial revolution and some developments reflected its earlier history and its new accessibility. About 1850 Jacob's biscuit bakery was founded – a normal enough development in an urban centre, but this firm expanded into a large factory whose growth was made possible by export to the British market as well as by the slow growth of prosperity at home. During the nineteenth century, too, Guinness's brewery began to invade the British market as well as to dominate that of Ireland, with the result that the firm eventually overshadowed all other Dublin manufacturers, not just brewers. The growth of trade was indicated, as in Belfast, by the further development of the dock system in the 1870s and 1880s.

Its growth of population and its physical expansion belies the suggestion that Dublin was a city in decline in the nineteenth century. Its population in 1800 was about 170,000 and by 1901, according to the census, it had reached 290,000. To that must at least be added the census populations of Kingstown, Blackrock, Balbriggan, Pembroke, Rathmines and Rathgar, all of which were effectively part of the geographical city, giving a total population of over 381,000 (see Table 9.1).

Table 9.1 Population of Dublin, 1821–1911

Date	Population
1821	188,662
1831	211,941
1841	252,663
1851	319,929
1861	311,805
1871	325,609
1881	345,002
1891	347,912
1901	381,277
1911	404,214

Statistics include Kingstown and suburbs outside the
legal boundary of Dublin city.

The outward spread of the built-up area reveals the same message. Early nineteenth century Dublin continued to grow, fingering out along main roads, in particular to the west, south and north-east; in 1837 the first edition of the Ordnance Survey maps shows how tentacles of housing had crept across the lines of the Grand and the Royal canals. In Dublin classical designs lingered on longer than was normally the case in England, with recognizably Georgian terrace housing still being built in the 1840s and elements of the style persisting almost to 1900. The physical expansion of Dublin continued in the second half of the nineteenth century. North Dublin expanded somewhat slowly, but to the south growth was more extensive. Building stretched along the coast and linked the continuous built-up areas of Dublin and Kingstown. The Pembroke estate to the south-east of Dublin, near Ballsbridge, was a particularly superior development in the 1870s. Development to the south-east of Dublin expanded further for the remainder of the century. Finally, the finger of urban growth which already pointed west close to the line of the Grand Canal continued to extend further.

The growth of fashionable suburbs and the relocation into them of middle-class people also contributed to the development of some of the worst slums in Europe. As well as middle-class employment, the urban economy of Dublin produced jobs for large numbers of unskilled or, at best, semi-skilled workers who trickled into the homes being abandoned by the better-off – the flight to the suburbs was not restricted to twentieth century North America. These substantial residences, originally intended for large individual families and their servants, were subdivided and their bigger rooms partitioned to house a population that was forced to live at remarkably high densities.

Slums in Dublin were no new phenomenon and in the eighteenth century had been concentrated in the old medieval city, but by the 1880s about 117,000 people – nearly 45 per cent of the city's population – lived in 10,000 tenement houses (McDowell, 1957). At least 30,000 of these people lived in accommodation deemed to be unfit for human use, even by the standards of the time. Later, a British parliamentary committee, which reported on the housing conditions of the working classes in Dublin, revealed that in 1914 the number of tenement houses had been reduced to about 5000 but the density at which they were occupied had risen and the proportion unfit for occupation had also increased somewhat. Some 12,000 families – perhaps 74,000 people – lived in one-room units, which produced zones of extreme poverty in various clusters around the city centre and north of the docks (Report of Departmental Committee, 1914). Sean O'Casey's most famous plays may have given a romantic patina to the cut and thrust of life in the Dublin tenements of this time, but the reality was one of miserable living conditions behind elegant but decaying facades. The architectural merit of many of the buildings heightened rather than reduced the planning problems involved in rehousing this slum population which eventually had to be addressed.

Dublin after independence

After 1922 Irish independence provided a new stimulus for Dublin's growth, producing a rapid expansion in its area and population, arguably at the expense of the rest of the country. Such a development was not surprising, since Dublin had acquired the additional functions of a capital city, with a less ostentatious way of life among the leaders of society than in the late eighteenth century, but with many more civil servants and diplomatic representatives. In spite of the development of a protected home market Dublin also became the principal location for economic growth in the new state, for which it possessed a number of distinct advantages: its growing population represented an increasing proportion of the domestic market for goods and services; it lay at the point of maximum accessibility to the rest of the Republic; and it was by far its largest port providing direct access to Britain – still the dominant source of imports and the destination of most exports.

The resulting growth in population led to the further expansion of middle-class areas to the south of the city and the broadening of the coastal belt between Dublin and Dun Laoghaire. New estates were also built to the north and north-east, linking the village of Howth to the continuous built-up area of the city. Dublin Corporation continued its task of sweeping away slum property, commenced before the First World War but given greater energy and resources in the 1930s. The corollary of slum clearance was the building of suburban council

Table 9.2 Population of Dublin, 1926–1991

Date	Population
1926	430,195
1936	513,993
1946	552,564
1951	636,831
1956	654,143
1961	669,553
1966	744,304
1971	801,298*
1979	900,884*
1981	915,115*
1986	1,021,449†
1991	1,024,429†

Statistics for 1926 to 1966 include Dun Laoghaire and contiguous Dublin suburbs.

* Greater Dublin (as defined by census authorities)

† Dublin county

estates, since rehousing at the existing density was impossible, as in most other inner city problem areas in other countries.

Implicit in the evolving townscape of Dublin has been the long-standing existence of extreme social polarization between rich and poor, but recent population movements within the urban area have produced a more complex social geography than must have existed in the nineteenth century. Kevin Hourihan's analysis of the 1971 census has indicated that socio-economic status, the age structure of the population and housing type are the three most important factors in producing distinctive social areas within Dublin (Hourihan, 1978). On the basis of 46 variables he found seven different types of social area in the city (Figure 9.2).

One was the inner city, made distinctive by the low socio-economic status of its population, the predominance of multiple-use housing, more elderly people, the worst housing conditions in the city, and population decline (Type 1). A second zone encircled the inner city and shared many of its characteristics, including many flat dwellers, delapidated buildings and many elderly people; its population was also declining but not as rapidly as in the inner city. A third area consisted of a concentration of young unmarried people, often students, office workers and junior government employees, living in conventional housing which had been subdivided into flats. The fourth type of social area was made up of corporation housing estates, mainly to the north and south-west of the city. Here social and economic status was low, but in contrast with the inner city there were few elderly people, although a slight fall in population numbers had been taking place, possibly because of the beginnings of a reduction in average family size. Fifthly, Hourihan recognized the older suburbs as distinctive. These still

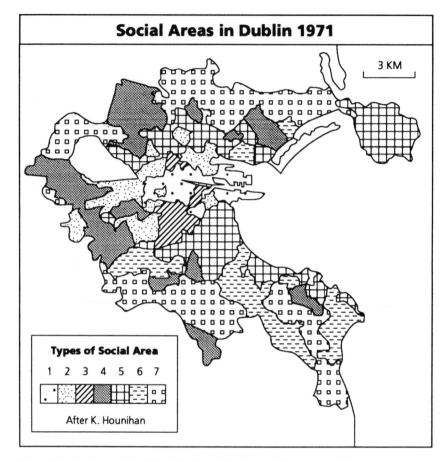

Figure 9.2 Social areas in Dublin, 1971. Kevin Hourihan (1979) has classified types of social area in Dublin by a statistical analysis of the 1971 census data. An explanation of the different types of area shown on the map is given in the text.

possessed high status and were without marked concentrations of elderly or young single people, but were also experiencing slight population decline. The newer suburbs, the sixth group, formed the highest status area in the city where housing was more recent and the population was predominantly middle aged; unlike the other areas of the city previously described, here the population was still expanding quite rapidly. Finally there were the most recently developed suburbs (Type 7), inhabited by young middle-class married couples with young children, living in new, privately owned homes in areas which had almost doubled in population in the five years before the 1971 census. These detailed complexities should not be allowed to mask the basic underlying contrast between, on the one hand, the inner city areas and also extensive tracts of council housing, where problems of social deprivation and poverty are commonplace, and on the other, the relative prosperity of the privately owned suburbs.

In spite of distinctive features related to the history of housing, the problems of the inner city in Dublin have much in common with similar areas in large cities throughout the British Isles. Those residents with the necessary credit-worthiness and a stimulus to move have relocated as owner-occupiers in the suburbs, thus leading to the out-migration of the more skilled, particularly if they have young and growing families. Those who remain are increasingly restricted to local authority houses, as pre-existing rented houses are replaced by council initiatives, either still in the inner city or in outlying estates if their family structure indicates a need for more space. As a result younger families again tend to move (or be moved), so that population in the inner areas has been declining because of lower levels of natural increase as well as because of out-migration. Increasingly council housing, wherever it is located, tends to be associated with concentrations of economically and socially disadvantaged groups. This is particularly marked in the inner city, where the replacement and upgrading of existing housing still remains a continuing problem.

Again, as in other large cities, the problem has been heightened by a changing economic base, producing much higher levels of local unemployment as inner city manufacturing has decayed and employment in the docks has declined and been relocated. It is difficult to find alternative openings for these surplus workers who live in inner city areas, partly because of their lack of appropriate skills. Often they do not have the training or the adaptibility to enter the expanding service sector; and they are also without the residential mobility to relocate closer to the limited number of suitable new suburban jobs which have been created. Certainly some reverse commuting to peripheral factories has grown up but, even where vacancies exist, travel costs are a considerable burden for the more poorly paid.

The pressures of contemporary change

The pressure on the Georgian core of Dublin has not been simply that of dealing with the problem of slum housing. The attitude of some Irish politicians has been one of apathy, or perhaps even antipathy, to the architectural heritage which may be said to symbolize the period of Anglo-Irish dominance in the history of the city, although, as Kevin Kearns has argued, such a point of view '. . . has obscured the reality that Georgian Dublin was an Irish achievement, imbued with an indigenous imprint worthy of being cherished and preserved' (Kearns, 1982, p. 274). That position has changed over recent decades, not least because of a growing recognition of the value which the original facades of central Dublin have for the tourist industry. Perhaps also, in the era of the European Community, there is a growing awareness that the style marks historic Dublin as having been a great European city as well as the centre of British rule. As a result a preservation policy has been spelt out in the Dublin City Development Plan of 1976 which lists a number of buildings, particularly to the east of St Stephen's Green, that are to be strictly preserved, and an area north of

Photo 18 Charlemont House, Hugh Lane Municipal Gallery of Modern Art, Parnell Square, Dublin. Parnell Square is the second earliest of the great Georgian squares of Dublin. Since 1932 Charlemont House has been occupied by what was originally called the Municipal Gallery of Modern Art. Other buildings in the square are now occupied by offices and institutions of various kinds. (Courtesy of Jean Johnson)

the Liffey, where buildings cannot be altered or demolished without planning permission. Yet it has to be said that protection has largely come too late and that modern pressures are considerable. Interiors are not protected; there is no central government financial assistance for preservation; and existing codes for protection have not been strenuously enforced. As a result preservation has often depended on individual and corporate initiatives; but at the same time similar initiatives have also been active in destroying the Georgian heritage of the city.

The loss of buildings as a result of slum clearance is now largely a matter of past history and probably an inevitable process, bearing in mind the structural condition of the buildings and their inappropriateness for modern residential use by the less well-off. In the modern city the pressures are largely commercial and reflect the economic growth of central Dublin since the 1960s. The increased demand which this has produced for office space and other commercial property in the capital city has meant that these uses can clearly outbid the conversion of the existing structures for superior residential flats, although some residential development has taken place.

The result has been the operation of a number of processes. One is the restoration and conversion of decrepit buildings, particularly for use as offices, but also as part of a limited amount of gentrification. Demolition and replacement is a quantitatively more common and, perhaps unfortunately, a financially more rewarding process. The Georgian districts immediately around the central business

Photo 19 O'Connell Street, Dublin. O'Connell Street is now the main popular commercial thoroughfare in Dublin. Once the centre of fashion, it is now more down-market, with fast food outlets, ice-cream parlours, cinemas and chain stores. A hint of its more elegant past is captured by this nighttime scene, although the destruction of Nelson's Column, formerly located opposite the General Post Office (on the left with a columned classical facade) has robbed the street of an important visual focus. (Courtesy of Bord Failte)

Photo 20 Interior of shopping mall, at St Stephen's Green, Dublin. Suburban shopping centres have sprung up in outer Dublin, but there have been central developments as well. This extensive and rather dramatic shopping mall, largely occupied by branches of well-known chain stores, has been quite tastefully fitted into one corner of St Stephen's Green, without drastic damage to an attractive corner of central Dublin. (Photo: J.H. Johnson)

district were particularly ripe for redevelopment of this kind. One estimate is that between 1960 and 1980 the number of Georgian buildings was reduced by 40 per cent. Some have at least been replaced by new buildings on an appropriate scale and sometimes with a facade which provides a sympathetic neighbour for the surviving structures. Others have simply destroyed the existing vistas and although these are now banned in the core areas, the damage is common elsewhere. Finally, some have been replaced by partial facsimiles of the originals or by mock-Georgian pastiches, a solution which may well prove to be a sterile exercise in window dressing.

The future of Georgian Dublin is an important planning problem, although it is one to which effective and long-lasting solutions are far from clear. But to keep a sense of balance it must also be recalled that this section of the city is estimated to occupy only one per cent of the continuous built-up area of greater Dublin. A preoccupation with the preservation of visual appearance, important though it may be, is something which should not be allowed to predominate over a concern for the material well-being of the local and national population. For example, the social polarization which has already been discussed would be further sharpened if the encouragement of middle-class gentrification turned out to be the only way of rescuing surviving Georgian residential terraces.

Indeed the modern city is undergoing important functional changes, which tend to be missed by the tourist gaze. For example, over the last 25 years more than 2.5 million square feet of new, planned shopping space have been opened in Dublin. These are developments which, taken together, are larger than the whole of the city centre shopping area in 1977 and 80 per cent have been located in the suburban and commuter areas of the city. This expansion has to be set in the context of a rapidly growing market of over one million people in greater Dublin, and a city in which the outward movement of population to the suburbs and to settlements beyond the continuous built-up area is taking place very rapidly. Around the Dublin suburbs over 40 planned shopping centres of at least 20,000 square feet each have been opened since 1966; others have been established in outlying centres (Parker, 1987).

Such developments have also brought parallel changes in the city centre. Convenience goods stores have declined, but investment has been made in a number of central shopping malls, the most extensive being one which has been inserted at the edge of St Stephen's Green and has allowed the introduction of a large number of chain stores without undue injury to that important element in the Dublin townscape. A contrasting example is provided by the refurbishment of Lord Powerscourt's dignified town house (built between 1771 and 1774 but even by the end of the nineteenth century merely used as a warehouse) to create a distinctive development of small craftshops, boutiques, art galleries and bistros for which tourist purchases and occasional extravagances by local residents play an important role. A development of this kind gives an indication of the specialist niches which increasingly must be exploited in central locations.

There are features of the existing shopping facilities of central Dublin which offer considerable advantages, since the area currently offers a range and variety of goods for a wide spread of tastes and incomes, of a kind with which no current suburban centre could possibly compete. Unfortunately, it is doubtful whether this diversity can be maintained in the face of the relative reduction in buying power among the population which immediately surrounds the central business district, a population which in any case is falling in number. To this difficulty must be added the lack of easy accessibility to the congested centre of Dublin for a more widely dispersed, car-dependent, middle-class population, who now have convenience goods readily available in large suburban outlets and, increasingly, can make a growing number of their more expensive purchases there as well. Finally, those shops which offer less profit per unit of area are increasingly unable to keep their central sites in the face of competition from the more profitable chain stores and from commercial offices of various kinds – central Dublin without its second-hand bookshops, for example, would be a poorer place for tourists as well as local residents.

The control of outward expansion

A second problem which reflects a general process which has been going on for many years is that of the control of the outward expansion of Dublin. Myles Wright's advisory plan for the Dublin region in effect positively encouraged the further growth of Dublin along the main roads, although these proposals were wrapped up in the jargon of the planning trade (Wright, 1967). The actual urban expansion which has taken place has been considerable, but has been much more undisciplined than Wright envisaged.

New suburbs like Clondalkin, Tallaght and Blanchardstown have sharply extended the built-up area to the west, and the recently opened M50 motorway has linked these western suburbs together and is in process of restructuring the accessibility map of greater Dublin. Further afield, longer-distance rail services have been developed which can bring passengers into central Dublin in time for work and have pushed the potential commuter hinterland for better-paid professional workers some 30 miles away. More local commuting by rail from the north and south-east of Dublin has been improved by DART (Dublin Area Rapid Transit), a development in 1984 which involved the electrification of 38 kilometres of existing railway track, although only a restricted sector of the city is currently influenced by this development. More important, car ownership and the location of an increased number of jobs and services in the suburbs, thus avoiding the tedium of car travel into the centre, have allowed the development of a broad fringe of population growth around Dublin, which has affected apparently rural as well as more clearly defined urban areas on the periphery. The map by Patrick Duffy (1987) of population change in the Dublin region between 1971 and 1981 reveals the importance of that change in a recent decade (Figure 9.3), and the process continues (Horner, 1990).

Attitudes to this type of development tend to be ambivalent. The British planning tradition, exemplified in Ireland by the so-called 'stop-line' implemented

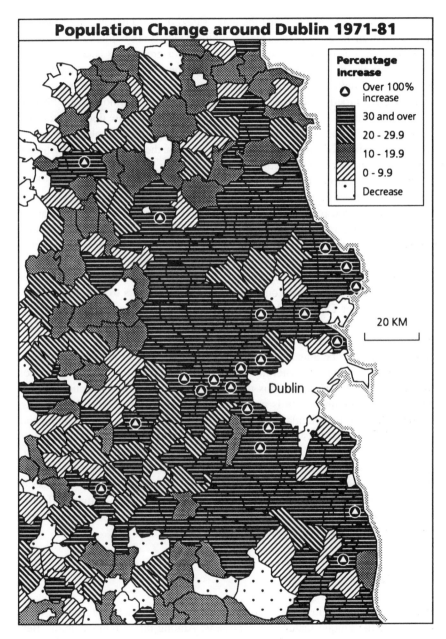

Figure 9.3 Population change around Dublin, 1971-81. James Duffy (1987) has demonstrated the considerable population growth which took place in a wide belt in the periphery of Dublin in the 1970s, a growth which has continued in the next decade.

around Belfast, has been to resist the unrestricted outward expansion of the continuous built-up areas of cities. This is a policy which is not without its difficulties in Britain, since leap-frogging of development over green belts is commonplace. Even within the preserved rural areas pressures on the existing population have not been removed by restricting new residential building, since these restrictions increase the competition for existing housing, a competition almost invariably won by urban-based incomers. The policy is also brought into more doubt by the new policy in the European Community of reducing agricultural surpluses by taking land out of cultivation. In such a context why increase the costs of providing homes and sites for industry by restricting the availability of land for building?

The case of Dublin is somewhat different, since in Ireland there have been fewer really effective restrictions on building non-rural houses of a variety of kinds in what were purely rural areas. This lack of restriction has implications for all parts of the urban area, not just the urban fringe. For example, there is the problem of encouraging development in inner Dublin, since the older suburban areas are now reaching a stage where investment will increasingly be needed to maintain their quality. Similarly, some restriction on the availability of industrial sites in the suburbs might encourage smaller manufacturers to consider possible locations in inner Dublin and reverse the decline in blue-collar work there. In other words, some control of outward expansion would assist in redressing the balance between the inner city and suburbs.

There may also be advantages for other areas as well. Much of current outer fringe development is at wastefully low densities, so that some greater restriction might increase densities and thus make easier the provision of public transport and the infrastructure which is necessary to serve the new residential building. In addition, there is particularly good agricultural land to the north of Dublin and, taking a longer view, it would seem inappropriate to allow permanent developments which would take it irreversibly out of cultivation. Finally, although Dublin is not without its own economic problems, it might be argued that there is a case for restricting its expansion if this is taking place at the expense of the rest of the nation. That is a policy, however, which would demand effective regional economic planning, not just simply local land-use controls, a matter to be considered in the next chapter.

Conclusion

Belfast and Dublin in their individual ways are intensely interesting cities because of the unique features they possess. Among other things Dublin offers its remarkable collection of fine buildings, the contrasting lifestyles of its rich and poor, its function as the centre of former colonial power and now as a capital city, and its role in the development of Irish national consciousness. There seems to be a dramatic contrast between Dublin's heritage and that of Belfast – in its own way just as stimulating – where the declining relics of a famous industrial past are surrounded by often brash twentieth-century developments, in a city which is divided more by religion than by class, but which has also acted as a centre for the development of regional awareness.

Yet in many ways the underlying geographical similarities are profound. Their sites provided direct contact with Britain, access to the interior of Ireland and space for urban expansion, both in their central areas and at their peripheries. In the modern world, the similar size of their populations and their parallel functions as centres of administration, education, shopping and political activity give them a greater likeness than their citizens might be prepared to acknowledge. So too does their complete domination of the economic and social life of the two political units in which they are located.

Further reading

The physical structure of Dublin, and especially the survival of the past in its modern urban landscape, is particularly well illustrated in N. McCullough, *Dublin: An Urban History* (Anne Street Press, Dublin, 1989). A more formal presentation of the architectural history of Georgian Dublin and its antecedents is M. Craig, *Dublin, 1660–1860* (Allen Figgis, Dublin, 1980).

The economic history of Dublin in the last quarter of the nineteenth century is effectively surveyed in M.E. Daly, *Dublin the Deposed Capital: A Social and Economic History, 1860–1914* (University Press, Cork, 1984). The problems of preserving the Georgian heritage of Dublin are surveyed in K.C. Kearns, *Georgian Dublin: Ireland's Imperilled Architectural Heritage* (David and Charles, Newton Abbot, 1984). A survey of contemporary Dublin by an informed group of local geographers is A.A. Horner and A.J. Parker (eds), *Geographical Perspectives on the Dublin Region* (Geographical Society of Ireland, Special Publication 5, Dublin, 1987).

Projections for the future growth of the Dublin region are discussed in the *Eastern Region Settlement Strategy 2011*, 2 vols (Eastern Regional Development Organization, Dublin, 1985). The most recent study of Dublin, published after this book was written, is A. MacLaran, *Dublin* (World Cities Series), Belhaven Press, London, 1993).

Chapter 10

Economic planning in the Irish Republic

With less than 3.5 million people in the Republic of Ireland and 1.5 million in Northern Ireland, these form two of the smallest units in western Europe measured by their total populations. Many of their economic problems are very difficult to solve within the confines of their local economies, since their small domestic markets greatly restrict the kinds of industry that can flourish without recourse to the greater uncertainties involved in the export of goods and services. The small total populations also make it surprising that there is judged to be a need for any regional dimension to economic planning in Ireland: looked at dispassionately the whole island of Ireland might seem an appropriate 'regional' area for planning and, indeed, the European Community has classified Ireland as an undifferentiated area, all of which is appropriate to receive regional aid from Community funds. But, even leaving on one side the special case of Northern Ireland where political division makes separate economic planning obviously necessary, there are many other local loyalties found among the Irish people – certainly enough to develop a parallel awareness of local economic problems among administrators.

The period of national self-sufficiency

Over the years policy makers in the Irish Republic have often been obsessed with population numbers, although that concern is not surprising when the downward trend since the 1840s is recalled. The many years of population decline have left an indelible mark on Irish political consciousness and influenced the economic stance that was adopted in the Irish Free State in the 1920s and 1930s. As was noted in Chapter 6 various policies were designed, not unnaturally, to promote economic independence from Britain, to parallel the political independence that had already been achieved; but they were also intended to create local employment and thus reverse population decline. By the early 1930s a tariff wall had been erected to provide an economic environment where new manufacturing industries could take root – industries which, to start with at least, were primarily intended to serve the home market.

The limitations of this policy only became clear in the 1950s. The basic problem was that the population of the Republic, which was then less than three million, could only provide a very restricted base for employment growth in manufacturing industry, particularly when set against an inevitable decline in the agricultural labour force. Two other difficulties also emerged. The policy of protection had no explicit regional component and contrasts in prosperity between the Dublin region and many parts of the rest of the country were emerging alarmingly. In addition, the quality of many of the products of the protected manufacturing industries, lacking the stimulation of effective competition in design as well as in price, not only provided a cause of concern for Irish consumers but also inhibited the expansion of exports.

A decisive change in direction was spelt out in 1958, when the government initiated its First Programme for Economic Expansion to cover the five years to 1963. The aim of the programme was an already familiar one of revitalizing the Irish economy in order to halt the emigration of those displaced agricultural workers not being absorbed by other sectors of the economy. What was new was that this goal was to be achieved by opening up the economy to outside influences. For example, the government dropped its insistence that all industries should be under the nominal control of Irish citizens and a concerted attempt was made to attract foreign capital, particularly if it was to be invested in export-orientated industries. Credit facilities and industrial grants were improved and, most important, significant tax reliefs were given on increased export earnings, a concession which in practice gave greatest benefit to newly established industries coming from outside Ireland. What turned out to be a modest economic growth target of two per cent per annum was set – in practice easily exceeded, with most of the increase coming in manufacturing. The most obvious result was a considerable reduction in net emigration and in the rate of population decline, already discussed in chapter 6.

The first programme was followed by a second, which was to operate from 1964 to 1969. Entry into the European Economic Community was expected during the operation of the second programme; and as a preparatory step into a more competitive environment, an Anglo-Irish trade agreement was signed in 1965, the same year as applications for membership of the European Economic Community were submitted by both the United Kingdom and Ireland. The Anglo-Irish agreement abolished duties on Irish exports to the United Kingdom, thus giving foreign firms an additional stimulus to establish plants in the Republic, because of the access which an Irish location would immediately give to the British market and (it was assumed) to the European Economic Community in the near future. In turn the protective duties on Irish imports from Britain were to be progressively removed over a ten-year period. What the agreement signalled was a willingness to dismantle the protected home market and a confirmation of the changed orientation of economic policy.

Britain's failure to be accepted for entry to the European Economic Community during the 1960s meant that inevitably the Irish Republic could not proceed alone because the two economies were so tightly knit together. As a result a third programme was initiated in 1969 with somewhat scaled-down targets for economic growth, designed to cover the period to 1972. In spite of this setback the 1960s can be seen as a period of remarkable success for the economy of the Irish Republic. This success was demonstrated by continued economic growth and by falling levels of net emigration, which were reduced from over 40,000 per annum in the 1950s to just over 16,000 a year between 1961 and 1966 and 12,000 a year between 1966 and 1971.

Underlying this achievement was a rapid reorientation in the relative importance of different sectors of the economy during this critical decade. Employment in agriculture, forestry and fishing decreased by over 25 per cent, but employment in services grew by nearly 11 per cent and the industrial sector showed an increase of over 27 per cent. During the same period there was a 198 per cent increase in the value of exports, particularly of manufactured goods, which by 1971 had replaced agricultural products as the main component and the driving force in Irish exports. About 550 new industrial enterprises were established during the decade, 68 per cent as the result of foreign participation.

One disturbing indicator was that, although the rise in national production was impressive, the growth in the number of people employed was much more modest. In fact it was a mere 1.9 per cent, or just over 18,000 people, between 1961 and 1971. The unrestricted entry of Irish workers to the British labour market had continued after political independence and wage aspirations therefore tended to be set by the levels available in Britain. Hence an underlying problem for successful new industries was that they usually had to attain high levels of productivity, and as a result employ relatively few people in relation to their turnover, if they were to compete internationally, given the wages that were acceptable to workers in Ireland.

A second reservation was that, if attention is shifted to individual regions within the Republic, the success of the policy in altering the longer-term pattern of population change was much less impressive. Areas in the north and west continued to experience decline, if at a less remarkable rate. Indeed, it is probably fair to say that although the first two programmes of economic expansion paid lip service to the needs of the less favoured areas, a fully-fledged concern with regional development came relatively late in the process of creating new employment.

Early regional dimensions in economic planning

Formal regional support for modern industry in the western counties of the Republic began in 1952, when a broad segment of the north and west was delimited as an area where government grants were to be made available for small-scale manufacturing industries. This first step had little effect on job creation in the Undeveloped Areas, later given the more politically correct title of 'Designated Areas' (Figure 9.1), because the range of employment assisted was limited, potential employers had more complex needs than a relatively small

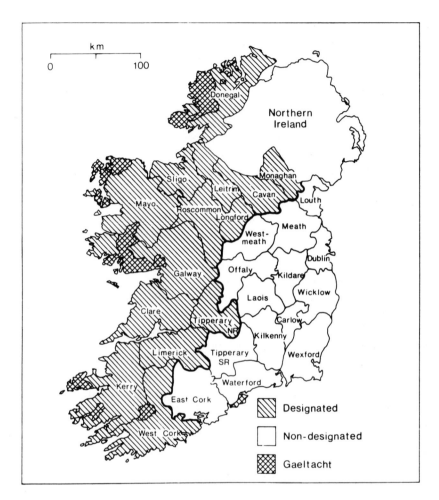

Figure 10.1 Republic of Ireland: Designated Areas and Gaeltacht

capital subsidy and, at that time, the general economy of the Republic was not conducive to economic growth. Later the initiative was expanded to develop the tourist industry and to attract larger firms; but, paradoxically, increased grants did not necessarily bring any real advantage to the Designated Areas. For example, the Industrial Grants Act of 1956 certainly gave higher grants to firms in this region, but somewhat lower grants were now also to be paid to new businesses locating in the rest of the Republic, with the net result that the relative financial advantage of the Designated Areas was in fact reduced. When the policy of general economic expansion was launched much more energetically in the late 1950s the main thrust, almost inevitably, was to obtain growth in any possible location.

If an effective general strategy was missing, two local initiatives provided sharply contrasting steps in the direction of regional development. In 1957 a state-sponsored board, *Gaeltarra Eireann*, was established to increase employment in the *Gaeltacht* – those rural areas where Irish was still actively spoken as the language of daily life (Figure 10.1). The problem was a considerable one and success was limited. Most modern industries that were likely to be successful would almost inevitably find themselves doing business in English and rural craft industries, where Irish might be used in day-to-day activities, would only be likely to employ a small number of people. Other possible activities had similar problems. The tourist industry might be expected to do well in the appealing scenery of the *Gaeltacht*, but its highly seasonal nature would be as likely to attract temporary employees from outside the region as to offer permanent work for local people. At the same time the growth of tourism would bring pressures which would tend to reduce the chances of the survival of the language. As a result the range of satisfactory new employment that could be encouraged was very restricted. In any case, the activities of *Gaeltarra Eireann* were only relevant to a very small proportion of the total population: in 1981 there were about 75,000 people living in the officially designated *Gaeltacht*, of whom only 58,000 were returned as Irish speaking.

In terms of creating a far-reaching strategy for regional development a more directly important step was the establishment of the Shannon Free Airport Industrial Estate in 1959. The original reason for creating this industrial estate was to boost the declining traffic of Shannon Airport, which was being increasingly by-passed by longer-range jet aircraft. The facilities of the international airport allowed the handling of air freight and the easy transit of visiting executives, and to add to these advantages a free-trade zone was established to reduce the bureaucratic problems involved in import and export. These very real advantages attracted a large number of overseas firms, producing a wide range of goods as diverse as pianos and transistor radios.

The development of Shannon Free Trade Area was important in that it illustrated the feasibility of creating employment for 5000 people (more than half of them men) in an area adjoining the underdeveloped areas to the west. Its success certainly influenced later proposals which emphasized the advantages associated with the concentration of investment in a limited number of places; but there were particular circumstances operating at Shannon. The existence of an already established international airport with surplus capacity provided a unique environment which could not be replicated elsewhere. The free trade area was again a local feature, again difficult to reproduce generally. Finally, the success of the industrial estate owed much to a special concentration of managerial talent and to a disproportionate amount of promotional effort, directed at making the estate a showpiece for the new expansionist industrial policies that were being developed.

The critical matter was that the undoubted success of the Shannon estate came just at a time when the idea of growth poles was making a general impact on regional planning theory and this was an important factor in popularizing a new policy of concentrating government assistance in a limited number of centres. It tended to be overlooked that few of the industries on the estate established links with each other or with other firms elsewhere in Ireland, although the concentration of activity certainly encouraged the improvement of educational, shopping and training facilities in the city of Limerick. The estate remained an enclave which assisted the balance of payments and provided local employment, but hardly could be said to have induced much self-sustaining growth in the national economy or extended any substantial influence outside the local labour market centred on Limerick.

The emergence of more formal regional plans

Indications of a new policy of concentrating investment can be detected in the findings of a variety of governmental committees and quangos in the early 1960s. The outcome was a government statement in 1965 accepting the concept of development centres as a means of promoting further expansion of economic activity. Somewhat earlier, in 1963, the State was divided into nine planning regions, formed by grouping together existing counties in a rough and ready way. A government regional development committee was set up and *An Foras Forbartha* (The National Institute for Physical Planning and Construction Research) was established. Under its auspices consultants were appointed to prepare three regional plans based on the new planning regions. The three reports which emerged, although each was very different, translated the growth centre idea into more tangible proposals.

The first was a study of the Mid-West Region by Nathaniel Lichfield and Associates (1966). This particular region was chosen because of the need to marry economic and physical planning in a region which included the then rapidly growing Shannon Airport Estate. Lichfield wrestled with the problem of whether to concentrate investment in part of the region or to spread it more widely, mirroring a problem which also applied to Ireland as a whole. His solution (an almost inevitable one in this region) was to designate the city of Limerick and the much smaller town of Ennis, together with the Shannon Estate as forming a central growth area where investment should be concentrated. The problem of how much investment was appropriate was impossible for him to answer effectively in the absence of any central government plan for the allocation of money to the various regions.

The second plan was prepared by Myles Wright and Partners (1967) for the Dublin Region, essentially the East Planning Region. This plan followed more closely the conventional mode of the time, by being much more directly concerned with physical planning. The Wright plan assumed that the continued growth of greater Dublin was inevitable, a reasonable enough assumption since it could be argued that, within the Irish Republic, Dublin was the only urban settlement large enough to offer the external economies which would attract self-sustaining economic growth. His proposal was that the continued expansion of the metropolitan area was to be accommodated by a westward growth of the built-up area, fingering out along the existing road pattern. There were few substantial towns nearby which could form significant counter-attractions to Dublin, but it was proposed that the populations of Drogheda, Arklow, Naas/Newbridge, and Navan should be approximately doubled to produce outlying subsidiary growth centres.

The third and most influential report, prepared by Colin Buchanan and Partners in association with Economic Consultants (1968), was quite different in concept. Although published last of the three, it would have made much more sense for it to have been issued first, since it proposed a strategy for the whole State and regional details were not worked out with any precision. The outstanding contribution of the Buchanan report was to present the argument for growth centres in a persuasive manner and to propose specific locations for their development. The argument was that economic growth should be concentrated because it could then be backed by good training facilities, effective communications and a reasonably diverse labour market. It was argued that the greater ease of movement which the expansion of private transport was bringing to the Irish countryside would allow these centres to develop more extensive journey-to-work areas around them, so that their economic benefits would be more widely diffused and trickle down to smaller communities.

Buchanan designated nine major centres where growth should be concentrated (Figure 10.2). Three of the centres already had quite virile growth: Dublin, Cork and Limerick (including the Shannon development). The dominance of Dublin in all aspects of Irish life was so great that it was impossible to modify, even if that was thought to be desirable. It was therefore suggested that no attempt should be made to stop Dublin's economic growth, although it was suggested that industrial expansion there should not be given any special inducements. Cork and Limerick/Shannon were also designated as national growth centres, to be allocated a major share of the country's economic growth, with a special effort being made to ensure their success. Buchanan added – somewhat reluctantly, a reading of the report would suggest – that there might be advantages in 'a certain amount' of industrial development taking place in other centres as well. These were what he called regional growth centres: Sligo, Galway, Drogheda, Dundalk, Athlone and Waterford. That left gaps in the regional coverage, hence Letterkenny was added as a local growth centre for Donegal and Tralee was given a similar function for the south-west. Castlebar was more tentatively recommended as a local centre for Mayo, much to the annoyance of the citizens of Ballina; and Cavan (with a population of just less than 4000 when the report was prepared) was picked out from a number of small towns of a similar size as a somewhat unlikely centre for the difficult small-farm area close to the Irish border, which embraced counties Longford, Cavan and Monaghan.

The recommendations in the Buchanan report reflected the fashion of the time and were quite eagerly seized on by the Irish chattering classes, as the report seemed to be underpinned by a sensible theory and broke away from the politically convenient, if economically illiterate, policy of spreading scarce resources evenly or, still worse, distributing them according to the relative strengths of competing lobbyists. But the strategy was not without its defects, some immediately obvious and some which emerged with the passage of time.

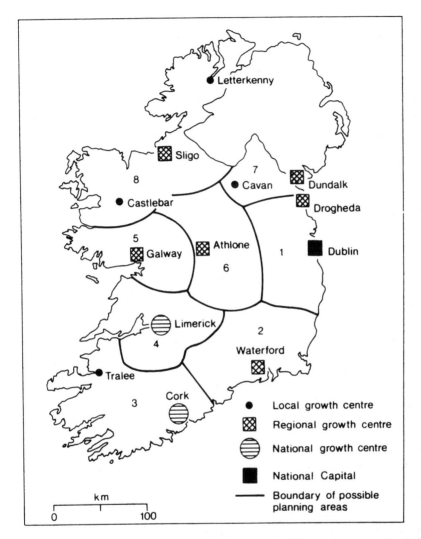

Figure 10.2 Buchanan proposals for the Republic of Ireland. The 1968 consultants' report by Colin Buchanan and partners proposed a general strategy for economic growth in the Irish Republic by concentrating investment in a series of growth centres.

Buchanan's national growth centres might well be viable, although it requires a considerable stretch of the imagination to see Cork and Limerick as comparable with the economist's concept of a growth pole, characterized by such a cluster of interlinked services and activities that self-sustaining economic growth would be an inevitable consequence. All the other centres were very small by West European standards and it was very unlikely that these centres could develop sufficient local networks of economic linkages to make them distinctively attractive to incoming employers. Their local labour markets would always be limited, with the result that large firms would have problems in recruiting sufficient skills and there could only be a restricted number of industrial units in each town. Even if it were possible to create external economies by concentrating industrial growth, this effect would always be limited. In addition, even allowing for the growth of greater personal mobility in the countryside, it was not clear how the benefits from these growth centres could trickle down to many smaller towns some distance away or penetrate far into the rural population. For example, Mary Cawley (1980) has shown that the new industrial estate that was created in Galway certainly recruited workers from the surrounding countryside and that a variety of contacts between countryside and town have increased as a result; but she also demonstrated that not all of the rural population was involved and that there was quite a modest limit to the distance that workers were prepared and able to travel.

A further problem was to do with the nature of the employment that might be attracted. The firms that were likely to do well in the smaller, more isolated growth centres would probably be small independent units particularly concerned with export overseas. Those that involved high technology (in, for example, the growing computer industry) would probably have to import many of their components. Few of them were likely to need complex links with other local firms. As a result some critics of the proposals wondered whether there was any real economic advantage in discouraging the establishment of new industries in other centres where they might do just as well.

An inevitable result of the proposals would have been that, as well as some towns being encouraged to grow, others would be actively discriminated against. As a result, other critics highlighted the moral problems involved if the central government was seen as arbitrarily depriving some of its citizens of the benefits of increased employment, simply because they happened to live in towns which were not singled out for development. This was not just an abstract moral issue, but also reflects a major political problem in a small nation, where local loyalties are strong and where the combined resistance of those towns not chosen for development could well be sufficient to overthrow the whole policy. As a result, although the Irish government made welcoming noises on the publication of the report, in the longer run it found difficulty in facing up to its more unpleasant implications.

Immediately after its publication industrial estates were sanctioned for many of the regional centres and industrial expansion was seen as the principal means of reshaping the economic map of the Irish Republic. To this end, the Industrial Development Authority (IDA) was reconstituted in 1969. In fact the IDA had its origins in 1949 when it was established to promote new industrial firms but not given any real economic clout. In 1952 a parallel organization, *An Foras Tionscail* (The Grants Board), was set up to administer grants in the under-developed areas. Then in 1969 these two bodies were brought together in the new IDA, which was given greater resources and was sensibly required to combine both financial and promotional functions. It was now made responsible for national as well as regional industrial development; it had powers to develop

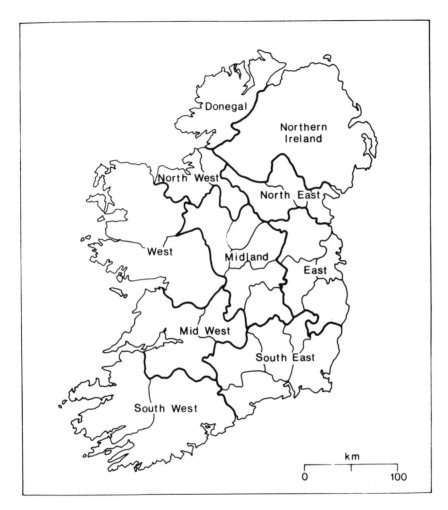

Figure 10.3 Industrial Development Authority Planning Regions

industrial estates, to administer grants and incentives for industry and to provide housing where it was needed to attract key employees. Not least it was required to foster regional economic development, which was now given a much higher national priority. Curiously the IDA was made directly responsible for only eight of the nine planning regions, with the Mid-West being subcontracted to the Shannon Free Airport Development Company – an existing vested interest, albeit a successful one. The IDA planning regions (Figure 10.3) were very similar to the 1963 regions, rather than the more radical recasting of regions which was also a feature of the Buchanan proposals; and as time went by other recommendations were watered down. This became manifest in 1972 with the first publication of detailed regional industrial plans.

The interest of the IDA plans lies in their specificity and their ambition, their combination of a grasp of the real world with flights of fancy (Industrial Development Authority, 1972; 1979). In theory, the IDA was concerned with manufacturing employment only, but fortunately its plans also examined the contribution to regional development of agriculture and services, although strictly speaking these fields lay outside its competence. The politically accept-able and probably quite sensible demographic objectives that the IDA took upon itself included the increase of population in all regions in the longer term, the reduction of emigration rates in all regions and the restriction of Dublin's growth to the equivalent of its natural increase. To this end, with considerable bravado, the IDA specified job targets in great detail for various small sub-regions of the State. Almost inevitably these local targets were impossible to achieve, even if larger regional totals worked out approximately right.

The IDA also specified very ambitious social goals, possibly a sop to its political masters. The existing pattern of communities was to be maintained but, remarkably, at the same time the clustering of geographically and functionally related towns was to be encouraged (whatever that might mean). A number of centres providing higher-order services were to be provided in each region, while at the same time the development of smaller centres also was to be encouraged and additional employment was to be found for the *Gaeltacht*. Selected towns were to be made growth centres, but employment opportunities were to be provided for the population within a travel-to-work time of not more than 30 minutes. Admirable though these goals may have been, it is difficult to see how they all could be fitted together in a real world where new employment and resources were becoming increasingly scarce.

The IDA's description of the kind of industries it wished to attract had a similar air of unreality. Such industries would have low capital intensity, use Irish materials and services, employ men and link with other Irish industries. They would also be highly profitable, be likely to grow, demand highly skilled labour and be involved in international trade. For good measure they would be Irish owned, or have substantial participation by Irish directors, or they would be international companies, with high commercial stability and strength, which were prepared to allow their Irish subsidiaries a high degree of independence. Suitable firms would originate outside the European Community, but would wish to trade with it. It was not clear how many of these admirable attributes an individual firm should be required to possess, but this certainly seems a counsel of perfection in the light of the effort involved in attracting any kind of new employment to the more remote parts of Ireland.

Leaving on one side the *Gaeltacht* and the Mid-West region, where other authorities carried the direct responsibility, the IDA proposed job targets for 177 towns. For the five years starting in 1973 55,000 new jobs were to be created. In all 50 per cent of these jobs (rather than the 75 per cent tentatively suggested in the Buchanan report) were to be located in Dublin and the major growth centres, with the rest elsewhere. These proposals were formally adopted by the Irish government in 1972 and, simplifying the details, four strands of policy could be distinguished.

Photo 21 Intel (Ireland) at Leixlip, County Kildare. The small town of Leixlip is 10 miles from Dublin. Here is located an example of one of the branches of multinational firms that have been attracted to the Irish Republic in the past 30 years, in this case in the growing computer industry. (Courtesy of the Industrial Development Authority)

First, the future development of Dublin was simply to accommodate the natural increase of its existing population and the population of other regions was to be at least maintained. Second, there was to be expansion centred on eight other urban areas. Third, there was to be the development of county or other large towns in each region. Finally, special measures for the development of the Irish-speaking *Gaeltacht* areas were to be continued. In short, the Buchanan proposals were far from being completely ignored – there was an inevitable quality about their main outlines which prevented that – but government officials were also interested in touching various other political bases. In effect, what had been produced was a policy which blended political constraints and economic realities to form some sort of a workable compromise – a situation not unknown in other countries where a regional dimension has been given to economic planning.

It is not easy to assess the detailed success of these plans for a variety of reasons. One hostage to fortune was given by the very detailed targets that were produced for 48 sub-regions, in practice very difficult to hit exactly in every location. Perhaps fortunately, these details seem to have largely been forgotten with the passage of time. A second problem was that running parallel with the creation of new jobs was a fall in the number of existing jobs. This was partly because the opening up of the Irish market to imports, an inescapable aspect of the new policy, led to the decline of some existing firms which could not adjust to the new economic regime. The new firms themselves contributed to the decline, occasionally because of the competition their products offered, but more commonly because they attracted the best workers. Indeed some small employers themselves found it more worthwhile to work for incoming firms rather than to continue with their own struggling businesses. Finally, policy could not be isolated from what was happening in the rest of the world; and very soon after the new plans were initiated a severe economic shock was administered by a massive rise in world oil prices after 1974.

The success in attracting new employment was clear. For the five-year planning period starting in 1973 57,500 jobs were created, clearly exceeding the overall target, but the parallel decline in existing jobs was much greater than the 17,000 possible redundancies originally expected. In fact the absolute number of job losses reached 55,600, so that the net increase in manufacturing employment was only 1900. However, this was a better result than might be thought at first inspection, since a contribution was made to a rise in disposable incomes, with the result that service employment of various types also expanded.

The policy of bringing in outside capital and improving the balance of payments was also clearly successful. Over 60 per cent of the output of the newly created firms was directed at export and over 56 per cent of the employment generated was produced by projects originating in overseas countries. Most of this foreign investment came from the United States (38 per cent), followed by the United Kingdom (20 per cent) and what was then West Germany (13 per cent). As 50 per cent of the fixed assets of new Irish registered companies were also owned by foreign enterprises (often British), even these impressive statistics tend to understate the importance of external influences.

Measured by population change – one of the chosen yardsticks when economic policy was being promulgated – the 1970s showed a remarkable success. As has already been recorded in chapter 6, between the censuses of 1971 and 1981 the total population of the Irish Republic increased by 15 per cent and it was notable that all the planning regions shared in that increase, although at varying levels. It has to be said that in the late 1970s the relative attraction of the British labour market had been falling, so that outward migration was reduced and return migration encouraged; but at least the kinds of jobs had been created which were attractive enough to bring back some of the workers who had left earlier.

The optimism of the 1970s was replaced by the reality of the 1980s. Increased expenditure on social security accompanied by world recession and rising fuel costs produced a situation in which, at the beginning of the 1980s, the Republic was deeply mired in international debt. From 1980 to 1984 numbers at work decreased by 40,000 and unemployment rose to 19 per cent. By the mid-1980s the cost of servicing the national debt was using 90 per cent of revenue from income tax. Tax rates had to be increased and a reduction of unemployment in Britain caused emigration to soar again. In the light of this situation the National Economic and Social Council commissioned the Telesis Consultancy Group in

1982 to produce *A Review of Industrial Policy*. This government-sponsored study, undertaken in a context in which government funds were becoming increasingly scarce, encouraged the development of a more selective industrial strategy.

This strategy placed greater emphasis on finding firms which would add high value as a result of the manufacturing process, with products aimed at specialist markets and requiring high quality and good design. In the face of increased competition from new industrial areas in the developing world it seemed sensible to emphasize the positive attributes of a labour force that was relatively well-educated, English-speaking and served by a well-developed business and institutional infrastructure. Greater selectivity also reflected a related problem: foreign firms tended to concentrate on manufacturing and, as well as components, imported design, research and marketing expertise from headquarters elsewhere. As a result they have not employed a proper share of the more advanced skills produced by the Irish higher educational system, with the consequence that many graduates are lost to the Irish economy. As a result some commentators have been expressing worries about the relationship of dependency associated with the branch-plant economy, although in fairness it would be very difficult for the IDA to find many indigenous firms that could provide these more specialized types of employment and sophisticated linkages with the rest of the economy.

Although more stringent criteria are being applied to the firms being assisted, the intention is not to abandon the Designated Areas of the west and the IDA continues to steer footloose firms in this direction using differential grants and presentational methods, although as funds are restricted the clout of the IDA in controlling location may be reduced. What certainly lies outside its control is the pattern of closures and redundancies that may affect already established firms. There must be a real concern that in the longer term the successful and lasting employers will be those which benefit from the business services available in limited areas, particularly those found in and around Dublin. In this context it is perhaps significant to note the abolition in 1987 of the nine Regional Development Organizations, which served each of the planning regions. These were non-statutory coordinating bodies which were responsible for producing a number of strategic planning documents. More importantly, they facilitated local initiatives, brought together representatives of various sectors of the economy, and acted as a bridge between local and central interests. Their disappearance does not signal the end of a regional dimension in job creation, but does seem to leave a vacuum in the planning process.

In conclusion it must be said that, measured by international comparisons, the economy of the Republic of Ireland has had considerable successes since it took a radical change of direction in the 1960s and, in a sense, these still continue. In spite of the problems of the early 1980s, from 1985 to 1990 the Irish Republic maintained an annual average rate of growth of 4.6 per cent. From 1990 to 1992 that growth has been maintained, if at a slightly lower average level. Economic growth has been based on particularly strong exports in recent years. This improvement has led to trade and balance of payment surpluses, reversing the substantial trade deficits experienced in the 1980s, although problems of national indebtedness still remain. The downside is in unemployment which in July 1992 stood at 17.5 per cent, with over 290,000 people out of work. As the current recession in Great Britain continues, thus checking emigration from Ireland, further rises in unemployment seem inevitable. It appears that a more selective attitude to financing new industry has also produced a low rate of employment creation: indeed over the 1980s the Republic was the only country in the OECD to experience an actual fall in employment overall. Hence the rather sour description by an Irish journalist of the situation in August 1992 as 'a country where the economy works but the people do not'.

Further reading

A general survey of various initiatives is J.H. Johnson, 'Republic of Ireland' in H.D. Clout (ed.), *Regional Development in Western Europe* (Fulton, London, 1987), 285–305. An effective critique of the concentration of investment in a limited number of centres is P. Breathnach, 'The demise of growth-centre policy: the case of the Republic of Ireland' in R. Hudson and J.R. Lewis (eds), *Regional Planning in Europe* (Pion, London, 1982), 35–56. An exposition of some of the moral issues involved in concentrating investment is provided by J. Newman, *New Dimensions in Regional Planning* (Stationery Office, Dublin, 1967).

The detailed historical background is provided in K.A. Kennedy, T. Giblin and D. McHugh, *The Economic Development of Ireland in the Twentieth Century* (Routledge, London, 1988). A short but effective account of industrial expansion and change over the past half-century is given in L. Kennedy, *The Modern Industrialization of Ireland, 1940–1988* (Economic and Social History Society of Ireland, Dublin, 1989).

Before its unfortunate demise An Foras Forbartha produced two relevant overviews: *Regional Planning in the 1990s: a Discussion of Issues* and *Regional Planning: a Review of Regional Studies* (An Foras Forbartha, Dublin, 1987).

Chapter 11

Economic planning in Northern Ireland

Although currently lower than in the Republic, one of the characteristic features of the Northern Ireland economy has been its high unemployment in recent years. In common with other economically marginal areas in the United Kingdom, Northern Ireland's unemployment rate has not only been higher than the national average, but in periods of economic recession the number of people out of work has also tended to rise proportionally more.

Many of the problems of unemployment in Northern Ireland result from the manner in which manufacturing industry has developed in the area, a matter which has already been discussed in chapter 8. The varied industries that grew up in the second half of the nineteenth century had a number of features in common – features which still remain relevant for modern employment in the area. Since the local market was static they were dependent on export sales for expansion. In addition, imported raw materials and imported fuel played an important role in production. In this economic environment the successful industries were those in which fuel costs, import costs and final delivery costs were low in comparison with the price of the finished product. As a result the Industrial Revolution did not penetrate effectively very far from the port of Belfast. These industries were also particularly susceptible to economic fluctuations, since ships and heavy machinery were expensive capital goods and linen sold at the luxury end of the consumer market.

In the twentieth century these fluctuations became more serious. The Great Depression of the 1930s brought general industrial decline, but economic recovery came with the Second World War. This was a period when the Belfast shipyard produced many British warships; the aircraft manufacturer, Short, relocated production away from its strategically exposed location in south-east England to a site adjoining Belfast Harbour Airport and Belfast Lough; and the textile and clothing industries were stimulated by the demand for uniforms and other materials. Farmers also enjoyed previously unknown prosperity, supported by subsidies and the demands of the wartime British market from which many overseas imports were excluded by the German blockade. In a situation of full and well-paid employment, service industries also did well, within the limits imposed by wartime shortages. In comparison with the neutral Irish Free State, where shortages of imports produced a considerable decline in industrial production and higher unemployment, the citizens of Northern Ireland found that, although the war brought death and injury to some, their average per capita income had moved sharply higher than that found in the South.

As the immediate impact of the war gradually disappeared previous problems of falling demand reasserted themselves, not because of a temporary recession but the result of more fundamental technological changes. The rise of long-distance air transport destroyed the market for large passenger liners, in which the Belfast shipyards had made their reputation. Competition from man-made fibres became irresistible. Economic growth was more strongly tied to consumer goods industries, in which being cut off from the British market by sea produced a competitive disadvantage – a disadvantage emphasized by the relative economic decline of the United Kingdom, which disproportionately affected Northern Ireland. Rural areas had similar difficulties. Underemployment among rural workers was long standing and, in common with rural areas throughout western Europe, population decline was an inescapable concomitant of a higher per capita standard of living in the countryside. Small towns which served the surrounding countryside, particularly those in the west of the Province without much manufacturing industry, had static or declining economies, with local labour markets characterized by a lack of turnover. The net result was that Northern Ireland found itself dominated by industries in decline or industries with falling labour forces. At the same time the Province had a high rate of natural increase, somewhat higher than in the Republic and considerably more rapid than in other regions of the United Kingdom.

Unemployment at different scales

As a result the problem of unemployment has taken a dominant role in considerations of economic development in Northern Ireland. Unemployment is unevenly distributed and constitutes a problem at three different levels. First there is the general problem of unemployment in Northern Ireland. Currently in the early 1990s the number of unemployed has remained over 100,000. In August 1992, for example, there were 111,390 people without work – 15.4 per cent of the work force (14.9 per cent if seasonally adjusted). This represents an upward trend, with an increase from 14.4 per cent (13.9 per cent seasonally adjusted) in the previous year. The situation in Northern Ireland has to be placed in the context of what is happening in the general United Kingdom economy, since macro-economic policy in Britain also applies in Northern Ireland. There are two possible interpretations. On the one hand unemployment in the Province has consistently been worse than the national average in the United Kingdom; and the nature of the industrial structure and the marginal location of Northern Ireland in the British economy make this unfortunate but unsurprising.

From another point of view, however, Northern Ireland has so far escaped the

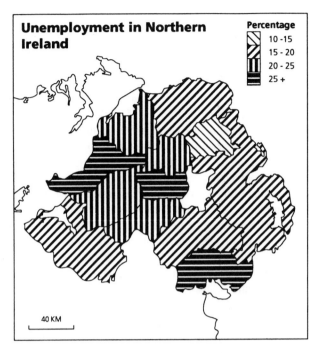

Figure 11.1 Unemployment in Northern Ireland. The map shows percentage unemployment by travel-to-work areas in August 1992, when the overall level of unemployment in Northern Ireland was 15.2 per cent of the workforce.

worst impact of the huge rise in unemployment which has spread across the United Kingdom since 1990. Along with other areas which have traditionally suffered the largest increases of unemployment during economic downturns, Northern Ireland has experienced the smallest increases in unemployment in comparison with other major regions of the United Kingdom. This can be explained in a number of ways. Firstly, there may be structural reasons why the Northern Ireland economy has been less affected. Employment in the public sector here is particularly significant and spending in this area has been maintained; manufacturing industries like food, drink and clothing are also relatively important and demand for these purchases has been less severely reduced than for some other goods; and house prices in Northern Ireland are the lowest in the United Kingdom, so that mortgage interest payments have had a less detrimental influence on local demand. Secondly, it may simply be that the British recession is having a lagged effect and that unemployment may continue to increase in Northern Ireland after it has started to fall elsewhere in Britain. Finally, the situation may simply reflect the fact that the unemployment situation in Northern Ireland as a whole was bad to start with, so that there was less scope for the situation to get much worse.

At a second scale, there is also an uneven distribution of unemployment within Northern Ireland (Figure 11.1). When the situation is analysed by travel to work areas the detailed picture changes from time to time, but the general pattern is remarkably consistent. Unemployment rates are much higher to the west of a line running through Lough Neagh, although in the south-east, in the Newry region, there is another area of permanent high unemployment.

Percentage levels do not capture the whole picture, and there are at least three other aspects which are worth noting. First, several local areas with high unemployment rates have many fewer people out of work than some areas with much lower rates, simply because of great variations in the total number of people available for work. To illustrate this, the Belfast travel-to-work area stands out quite clearly in having the largest number of people unemployed (51,734 at the end of 1992), but the percentage figure for the Belfast region was 13 per cent of the workforce. Compare this with the Strabane travel-to-work area, which had 22.6 per cent unemployed, although this high figure was produced by only 3200 unemployed people. Second, experience over the years reveals considerable fluctuations in the levels of unemployment, but fluctuations have usually been greatest in the east, while the west has displayed greater stability, albeit at a higher level – a long-standing feature of the geography of unemployment in Northern Ireland (Salt and Johnson, 1975). Finally, unemployed workers under 45 years old have tended to have been out of work for much longer periods than comparable workers in Great Britain.

The third and most detailed scale is at the level of individual travel-to-work areas, which show considerable internal variations. These local differences may be found at the level of, say, local residential areas in various locations where unskilled workers and young adults are particularly concentrated. Local contrasts are most extreme and most important in Belfast, by far the largest centre of employment (and unemployment) in Northern Ireland. The Belfast travel-to-work area has experienced quite extreme fluctuations in its total level of unemployment in the last decades, but hidden behind the total figures were much higher extremes, with local districts having over 40 per cent male unemployment and it is very likely that this figure was easily exceeded at the level of individual streets. The problem in Belfast is given a sharper edge by the fact that highest levels of unemployment are found in Catholic unskilled working-class areas, although Protestant areas with similar social and economic profiles are also suffering severely (Doherty, 1990, Table 2).

Strategies to alleviate unemployment

Unemployment, although currently particularly high, has been a long-standing problem in Northern Ireland and constant efforts are required to make any impact on it. Over the years a triple strategy has been adopted, involving alleviation of the problems of existing industries, the production of a more diversified base for the economy and the creation of additional jobs. Unfortunately these three aims have not always blended together to form a unified solution to the unemployment problem. The application of the first aim to agriculture, for example, had involved subsidies, guaranteed prices and various marketing schemes. Entry to the European Community has changed the basis of assistance, but has involved continued, and in some cases, enhanced subsidies, although of a different kind. As a result the prosperity of farming has increased considerably, but no further expansion in agricultural employment can be expected. Indeed, a continued reduction in rural population is still necessary if the incomes of individual farmers are to keep pace with the growing expectations encouraged by a more commercial way of life in the countryside. The decline in agricultural employment is particularly felt in the western areas of Northern Ireland where alternative jobs are not easily obtainable.

The shipbuilding industry reveals a similar pattern. With government assistance new equipment was installed in the 1960s to allow the building of supertankers to replace the passenger ships which were no longer in demand, but continuing orders were not forthcoming. Bankruptcy was headed off by government intervention and restructuring of the firm, followed eventually by privatization; but an essential element in attempting to rescue the industry has been a considerable reduction in its labour force, since international competition is intense and high productivity essential for economic survival.

In the same way, the adoption of new machinery by the textile industry has led to greater productivity but fewer workers. In this sector, too, substantial capital grants were made by the Northern Ireland government, starting in 1958, towards the construction of six large plants producing man-made fibres of various kinds, but once construction was complete the total number of workers they employed was relatively small in relation to the large amount of capital employed. Nevertheless this development seemed like a logical extension of the textile industry and by 1973 these factories produced one-third of the synthetic fibres used in the United Kingdom and made an important contribution to employment, particularly in south Antrim. Unfortunately the oil price rises of the late 1970s and overseas competition almost wiped the industry out, so that all but one has now shut down.

It is difficult to quantify the amount of aid made available to create new jobs, since there are complex levels of assistance of various kinds and substantial government intervention has taken place since the end of the Second World War. In more recent years, with considerable success, a Local Enterprise Development Unit was established in 1971 with the task of promoting employment in local firms with less than 50 workers. In 1976 financial assistance was consolidated under the direction of the Northern Ireland Development Agency and the package of assistance was upgraded. Later, in 1982, the Industrial Development Board was created by amalgamating the Northern Ireland Development Agency with a section of the Department of Commerce concerned with industrial development. The stated objectives of the IDB are not unlike those of the IDA in the Irish Republic: to develop profitable and productive companies; to encourage exports from Northern Ireland; and to introduce profitable and productive investment from Great Britain and abroad.

The end result is that it is likely that more government funds are now being made available in Northern Ireland than in any other assisted area in the United Kingdom. Advance factories are obtainable at cheap rents, selective grants are possible for up to 50 per cent of capital investment, research and development grants may be applied for and practical help is provided with the training of employees. Following the initiative begun in Britain involving the establishment of local areas where planning procedures are simplified and tax concessions given, the Belfast Enterprise Zone was established in 1981 and a further Enterprise Zone was located in Derry in 1983.

Unfortunately, as in the Irish Republic, new jobs do not necessarily mean additional employment, since traditional industrial employment has continued to decline. Nor have all new jobs turned out to be permanent in the long run, since branch factories of parent companies with their headquarters in Britain or overseas tend to be the first to catch cold when the chill wind of economic difficulty is blowing. Bad luck (or bad judgement) has also played a part: for example in the financial support given to the disastrous De Lorean car plant, which it was hoped would generate highly needed jobs in west Belfast, and in the failure of the Lear Fan aircraft project. The high rate at which young people have been coming on to the labour market (ultimately the result of relatively high rates of natural increase) is a further special problem in Northern Ireland. The terrorist campaign of the last two decades has also been a negative force on balance. Certainly the necessity to rebuild after destruction and employment in security work of various kinds has generated many jobs. Against that must be placed the problems which civic disorder have placed in the path of recruiting new industrialists to come to Northern Ireland. In fact industrial production has not been very badly affected, but perceptions rather than reality have produced an adverse impact which cannot be accurately quantified. To this must be added the handicap which these problems have also placed on the growth of the tourist industry, for which the Province had considerable advantages in more normal times.

These considerations make any reasonable assessment of the efforts that have been made very difficult to undertake. On the face of it the current levels of unemployment suggest that the policy of job creation has been a failure. The imponderable element, however, is the question of what would have happened if these efforts had not been made. It seems certain that, over the years since the 1950s, unemployment would certainly have been worse and the level of emigration higher. In the 1960s there was a net addition of about 40,000 manufacturing jobs and sponsored employment accounted for 45 per cent of all manufacturing employment in 1970.

What is more difficult to assess is whether good value has been obtained for a public investment now running at approximately £200m per year, with grants thought to be more generous than in most other regions of the European Community. A recent study gives some feel for the results obtained, although they do not reveal the knock-on effects of these new jobs elsewhere in the economy (Northern Ireland Economic Council, 1990). Between 1982 and 1988 the IDB created nearly 9300 jobs, not a remarkable figure over a six-year period

Photo 22 Interior of part of Montupet Factory, Dunmurry, near Belfast. This factory which manufactures aluminium castings is a Northern Ireland example of a branch factory based on overseas investment, an important source of new jobs. In this case the firm involved is a French company, exploiting the long-established engineering skills which still survive in the Belfast region. (Courtesy of the Industrial Development Board)

and representing only 40 per cent of the target for jobs expected to be promoted. By far the greater number of jobs (6700) was created by Northern Ireland firms, illustrating the problems of bringing in foreign employers in the present political situation. The overall cost was an average of £15,570 per job, at 1985 prices; but these costs have fluctuated considerably from year to year. In spite of considerable capital investment the increase in productivity in Northern Ireland has lagged behind that in Britain. This leads to some reservations about the efforts made, although the situation would certainly be worse without them: at present unemployment is showing a stubborn tendency to increase more rapidly than jobs can be created.

Discussions of economic development tend to be dominated by concerns about manufacturing industry and the package of inducements that are provided seem to emphasize employment in this sector, probably because there is a greater possibility of employment for men. This tends to mask the great change of emphasis which has taken place in the Northern Ireland economy. With manufacturing industry particularly difficult to attract in the last two decades, most expansion of employment has taken place in areas like health, education and social services, largely but not entirely based upon public expenditure. The net result has been that employment is now dominated by services rather than manufacturing – a quiet revolution, but one which poses queries for the future. If the telecommunications revolution brings the results that some hope for, it may be possible for some workers in Northern Ireland to carve out for themselves a niche in providing modern clerical-style services for head offices elsewhere, using computer links: the beginnings of this type of secretarial work have already been established. On the other hand, so much employment in the Province is dependent on government expenditure on public services, on social security, on anti-terrorist activities and, indirectly through subsidy, on manufacturing, that an economic situation in which it is deemed necessary to cut government expenditure poses great worries for the future.

The framework of physical planning

The initiatives that have been taken to encourage economic growth (or, rather, to prevent further deterioriation) have been undertaken in a gradually changing framework for physical planning. In Northern Ireland, as in the Irish Republic, over the years there has been a more *laissez-faire* attitude to land-use planning than in Great Britain. Again, as in the South, a British consultant was brought into give advice in the 1960s, with the result that Sir Robert Matthew's *Belfast Regional Survey and Plan* was published in 1964. This plan was concerned not just with the problems of Belfast and its immediate surroundings, but in outline was also required to consider the implications for other towns in Northern Ireland. Matthew's recommendations bore the familiar stamp of the tenets of British town and country planning of the time. Belfast was to be limited by a 'stopline' to halt the expansion of its continuous built-up area, an equivalent of the green belt idea (Figure 11.2). Major amenity areas were defined close to Belfast, like the southern edge of the Antrim plateau and the Holywood Hills, as well as in more distant locations like, in particular, the Mourne Mountains. Relatively close to Belfast there were to be seven growth centres to absorb over-spill from Belfast and to intercept population loss from elsewhere in Northern Ireland (although quite how this latter aim was actually to work was far from clear). More radical in an Irish context, a new special development area, with a projected population of 100,000 in 1981, was to be established approximately 20 miles to the south-west of Belfast, based on the existing towns of Lurgan and Portadown. Finally, six key centres were to be established elsewhere, where further industrial expansion was to be concentrated.

As in most planning proposals the element of compromise was strong. The restriction of the growth of Belfast was to be assisted by demagnetizing its attraction by providing growth centres elsewhere. These could not be too far away, because it seemed that east Ulster, where the services available in Belfast could be more easily reached, was the area most likely to attract substantial numbers of new jobs. Craigavon, as the new regional centre was eventually and controversially named, was to be much larger than the other centres of expansion in order to derive some external economies, but it too was within easy reach of

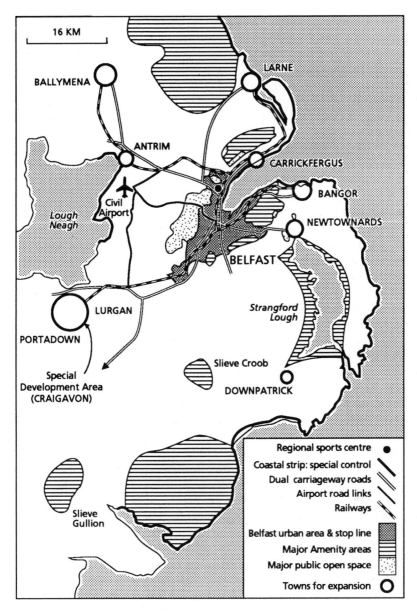

Figure 11.2 Matthew proposals for the Belfast region. In 1963 Sir Robert Matthew's report outlined development plans for the Belfast region, which in fact had implications for all of Northern Ireland.

the port facilities of Belfast. Little was said about the other key centres which, one suspects, were thrown in for good measure because it was politically convenient to mention them. Physical planning was followed by economic planning. In 1965 the economist Tom Wilson produced his study of *Economic Development in Northern Ireland*. Not unnaturally this report also advocated the concentration of investment in the greater Belfast region, but assumed that investment in Craigavon and Derry city would also trickle down to more remote areas in west Ulster.

The Matthew proposals have been criticized for their urban bias, with the Belfast city region being taken as synonymous with all of Northern Ireland. This criticism is unfair in the light of the brief that Matthew was given. It is probably also unfair in relation to the relative urgency of the various physical planning problems with which Northern Ireland was faced and the hidden agenda of producing planning proposals which would provide a framework for the maximum possible amount of job creation, which demanded an urban solution. What is more noticeable is the degree to which the proposals echoed the received planning doctrines current in Britain, whether or not they fitted local conditions. Green belts, provision for urban overspill and regional growth centres were very much a reflection of the spirit of the times, as was the underlying belief that sufficient additional economic growth and employment could be conjured up and located where planners wanted. Even more problematical was the assumption that these proposals, which would probably have been generally acceptable in an English context, would not be sucked into the sectarian political confrontation which characterizes life in Northern Ireland. As it turned out, the expansive optimism of the 1960s proved premature and the brave new world it forecast resolutely refused to emerge.

In the 1960s Belfast continued to grow, but Craigavon (and to a lesser extent the other growth centres near Belfast) did not attract sufficient overspill from Belfast nor intercept population migrating from west Ulster. In 1970 the *Northern Ireland Development Programme, 1970–75* was published by the Northern Ireland government, which modified the strategy somewhat, while maintaining its main outlines. Greater Belfast (which was by now taken to include Craigavon and Antrim), Ballymena and Derry were designated as centres of accelerated growth, strengthening the idea of a concentration in growth centres and no doubt influenced by the proposals in the Buchanan report for the Republic of Ireland. The development programme had one important innovation, which was to recognize that the problems of Belfast were similar to those of Glasgow and Liverpool, while the difficulties of the western counties were seen as more similar to those of the Highlands and Islands of Scotland.

One problem with the Matthew plan and other proposals for physical planning was the lack of any proper legislation to allow these to be implemented in any effective way. The dramatic events of the 1970s, however, brought drastic reorganization of local government with 26 local districts being created, but given very restricted responsibilities. In addition, planning legislation was changed to the British system, in which there was a legal requirement to prepare statutory plans. To avoid the machinations of local politicians publicly owned house building and allocation was centralized under the responsibility of the Northern Ireland Housing Executive in 1971 (Brett, 1986), and the Department of the Environment for Northern Ireland (1975) prepared a *Regional Physical Development Strategy 1975–1995* as a framework for these activities. Basically this strategy proposed the wider dispersal of resources. The number of key centres and growth centres was increased to 23, so that each of the new District Council areas was to have its own centre and some other small towns were also to act as local centres. Plans were also advanced for the expansion of some larger villages and unfit houses in the countryside were to be replaced by modest housing developments in a number of smaller settlements. What was proposed was certainly more equitable and gave greater emphasis to the more rural parts of Northern Ireland, but it appears to be concerned with physical planning rather than economic development and whether the plans make economic sense is something which cannot be tested until economic growth is re-established in the fullness of time. While publicly owned houses may be located by administrative fiat, private building is more likely to follow the pressures of personal taste and the location of employment, as the roadside development of rural bungalows already indicates.

Equity and industrial location

These changes in the physical planning proposals indirectly reflect the problem of equity. Whatever outlines are provided by physical planning, new industries which have been attracted to Northern Ireland depend on British and overseas markets and have exploited a plentiful and diverse supply of labour. Rightly or wrongly eastern Ulster is perceived by many industrialists as offering a more fertile seedbed for new investment. A.R. Hoare's analysis of the location of various facilities which employers look upon as useful and their zones of influence reveals the attraction of the greater Belfast region (Hoare, 1977). Here, in theory at least, there are greater possibilities of establishing local industrial linkages, although it has to be said that many industries currently have few significant linkages with other local firms and often have greater dependence on plants in mainland Britain. In this broad region there is access to a more diverse, more numerous and often better-trained labour force. These advantages apply to already established businesses as well as to immigrant firms, so that further expansion of successful indigenous employment is also likely to be in the east rather than the west.

Yet on the face of it, this gives rise to problems of social equity, given the higher percentages of unemployment in the west. In Northern Ireland this problem is greatly sharpened by the religious geography of the Province, with the highest percentages of Roman Catholics being located in the west. Two comments must be made, however. First, new employment is difficult to attract anywhere in Northern Ireland, so that in the real world of industrial negotiations it is often a matter of allowing firms to locate where they want or not having them in Northern Ireland at all. Second, as already shown, percentage figures conceal as much as they reveal, since the absolute number of unemployed is much higher in the east than in the west. Further, the percentage unemployed in some residential areas in Belfast is probably as high (if not higher) than in small towns to the west. In other words, there are problems of unemployment in eastern Northern Ireland just as grave as in the west, possibly made worse by the larger total of jobs required to solve the unemployment problem.

The level of religious discrimination in obtaining jobs in contemporary Northern Ireland is a matter of bitter debate. It is indisputable that unemployment rates among Catholics have been over twice that of Protestants and that there has been little apparent convergence in times of recession. It is hard to argue that there has been no job discrimination in Northern Ireland, but there are other factors involved as well as religious affiliation. Catholic families are still substantially larger than Protestant, their educational qualifications are lower and their geographical distribution presents more difficulties in job creation. These factors appear to be largely independent of discrimination and in a different context, say in Great Britain or in the Irish Republic, would produce higher levels of unemployment without any religious element being involved. Catholics are also more often unskilled manual workers, a situation in which admittedly an element of past discrimination must certainly have played some part, but which nevertheless makes the current problem more difficult to solve, in the short term at least. It is difficult, however, to pin much blame on regional development policy for the problem of discrimination, since the strategies adopted followed the prescriptions that outside observers suggested.

One more wide-ranging criticism is that economic policy was not sufficiently concerned with the more rural parts of Northern Ireland, although there is some evidence that since 1975 a higher proportion of new jobs have been more widely distributed. These have often been jobs for women in the clothing industry provided by local entrepreneurs, or work in the public sector whose location is more susceptible to government control. A major obstacle to the longer-term continuation of this situation is that the number of jobs from external sources has fallen quite sharply since the mid-1970s and that much further expansion of employment in the public sector cannot realistically be expected. Hence, it probably still remains true that if substantial private sector expansion by larger firms were to take place, the pressure to locate would most likely still be in the greater Belfast region, broadly conceived, where, after all, the majority of unemployed people live.

Convergence and complementarity?

In the 1920s, at the time of Partition, the economies of the newly created Irish Free State and Northern Ireland contrasted sharply. In fact both areas contained considerable internal contrasts, but the total picture for the Republic was of an economy predominantly based on agriculture and agricultural products, while the most important sector in Northern Ireland was export-orientated manufacturing industry.

Times have changed. Manufacturing and, inevitably, services have grown dramatically in importance in the Republic and agriculture has contracted, so that one tentative calculation is that the value of manufacturing output in the Republic is now 60 per cent higher per head than in Northern Ireland. Northern Ireland has seen a massive contraction in its formerly basic industries and the new diversified employment which has been attracted is basically similar to that which has been located in the Republic. Now there are about 102,000 people employed in manufacturing industries in Northern Ireland, compared with 196,000 in the Republic of Ireland. In both areas services employ the majority of people.

Many problems of both areas in the twentieth century are similar. Unemployment is serious in both, but new employment is difficult to attract in competition with the newly industrializing nations of the Pacific Rim. Each has a limited home market, so that exports are seen as essential for a substantial increase in employment, with the risks of fluctuation in demand which this implies. In both areas successful industry implies high productivity and hence fewer employees, so that greater output rather than higher employment is more easily achieved. Emigration provides an important safety valve for both, but fluctuations in the British economy spill over into both countries, more intimately in the case of Northern Ireland, but also significantly in the Republic. Both are dependent on flows of capital from outside, one on subventions from the British government, the other on attracting overseas industrial investment.

The similarities are sufficient for it to be possible to observe a clear convergence in the two economies, which may eventually have political implications to which it will be necessary to return later. Unfortunately, although they have become more alike, the two economies are not really complementary. In fact their greater similarity may mean that they are more in competition with each other for new employment and markets than was the case in the past.

Further reading

For a short but effective comparison of industrialization in Northern Ireland and the Republic see L. Kennedy, *The Modern Industrialization of Ireland, 1940–1988* (Economic and Social History Society of Ireland, Dublin, 1989). An authoritative study of employment discrimination is D. Eversley, *Religion and Employment in Northern Ireland* (Sage, London, 1989). See also the research by R.D. Osborne and R.J. Cormack, for example their brief, but objective and very clear article 'Unemployment and religion in Northern Ireland', *Economic and Social Review* 17 (1986), 215–25; and their much longer, more recent and wider-ranging, *Discrimination and Public Policy in Northern Ireland* (Clarendon Press, Oxford, 1991).

The effect of industrial linkages on the location of industry is discussed in A.R. Hoare, 'Industrial linkages and the dual economy: the case of Northern Ireland', *Regional Studies* 12 (1978), 167–80; and on the perception of various areas of Northern Ireland as a location for industry see his 'Why they go where they go: the political imagery of industrial location', *Transactions Institute of British Geographers* 6 (1981), 153-75.

Some planning documents mentioned in this chapter are: R. Matthew, *Belfast Regional Survey and Plan* (HMSO, Belfast, 1964); T. Wilson, *Economic Development in Northern Ireland* (HMSO, Belfast, 1965); Department of the Environment for Northern Ireland, *Regional Physical Development Strategy*, 1975–95 (HMSO, Belfast, 1975).

For recent, accessible summaries of employment and planning contexts see contributions to R.H. Buchanan and B.M. Walker (eds), *Province, City and People: Belfast and its Region* (Greystone Books, Antrim, 1987), especially J. Greer and P. Jess, 'Town and country planning', 101–124, and C.W. Jefferson, 'Economy and Employment', 191–214.

Chapter 12

Some aspects of the political geography of Ireland

This chapter does not seek to rake over once again the rights and wrongs of the present political division of Ireland. Nor is it concerned with a dull recital of the distribution of election results. It merely attempts to pick out some relevant themes which underlie the political geography of modern Ireland and to make some geographical comments on them.

Alternative interpretations of partition

John Whyte's review of the enormous literature that has accumulated on Northern Ireland since the current troubles began in 1968 attempted a classification of various approaches, based on their individual perceptions of the primary source of conflict in the North (Whyte, 1988). He recognized four contrasting interpretations: nationalist; unionist; marxist; and an internal conflict perspective. In fact there turns out to be overlap between some of these and in detail the writings of every author are unique; but most fall fairly neatly into these broad sets of interpretations.

A crude summary of the nationalist view is that all the people of Ireland form one nation and that the fault for keeping Ireland divided lies with Britain. In the past an extreme nationalist view was that the unionist resistance to an all-Ireland state was simply created by Britain for its own nefarious purposes, although the current strength of resistance to a unified Ireland among Northern unionists is so strong and their opposition to any compromise by the British government is so unyielding that it is difficult to accept that view today.

The unionist position is that there is no natural all-Ireland state and that there are no benefits in joining one. The argument against uniting with the Republic is partly economic: that Northern Ireland is far better off as part of the United Kingdom than it would be as part of the Republic. At an earlier time access to world (or at least United Kingdom) markets seemed important; and today it would be the availability of better social security payments and a higher average standard of living, to which subventions from Britain make important direct and indirect contributions. A second more intangible but arguably more important point is the strong unionist identity with British nationality and hence a strong antipathy to a state founded on anti-British nationalism, and which, to start with at least, was attempting to find national identity in the revival of Gaelic as a living language. Finally, there is fear of religious dominance in a Catholic state: in spite of the first stirrings of a wind of change in the Republic, more liberal unionist elements still point to current legislation in the Republic against divorce and birth control, to literary censorship, and to church control of education; and the cruder, more fundamentalist attitude that 'Home Rule is Rome Rule' continues to flourish at the grassroots.

The marxist interpretation originally derived from James Connolly, one of the martyrs of the 1916 rising. In his view the British Empire was a staunch defender of capitalism, and a workers' Ireland would therefore have to be independent of Britain. Many northern workers seemed reluctant to share that attitude but that was because 'with devilish ingenuity' the master class had mystified their view of the world. He forecast, as it turned out quite accurately, that the partition of Ireland would keep alive the national issue and 'all hopes of uniting the workers, irrespective of religion . . . will be shattered . . .' (Ryan, 1948, pp. 102 and 114). It was not until the recent troubles erupted that this interpretation was criticized in marxist circles. Just as manipulation by the British became a less convincing argument in nationalist discussions, so manipulation by the international capitalist class was not such a convincing view of what was actually going on in Northern Ireland. The traditional Irish marxist interpretation is still energetically advanced, but revisionist writers seem to accept the reality of the unionist workers' separate identity. Non-marxist criticism is more basic and simply rejects an economic interpretation of the Northern Ireland problem.

A fourth group of commentators gives primary responsibility for the political problems of Northern Ireland, not to the British or the Irish governments, but to internal factors within Northern Ireland. Such writing has emerged only relatively recently, in the 1960s and later. The delay is not surprising, since in earlier decades external forces were clearly of critical importance. In the beginning unionist politicians wanted all of Ireland to remain part of the United Kingdom and when that position became untenable a semi-independent parliament was imposed by Britain, not requested by them. Similarly, the nationalist cause in Northern Ireland was bolstered by the Irish government, for example by asserting a territorial claim for the six counties in the 1937 revision of the constitution.

By the 1960s, however, the Northern Ireland parliament, far from being temporary, had been in existence for over 40 years, its rule was indeed semi-independent and in truth its activities were not of much real interest to the British government. Similarly, in spite of occasional affirmations for electoral consumption, Irish governments in the Republic, facing political reality, increasingly took the view about Irish unification that St Augustine prayed for concerning chastity: 'Give me chastity and continency, O Lord, but not yet'. The remarkable underlying stability which characterized political life in the Republic after a most unpromising beginning would, after all, have been gravely disrupted by the introduction of Northern politicians and electors of all parties into the political processes of the Republic.

As a result the bulk of recent academic writing has looked at internal conditions within Northern Ireland, exploring the political, cultural and economic differences between Catholics and Protestants, essentially between nationalists and unionists, and implicitly looking for a solution of the present situation within the existing division of Ireland. Most writers note the existence of similar value systems in the two communities, but variously stress the role of separate educational systems, residential segregation, job discrimination and stereotyped attitudes in developing mutual suspicion. Unfortunately the solutions they offer (if any) are diverse and their conclusions pessimistic, at least in the short term.

A strict, quantitative analysis of the amount of ink that has been spilt in recent years on various interpretations of the Northern Ireland problem is misleading about the real position on the ground. As John Whyte pointed out, the emphasis in academic analyses is very different from the attitudes commonly found among the ordinary people of Ireland, North and South, where the traditional nationalist and traditional unionist interpretations of the partition of Ireland still hold firm sway, however meagre the acceptance of their validity among those who see themselves as academic experts on the situation.

As a result it is still relevant to examine from a geographical point of view whether the original partition of Ireland did in fact symbolize real divergences at the time that partition took place, and to assess the degree of genuine regional consciousness which existed in the northern counties at that time. Was this division something that was artificially imposed by the British government of the period or did it have deeper roots?

The location of the Irish border

Certainly an obvious initial geographical comment must be that the frontier between Northern Ireland and the Irish Republic bears little relationship to detailed geographical realities. When Ireland was divided Northern Ireland was produced by merely grouping together six north-eastern counties, which owed their origins and boundaries to events in the sixteenth century rather than to political attitudes and religious affiliations in the twentieth. The straight adoption of county boundaries meant that it is not surprising that the detailed location of the frontier is artificial in both a human and a physical sense, as a study of any atlas map will show. On the physical side, to quote just two examples, the basin of the river Foyle was split and the outlet of the Lough Erne drainage system was cut off; and on the human side, the zones of influence and the surrounding communication systems of Derry and Newry were broken by the border and the twin towns of Lifford and Strabane, on either side of the river Foyle, were split apart. Elsewhere a number of curious enclaves were produced without proper road access and more generally the daily movement of rural people to shops and schools was often distorted.

Presumably to deal with some of these potential problems a boundary commission was initiated in 1921 as part of the Anglo-Irish Treaty of that year, with the responsibility of 'determining in accordance with the wishes of the inhabitants, so far as may be compatible with economic and geographic conditions, the boundary between Northern Ireland and the rest of Ireland' (Report, 1969, p. xii). Its failure was pre-ordained by the impossibility of its task. Politicians in Dublin expected that considerable areas of Northern Ireland would wish to be included in the new Irish Free State. There were also districts in east Donegal and parts of Cavan and Monaghan that were likely to have voted for transfer into Northern Ireland, although the Free State government argued that the Commission had no power to make transfers from South to North. The slogan of Unionist leaders in Northern Ireland was that 'Not an Inch' of Northern Ireland could be sacrificed; but, privately, at least the more thoughtful would probably have accepted limited changes, particularly if they were balanced by the allocation to Northern Ireland of some areas with Protestant majorities living on the Free State side of the border. Such political pressures meant that, at best, the Commission was free only to suggest minor adjustments.

In any case, the work of the Commission proved futile. Some three weeks after the Commission had privately agreed on a boundary in November 1925 the results were forecast in the newspaper *The Morning Post*. It turned out, when the papers of the Boundary Commission were released many years later, that the forecast was a reasonably accurate leak of the Commission's findings, although the map published in the newspaper was highly generalized, contained some geographical inaccuracies, and may have been derived from a verbal account of the Commission's proposals rather than from an original map. These proposals have usually been interpreted by various commentators, rarely non-partisan, as involving a rape of territory from the Irish Free State, although a geographical analysis has come to much less dramatic conclusions (Andrews, 1960). This suggests that the *Morning Post* line would probably have given Northern Ireland about 55 square miles, with a population in 1911 of 7600 to 8000. The Irish Free State, on the other hand, would probably have gained 194 square miles and about 24,000 people, together with 53 more doubtful square miles and a further 3400 people. The actual line that was proposed is shown in Figure 12.1.

Such matters are merely of academic interest, since the Commission's Report was not officially released at the time. In the face of the storm of political protest from both sides which followed the press leak and its assumed implications, it was probably thought that official publication would have been counterproductive for any settlement. In the end the existing county boundaries were reluctantly accepted by the government of the Irish Free State in return for financial concessions from Britain, and this result was confirmed by treaty. Unionist politicians were also unenthusiastic about the settlement, since they were being criticized by many of their supporters for abandoning the then substantial Protestant minorities in Cavan, Donegal and Monaghan.

But although the border might have been tidied up in a variety of ways, in truth the Commission was faced with an impossible task in producing an

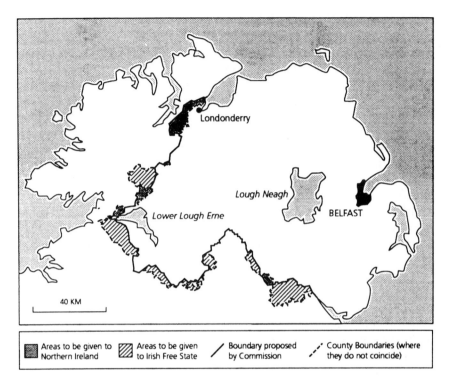

Figure 12.1 Boundary Commission Adjudication on Irish Border, 1925. Although there was heated and often geographically ill-informed comment on the results of the Boundary Commission adjudication, stimulated by a leak published at the time by the *Morning Post*, the authoritative map evidence, of which this is a greatly reduced version, only became available when the report of the Commission was eventually released in the British Public Record Office in the 1960s and was published by the Irish Universities Press in 1969.

acceptable line between those who wished to continue to live as part of the United Kingdom and those who did not. Such were the complexities of the distribution of nationalist and unionist people that, however a line was drawn, there would have been a substantial minority of Catholics in Northern Ireland; and the more land that was transferred to the Free State the greater would have been the number of unwilling Protestants who would have found themselves forming part of a minority there. There was also a hidden British agenda. In spite of contrary beliefs within Ireland it now seems clear that the then British government was sincere in believing the partition of Ireland to be a temporary compromise. The establishment of a regional government in Belfast was seen as a step away from Britain and a move toward a united Ireland sometime in the future. Given that context the existence of a larger nationalist minority in Northern Ireland was interpreted as meaning that the proportion of the population that would have to be won over to achieve eventual unity would be that much smaller.

Historical repetition and paradox

Nit picking about the location of the border, however, masks the much more fundamental question of why what are essentially two separate states should have arisen in a small island not marked by any major physical divisions. Does the existence of Northern Ireland merely represent a false state of affairs imposed by Britain, as some would argue, or is the political and other forms of distinctiveness which mark out the Province based on any geographical logic?

Certainly it is possible to illustrate the distinctiveness of the north at various times in the past. There was for example a close similarity between the Mesolithic cultures of north-east Ireland and south-west Scotland. Or again, in Neolithic times, when there were distinct communities in various regions of the British Isles, a similar culture was found in south-western Scotland and in northern Ireland, indicated by a particular form of burial chamber, the 'Horned' or 'Court' cairn, so-called because it incorporated in its structure a ritual unroofed court. These prehistoric links, of which these are just two examples, obviously have no direct bearing on the modern political geography of Ireland; but they serve to emphasize two important features of the physical geography of the island which were to prove of repetitive importance in later, more relevant historical events.

One was simply the remarkable geographical propinquity of Scotland and Ireland, which is often masked by studying the two countries in separate atlas maps. In fact at their closest they are only slightly more than 12 miles apart as the crow flies, and in the past the sea was more often a link than a division, in pleasant weather at least. The other was the relative difficulty of north–south contact by land within Ireland in the era before metalled roads. Glacial ridges in the Midlands tended to aid east–west travel; and lying to their north was the belt of drumlins, often with ill-drained, bog-covered hollows between them, which made the north of Ireland more independent of land influences from the south well into historic times.

That relative lack of access is illustrated at the time of the occupation of Ireland by the Normans, when in much of the north their hold on the country was only tentative. Certainly they succeeded in establishing a temporary hegemony over part of the north-east; but their more impregnable strongholds were almost invariably in coastal locations and their more superficial occupation is indicated by the absence of Norman urban foundations in the north, except at Carrickfergus and Downpatrick. Even their limited control of a restricted area in the north-east was shaken by Scottish invaders under Edward Bruce in 1315 and by the final overthrow of the De Burgh earldom of Ulster in 1333. By the later Middle Ages Norman influence was restricted to a few coastal toeholds: at Carrickfergus on the shores of Belfast Lough, in south-eastern county Down, and on Carlingford Lough.

In the south of Ireland, on the other hand, a powerful aristocracy was established, as Anglo-Norman lords established permanent family alliances with Gaelic leaders. Loyalties fluctuated confusingly, but at least there was a local nobility which recognized the existence of an authority operating from Dublin. In the north family feuds were vigorously pursued as if the English attempt to rule did not exist; and the north remained a stronghold of Gaelic resistance even as late as the end of the Elizabeth I's Irish wars. In 1603, at the beginning of the rule of James I, English settlement in Ulster was limited to the east coast of county Down, to the area of south Antrim around Carrickfergus, and to an area in the Newry district settled in the sixteenth century. In addition, a large part of north Antrim was under the control of Gaelic Scots – reflecting the ancient links to and from Scotland in this corner of Ireland – and Scottish influence extended informally beyond this area, since many Irish chieftains in the north employed mercenaries from the Scottish Highlands and stonemasons from the Lowlands.

The Scottish connection and the difficulty of penetrating the region from the south was clearly influential at this stage; and the northern part of Ireland certainly stood out as distinctive in its resistance to English colonial activity, paradoxically enough in the light of its more recent history. This situation contained the seeds of later developments, because it was clear that if all Ireland was to be subdued, a fresh policy would have to be developed, leading to a more permanent solution than temporary conquest.

The plantation of settlers

Two historical events made a more effective occupation possible. In 1603 Hugh O'Neill, earl of Tyrone, was defeated by the English after leading a rising of unprecedented scope. Much of the resistance in the north had been focused around this man and in 1607 O'Neill and his ally Rory O'Donnell thought it expedient to flee the country, in spite of a royal pardon, as the English Crown systematically tightened its grip on Ulster by the establishment of a series of fortified posts.

The second important event in 1603 was that under James I the thrones of Scotland and England became united, if not yet the two states. The geographical result was that the northern part of Ireland became more vulnerable to rule by the Crown of Great Britain. Thus, in the first few years of the reign of James much of the remaining territory of Antrim and Down was appropriated by a few influential Scottish and English settlers. New colonies were established in the Lagan valley, in part of south Antrim, and in the Ards peninsula, based on the private enterprise of a few men. Finally, a more radical process of settlement was begun, aided by the power vacuum left after the so-called 'Flight of the Earls', and involving an extensive, government-organized colonization of the area by the introduction of English and Scottish settlers.

The Ulster Plantation was not the first experiment of this kind. For example, the area which is now Leix and Offaly was allocated for settlement by English settlers or their descendants; but local resistance was strong, financial problems considerable and the process of settlement less effective than expected. Again, the Munster Plantation of 1586 involved considerable areas of south-west Ireland which fell under Crown control following a rebellion led by the Earl of Desmond and his subsequent defeat and execution. Although organized by the state, private entrepreneurs (or 'undertakers') were given land grants on which they were then expected to establish a representative cross-section of English society. In fact the Munster Plantation suffered from administrative difficulties, relatively few immigrants were induced to settle, and the various undertakers were forced to retain Irish tenants and use local Irish labour (Buchanan, 1986).

Past experience was brought to bear when a similar strategy was applied to Ulster. The Plantation involved six counties: Donegal, Londonderry, Cavan, Fermanagh, Tyrone and Armagh and again involved undertakers, operating under government direction, but allocated smaller blocks than in Munster and required to introduce a fixed quota of English and Scottish immigrants. In the rest of Ulster, counties Antrim and Down were being settled by private enterprise and Monaghan was not included in the scheme. As in Munster the labour of some of the native Irish was needed, but the scheme was successful in bringing in Protestant settlers of all levels of society, both landlords and tenants. Reflecting the context of the time, religious conversion had by then become an important motive in the plan of occupation and it was felt that the establishment of a Protestant community would act as a 'leaven' which would serve to convert the population as a whole. Thus Protestantism was more firmly rooted in the 'planted' counties and in Antrim and Down than elsewhere. Here it was not merely the religion of a numerically limited ascendancy, but that of a large proportion of the population.

The Ulster Plantation had other distinctive features which were to be important later. The firm unity of Protestant groups in modern Northern Ireland masks the much stronger division which earlier was found between the Presbyterian settlers who often came from lowland Scotland and the settlers from England who were often Anglicans. In the eighteenth century the religious disabilities suffered by the Ulster Scots nonconformists were one influence encouraging many of them to emigrate to America. Among those who remained a sense of grievance developed against the British government, illustrated by the fact that in due course a proportion of them participated in the 1798 Rising; and the egalitarian structure of their church government was reflected in a sympathy, among some at least, for republican political attitudes.

The Plantation also produced a new relationship between landlord and tenant – not the relationship of conquered and conqueror, but of joint partners in a common enterprise. Hence it probably made an important contribution to the development of the so-called Ulster Custom of tenant right which became important in shaping the demands for land reform throughout Ireland in the nineteenth century. In particular the Ulster Custom allowed an outgoing tenant the right to compensation for improvements and thus increased security of tenure. Its contribution to the development of a more prosperous class of industrial entrepreneur has been mentioned earlier in this book, but its existence was also important in reducing the chances of the small Protestant farmer being permanently won over to the cause of Irish nationalism, although it did not prevent the development of some cooperation between Protestant and Catholic farmers in Ulster during the so-called Land Wars of the 1870s.

Although there may have been sound economic reasons for the unity of Catholic and Protestant small farmers, and indeed a section of the Presbyterian church supported Home Rule for Ireland until the end of the nineteenth century, in the long run doctrinal differences were sufficient to destroy any such solidarity. Evangelical activity in the nineteenth century made an important contribution to this division, but even as late as 1908 the papal decree of *Ne Temere*, which laid down the conditions under which a Roman Catholic could marry outside his or her religion, caused a 'moral panic' among Protestants, now largely forgotten but with a wide impact at the time (Lee, 1985). The underlying problem was that the decree specified that a valid marriage in such circumstances could only be conducted by a Catholic priest and, in turn, this in effect meant that promises had to be made that all children of the marriage would be brought up in the Catholic faith. Among Presbyterians this questioning of the validity of marriages conducted by their clergy had particular impact, since it raised memories of their struggle as dissenters at the beginning of the nineteenth century to establish their right to supervise legally-accepted marriages. Their argument was: if a marriage between a Catholic and a Protestant was not valid if conducted by a Protestant clergyman, did this not also logically imply that a marriage between a Protestant and a Protestant was also invalid, based as it was on the same form of service? Rightly or wrongly this issue stoked up fears about religious freedom in a future Catholic-dominated Ireland. It had the immediate result of firmly consolidating opposition to Home Rule among Presbyterians and it has been argued that it was largely responsible for driving a wedge between all Protestant groups and Catholics at the beginning of the twentieth century (De Paor, 1971). Its longer-term effects were also important. Since that time the Catholic attitudes to mixed marriages have been seen by some commentators as one stumbling block to better community relations in Northern Ireland, as well as being a major factor in the numerical decline of the Protestant minority in the Republic of Ireland (Barritt and Carter, 1972; Walsh, 1970b).

Urban and industrial growth

The 'plantation' of manufacturing industry and the associated growth of Belfast and other urban areas with which it was associated have already been discussed in chapter 8. The industrial structure that was created in the second half of the nineteenth century coloured the politics of many influential Northerners. The products of the factories of the north-east were of necessity sold almost entirely outside Ireland and an inward-looking Irish nation with ideas of rural regeneration, speaking a revived Irish language, had no appeal to hard-nosed northern businessmen, who increasingly valued their British connection and the opportunities for trade that it brought.

It has been argued that their workers were hoodwinked by some sort of false consciousness into allowing their attitudes to be similarly influenced; but the anti-urban tone of much nationalist writing of the time was hardly attractive to the Belfast worker. Both employers and employees, perhaps closer to market realities than some political theorists, realized quite clearly that the idea of an industrial north which would be complementary to an agricultural south in an independent, self-sufficient Ireland was a myth. With the passage of time, the growth of manufacturing industry in the Republic has made that myth even more absurd, although it still surfaces from time to time in Irish political folklore.

The end product of the resulting geographical distribution of religious adherences and manufacturing industry was the concentration of substantial unionist support in the north of Ireland at the beginning of the twentieth century, in contrast with its scattered and numerically restricted support elsewhere in the island. In spite of this, it is very doubtful if a viable political unit could have maintained its connection with Britain and broken away from the official infrastructure of Irish administration, education and culture, still effectively centred in Dublin, except for one critical geographical fact. This was the rise of the city of Belfast, with its own communications network dominating the north of Ireland and providing links with Scotland and England, and with its local banks and other financial institutions as powerful as most of those with headquarters in Dublin.

The influence of the city was not limited to the channels which it provided for the flow of economic activity in the region. Many years ago Mark Jefferson noted the curious way in which every state tends to have a dominant urban centre, and he advanced the dictum that 'a country's leading city is always disproportionately large and exceptionally expressive of national capacity and feeling' (Jefferson, 1939, p. 231). The precise statistical validity of that statement in all cases has been debated, but certainly by the end of the nineteenth century Belfast exemplified his observation for the area that was to become Northern Ireland. As we have seen earlier, the city was the centre of professional life, it was the mecca for the local Presbyterian community, it possessed civic pride, and it had independent cultural and educational facilities. The newspapers published in the city, and the possibility for mass political action which it offered, provided mechanisms by which public opinion was formed, consolidated and disseminated. When the various disparate northern interests detached themselves from the leadership of Dublin, Belfast was available as a focus for the loyalties of the majority in the new political unit and as a large accessible centre around which it could be organized.

Clearly one source of the political separation of the six north-eastern counties from the rest of Ireland may be seen in the precise form taken by British colonization in this part of the island in the early seventeenth century, although it might also be argued that quite an important part of that colonial process was an independent activity, rather than one directly inspired by the English government. There is also a danger of projecting backwards ideas about the nature of nationality from the present to the more distant past: the original colonists certainly did not look upon themselves as 'British'; the existing inhabitants of the region had their own long-standing connections with Scotland; and the emotions associated with being 'Irish', 'English' or 'Scottish' were surely not those engendered by a modern nation state. Clearly, too, locational factors had their own independent part to play. In more recent times the Scottish connection sustained an important part of the Protestant community in the north-east; and access to the Clyde and to north-west England encouraged the form of industrial and commercial development.

In looking at the more immediate development of the modern situation, however, the more basic question is whether the political distinctiveness which became apparent as the nineteenth century evolved was sufficient to explain the wish to be separate from the rest of Ireland or whether it was contrived by the British government for strategic and commercial reasons. Certainly the existence of Northern Ireland as part of the United Kingdom proved to be of considerable military importance in the Second World War, particularly in the Battle of the Atlantic, and also as a somewhat safer haven for important wartime production and for the assembly of American forces before the invasion of mainland Europe. Yet these considerations did not seem to arise in discussions about the formation of Northern Ireland in the 1920s, although it has to be said that a British naval base was retained in Cork Harbour until 1938.

It is also true that the issue of Irish independence became a pawn in the domestic British political battle and that for some politicians party self-interest was more important than the well-being of Ireland. Yet there is no doubt that the slogan of the time, which pre-dated the First World War, that 'Ulster will Fight' against incorporation in an independent Irish state was no empty threat and was based on regional solidarity and on a local rather than an externally imposed perception of where the best interests of the majority of people in the north-east lay.

Redrawing the Irish border

Few people these days would not recognize the cultural, economic and political distinctiveness of the majority of the population of north-east Ireland. A more contentious issue is whether this regional consciousness is sufficient to justify the existence of a separate administrative entity in this part of Ireland, although most realists accept that the division of Ireland has become a rather permanent *fait accompli*. As a result some outside observers have from time to time wondered whether a sensible redrawing of the Irish border would reduce the current problems of Northern Ireland. To nearly everyone living in Ireland that would probably seem a naive proposition on both political and geographical grounds, but it is nevertheless worth some examination.

One problem is a simple one of the passage of time. What might have been possible in the upheavals of the early 1920s seems less acceptable when party structures and political positions have been in place for 50 years. It may be possible in due course for the territorial claim on the six counties of Northern Ireland to be eased out of the Irish constitution, but, given the years of rhetoric, it would not be politically possible for a government in the Republic to endorse what would have to be seen as a completely permanent division of the island based on a reconstituted Northern Ireland, reduced to a Unionist heartland. Northern politicians would be in a similar fix. In fact the Province would probably be able to function economically, given the industrial structure of the north-east and its dependence on Britain, but the institutional framework is well established and much more important than in the early twentieth century.

The problems of drawing an actual line are considerable, as has already been indicated, and could not be limited to minor adjustments of the border. The Catholic majority in Derry city sits alongside a Protestant majority in that part of Londonderry immediately east of the Foyle. The town of Strabane appears to have a Protestant majority, surrounded by a rural Catholic majority. Fermanagh, although largely Catholic, has important Protestant enclaves. Catholic south Down contrasts with Protestant north Down, south Armagh with north Armagh. Even staunchly Presbyterian Antrim has an area with a Catholic majority in the north-east.

But the greatest problem of all lies in Belfast, where division is sharpest and where 'ethnic' differences, if that is an appropriate term to use, are more strongly overlain by strong social and economic differences. Here the existence of a Catholic ghetto, with higher than average levels of deprivation, provides the major base for republican terrorism in Northern Ireland. As Doherty has pointed out, although '. . . deprivation is not the root cause of terrorism, and terrorism is not the root cause of deprivation, the two nonetheless feed on each other' (Doherty, 1990, p. 35). The problem is that Catholic parts of Belfast cannot be red-lined out of a compact, unionist Northern Ireland; it is hard to see how relative deprivation could be quickly removed, and revolutionary republican politics would be unlikely to go away in any case. Indeed, violence might be increased in such a restructured province, as political change by a democratic process would be that much more remote. The conclusion has to be (and this is probably quite generally accepted) that a political solution will have to be worked out within the existing boundaries, for better or for worse.

The bitter internal political divide which has existed from the formation of Northern Ireland and, in particular, the violent conflict of the past two decades have tended to hide an important aspect of life in Northern Ireland which in the long run may give a sign of hope. This is that the greater part of the population of Northern Ireland, of whatever religious or political persuasion, is not dedicated to violence. Separation of the religious groups has certainly increased in Belfast, but most people in fact live in peace with their neighbours and fellow workers. In discussions of the political situation it is convenient (not least because of the availability of census statistics) to relate sympathy with the nationalist cause with adherence to Roman Catholicism and a unionist attachment to membership of one of the many Protestant faiths. While such a generalization is broadly accurate it masks a range of shades of political opinion.

A sizeable proportion of the Catholic working-class population, for example, suspects that its standard of living might be lower in a united Ireland and, although it might certainly welcome greater active participation by the Catholic minority in government, would be happy to use the existing insitutional frame-work, suitably modified. The greater part of the Catholic vote goes to the Social Democratic and Labour Party which is dedicated to non-violent methods of bringing political change. Some middle-class Catholics probably find difficulty with the somewhat left-of-centre politics of the Social Democratic and Labour Party and, along with a number of Protestants who have also despaired of the sterile politics of the past, have associated themselves with the Northern Ireland Alliance Party. Although this party managed to command 9.2 per cent of the votes shortly after it was formed, it has been unable to build on this start, since it draws on a largely middle-class base and has been squeezed by the major groups. On the other hand public opinion polls suggest that its support is very similar to that normally achieved by Sinn Fein, generally recognized as the political wing of the Provisional IRA. Certainly Sinn Fein pushed its vote up to 13.4 per cent of the Northern Ireland vote at the British general election of 1983 (although it does not follow that all these voters necessarily supported every activity of the IRA), but at the most recent British general election in 1992 its share of the vote had dropped back to 10 per cent of the Northern Ireland electorate.

Similarly, divisions have emerged in the formerly staunchly united Unionist Party between the more extreme Democratic Unionists and the Official Unionists, a division which partly, but not entirely, reflects a class bias. This division has a regional distribution, with the Official Unionists being stronger in suburban Belfast and in the districts around the city, with the Democratic Unionists being stronger among small farmers in the rural areas away from Belfast where the balance between nationalists and unionists is closest, and also in working-class Belfast. Too much should not be made of this division, since the gap between the groups has appeared to close recently; but the general point that the Protestant group is not as completely monolithic as some outside observers would suggest is still an important one.

This is not to say that political compromise is immediately likely – in the context of Northern Ireland the art of compromise is not looked upon as the virtue that it is taken to be elsewhere. The conclusion is, rather, that the two communities in Northern Ireland – and certainly they have to be described as two separate communities – are not even the near equivalents of the murderous ethnic groups in, say, former Yugoslavia, or the Greeks and Turks of the eastern Mediterranean. As a result a solution based on the redistribution of population, which could so easily deteriorate into ethnic purification, is not needed, probably not possible, and, if an acceptable long-term political settlement is eventually to be built, not desirable.

Political distributions in the Irish Republic

To an outsider the ideological underpinning of political parties in the Republic of Ireland seems quite mysterious, since it is difficult to prise apart the differences between the major proponents in any convincing and systematic way. In Britain party divisions are mostly based on class affiliation; in Northern Ireland they are even more clearly attached to religious affiliations. In the Republic, however, the two major parties, Fianna Fail and Fine Gael, attempt to appeal to a wide cross-section of society. Partly this may be a reflection of the system of proportional representation with multi-member constituencies, since if political differences were made too clear-cut it would be difficult for the parties to slip in the odd successful candidate who does not fit into local regional patterns of dominance. It is also to do with party histories, in which political affiliation still has much to do with the sides taken by relatives (now quite distant) in the civil war which followed Independence. Nevertheless there are some regional contrasts in the importance of parties which have a geographical expression.

In its early years Fianna Fail traditionally drew support from small farmers rather than large, from rural areas rather than urban, from lower middle classes rather than upper middle, and from the west rather than the east, reflecting the core of militant republicanism in the west and south-west. Because of its greater emphasis on welfare and economic protectionist policies it gradually managed to recruit working class support from both rural and urban areas, and because of its hold on power for long periods it widened its appeal to medium-sized farmers and some businessmen.

Cumann na nGaedheal was more stongly supported by the business and propertied class of the newly independent state. The natural successor to this party, Fine Gael, inherited this constituency and traditionally drew on urban, middle-class support. With the passage of time Fine Gael put together a coalition of larger farmers, of the business and commercial classes and of the relicts of the Protestant community to add to its white collar support, although the quality of the local candidate may well be important in drawing in additional support in particular cases. The relatively pale pink Labour Party originally drew much of its backing from farm labourers and was therefore stronger in the south and east of the country. Although it lost rural support to Fianna Fail, in recent years it has managed to make inroads into the urban, working class vote; but because of their loosely defined policies Labour has been in competition with Fianna Fail and even with Fine Gael for the votes of this group. A gap was thus left for the small, more radical left-wing Workers' Party, where a class-based, urban vote is most clearly demonstrated, although this is still a minor party and, although renamed the Democratic Left, in fact lost considerable ground to Labour in the 1992 general election. The Progressive Democrats are much more difficult to differentiate, since this is largely a group which broke away from Fianna Fail in the 1980s, probably for reasons of clashing personalities than because of discernible policy differences and showing little regional pattern. Yet, in spite of the complications brought by the smaller parties encouraged by proportional representation, the current dominance of the two leading traditional parties remains clear. Traditional associations, with some hints of a distinctive geographical distribution but no really clear-cut regional affiliations, are still a dominant force in the political groupings in the Republic and effective class-based politics are still some way away.

But this is not to say there are no hints of eventual changes to come. One straw in the wind, perhaps, was the election of Mary Robinson as President – a seven-year appointment based on a direct vote. Her election broke new ground in a number of ways. Most notably she was a woman President, the first in the history of the State. Second, she was the first non Fianna Fail politician to win a presidential election. Third, she had earlier resigned from the Labour Party on the grounds that it was inappropriate to impose the Anglo-Irish Agreement on the Northern unionists – a position which one would have thought heretical (and electorally suicidal) in the political context of the Irish Republic. Finally she won in the face of general expectation to the contrary, producing a remarkable late swing in public opinion.

There were also geographical dimensions to her victory, although these are difficult to tease out because of proportional voting (Pringle, 1990). However by far the bulk of her first preference votes were cast in the greater Dublin region, and in and around the three urban areas of Cork, Limerick and Galway. Although Robinson had been a member of the Labour Party it is hard to interprete her support as class based. Rather it seems to have more to do with a more modern view of appropriate political behaviour. As Pringle has argued, the significance in an Irish context may be, not that she did well in attracting women's votes, but that there were a substantial number of men who were prepared to vote for her, or at least allocate their second preference votes to her.

In terms of geographical distributions it could also be argued that this election may be interpreted as a change to a 'new' Ireland from an 'old'. The pattern of her first preference votes correlated strongly with those who voted for the possibility of divorce in the 1986 referendum on that topic, and also who voted 'no' in the Pro-Life referendum on abortion in 1983. There are, of course, very difficult statistical problems in coming to a conclusion simply by comparing broad geographical patterns of this kind, particularly as the results of the presidential election in the end came out quite differently from what would have been expected from the overall outcome of those two referenda. Given the particular political situation in 1990 when there was considerable disenchantment with the two dominant parties, it is much too early to see this result as a radical change in Irish political attitudes. Yet nevertheless, there is a feeling abroad that more class-based politics may be evolving and also that the voting pattern of women may be taking a more independent path.

That change was afoot was confirmed by the Irish general election of 1992, in which the Labour Party made important gains in its share of the vote and in the number of members returned. Fianna Fail saw its share of the vote slip, but its traditional rival, Fine Gael, was unable to exploit widespread lack of faith in the dominant party of government in an election fought during a period of high unemployment, currency instability in Europe and considerable worries about the economic future of Ireland. After the machinations of forming a government, which in recent decades have accompanied the inconclusive results produced by proportional representation in the Republic, the curious outcome has been the return of Fianna Fail to power in coalition with Labour. The resulting government may be seen as one which marginally leans left of centre but the obvious conclusion is that real change is a slow process in the Republic. Perhaps one important new strand may turn out to be the revised and more constructive approach to the Northern Ireland problem that has been promised in a statement of intent by the new government. Unfortunately, the basic elements of a solution to that particular problem lie north of the Irish border, rather than in the hands of the Dublin (or London) governments.

Underlying these political changes there are also longer-term geographical developments which are beginning to stir the electoral pot in the Republic. More white collar workers are living in the countryside, at least in the environs of the larger urban areas. More industrial and administrative workers are being located in the western counties. Increasing numbers of middle-class people are choosing to retire to the more attractive country towns. The Republic of Ireland is also a country with a notable proportion of young people in its population whose attitudes to such matters as moral guidance from the Church are more question-ing than they have formerly been. Finally, economic change and entry into the European Community have produced an electorate which is much more outward looking and more aware of social change in Europe than was the case in the past. As a result it will be extremely surprising if, during the next few decades, the electoral pattern does not alter much more sharply than it has done during the first 70 years of the State, as more secular attitudes become established, as traditional loyalties weaken, and as urban-based concerns become politically more important. It is to the future that attention must now be turned.

Further reading

The anti-urban bias among late nineteenth century opinion in Ireland and, among other things, the resulting inability to incorporate Belfast within the image of Ireland that was being created, is examined in M.E. Daly, 'An alien institution? Attitudes towards the city in nineteenth and twentieth century Irish society', *Etudes Irlandaises* 10 (1985), 181–94.

Those with a high boredom threshold might care to look at the report of the Boundary Commission which was eventually reproduced from British government files in the Public Record Office: *Report of the Irish Boundary Commisssion, 1925* (Irish Universities Press, Shannon, 1969).

A summary of geographical factors which have contributed to political separation of the northern counties is J.H. Johnson, 'The political distinctiveness of Northern Ireland', *Geographical Review* 53 (1962), 78–91. Written about the same time, a more wide ranging and controversial attempt to put the political separation of Northern Ireland in a European context is M. Heslinga, *The Irish Border as a Cultural Divide: a Contribution to the Study of Regionalism in the British Isles* (Van Gorcum, Assen, 1962). An excellent overview of contemporary political problems in Northern Ireland is J. Whyte, *Interpreting Northern Ireland* (Oxford University Press, London, 1991).

Chapter 13

The future geography of Ireland?

It is offering a hostage to fortune to speculate about the future, even in Ireland where the past is a stronger force than in many other places in shaping the present and, no doubt, the future as well. Yet there is some responsibility to highlight some of the possible developments which lie ahead, based on current processes. No attempt is made here to explore this theme in a comprehensive manner: what is offered is a personal perspective on some features of the evolving geography of Ireland which have already been discussed in earlier chapters.

Handicaps and resources

Certainly it is possible to list a number of handicaps which Ireland, North and South, is currently facing and which will continue their influence in the future. Most obviously, the activity of terrorists of various persuasions in Northern Ireland, besides distorting everyday life and sharpening community bitterness there, has certainly handicapped economic growth in Northern Ireland and probably also has had adverse economic effects in the Republic of Ireland. A second, inescapable drawback is the fact that the two Irish 'home' markets for agricultural output, manufacturing and services – the base on which indigenous producers might expect to build effective penetration into export markets – are strictly limited and, in addition, exporters suffer the extra costs in time and money of having to ship overseas. Finally, it can be reasonably argued that emigration has tended to remove the most energetic and, increasingly, the better qualified young people. Some of these problems are insoluble; others require time, patience and good fortune to resolve.

Yet Ireland also possesses resources for the future. The importance of emigration in Irish life implies that a surplus labour force is available, often quite well educated, youthful, ambitious, English speaking, and willing to learn new skills. The Irish landscape, rural and urban, offers potential for the further growth of the tourist industry, not for mass holidays by sun-seekers perhaps, but for special interest activities, conferences and touring. The rich farm lands of some regions indicate that, given the will to institute necessary changes, agriculture can continue to make an important contribution to total output. The infrastructure is steadily improving: for example, those who remember the Irish telephone system some decades ago cannot fail to be impressed by the developments that have taken place; investment of EC funds is bringing improvements to the road system, if at present in a somewhat piecemeal fashion; and competition has reduced the relative cost of air travel to Britain. Finally, the Irish Republic offers political stability of a kind that is rare in many other parts of the world. Unfortunately the same cannot be said of Northern Ireland at present, but even there politicians at least agree in welcoming inward investment and their various policies do not offer any threat of a government take-over of private firms.

As a result there is no reason why economic growth should not flourish in the Irish Republic given an appropriate international economic regime. Northern Ireland can also offer similar advantages, given some kind of stable political settlement and, even more difficult to achieve, the end of terrorism by a very small violent minority. Whether the resulting economic development will be of the kind that will maximize incomes in Ireland is quite another matter.

Rural and urban change

The survival of unhurried and traditional ways of life which the tourist industry markets energetically as an attractive Irish characteristic masks the rapid change which is a feature of modern Ireland. There is no doubt that elements in the rural landscape are altering quite rapidly. Traditional houses which were not uncommon forty years ago, particularly in the west, are now being swept from the landscape. The demise of the thatched single-storied cottages must be regretted by all who have affection for the Irish landscape, but not by those who had to live within their often damp walls (nor, presumably, by the fire insurance companies which charged extra premiums for buildings with thatched roofs). Piped water and the universal availability of electricity, together with increases in real incomes and exposure to the attraction of consumer goods have brought inevitable changes to house and farm design. The practice of building afresh rather than restoring the old – many traditional houses were not very ancient in historical terms – has meant that older houses throughout rural Ireland have gone and will continue to disappear in the future, in spite of the sentimental regrets of urban-based scholars.

The changing design and appearance of rural houses is a visible expression of deeper social changes in the countryside. The wide diffusion of industrial employment to towns throughout Ireland has also brought urban places of work for many of those who continue to live in the countryside and travel daily to the town. Continued population decline in rural areas has produced larger effective farm working units partly expressed in the removal of field boundaries in some agricultural regions where they impede the use of machinery; and the peasant farmer for whom agriculture was more a way of life than a source of the maximum possible income is rapidly becoming rarer. The inevitable reform of the Common Agricultural Policy will continue that process further, so that the larger, more highly capitalized farm units will become even more dominant.

This will be resisted most strongly in the north-west and west of Ireland, but further changes there are also inevitable. The age structure of the population is such that older farmers will disappear from the scene and many of the younger people who will inherit may not be prepared to struggle on in an area of environmental difficulty for agricultural production. Tourism and urban employment, rather than their farming activities, may allow people to stay on the land, but overall it seems likely that rural population numbers will continue to decline. Some farmers who remain will cooperate with kin to work what are, in effect, larger units, although perhaps not shown as such in agricultural statistics. Others may find niches in the intensive production of poultry, pigs and cattle, although distance from market and capital requirements may erect formidable barriers for small farmers who wish to undertake such developments.

Whatever changes actually take place it is difficult to see any lessening in the contrast between farming in the south-east and east, and farming in the west and north-west. If anything, social, environmental and locational factors point to a sharpening of these differences. Farmers generally will aspire to the material standard of living achieved by urban businessmen and many may take a jaundiced view of rural life, as in fact Irish small farmers have been doing for many decades. The modernization of the countryside is no new feature of Ireland, nor is a hard-nosed personal assessment of future prospects which flies in the face of long-standing political rhetoric about the moral superiority of rural life.

More people now live in Irish towns than in the countryside and that trend will certainly continue. Economic growth recently in Northern Ireland has been slow, but when it increases again the greater Belfast region will undoubtedly resume its upward trend, although much growth may be associated with satellite towns around the perimeter, rather than with the continuous built-up area of the city. Dublin also will continue its expansion, probably also in a more dispersed, less continuous form. Other towns away from the two major cities will also share in that growth, partly because it is likely that suitable new employment will continue to be steered towards them to relieve local pockets of unemployment, and also because tourism and a retirement population will be attracted to those smaller towns which offer what is perceived to be an attractive urban environment. But urban life is not merely a matter of location: it also implies changing attitudes and aspirations and will therefore be a stimulus to further social change in Ireland.

Ireland in an integrated Europe

As the links between the countries of the European Community continue to tighten and as a single market is created, the question arises as to what will be the effect on Ireland, North and South. Leaving political implications on one side for the moment, two contrasting views may be advanced.

In a real sense Ireland already lies at the periphery of the European Community and if the centre of gravity of its markets, still very strongly influenced by Great Britain, moves further into mainland Europe, that marginal location may be emphasized further. There is no equivalent of the Channel Tunnel in prospect for Ireland, nor is one even technically or economically feasible at some remote future date. As a result Ireland is separated from its present and potential export markets by barriers of time and cost and it is possible that it may be put at even more of a disadvantage by the future development of the single market. In both parts of Ireland the average size of indigenous firms (as opposed to branches of multinational businesses) is small by international standards and their productivity relatively low. There is a very real question of whether many can survive in an integrated market.

But the problem is not merely locational. Developments in the technology of transport and communication may be making the idea of agglomeration economies within the confines of a single city an old-fashioned concept, but this is much less clear at a regional scale. The higher levels of political and economic decision-making are likely to be concentrated in the heartland of European economic activity, to which part of Great Britain may aspire, but probably not Ireland. In the same way, the research and development which produce technical innovations may be similarly concentrated, which means that the industrial future for both parts of Ireland may be focused on assembly and sub-contracting. This fate may not represent a decline in present standards, since a pressing contemporary need is for employment of any kind; but in the longer run it offers less hope of retaining within Ireland many able and technically trained young people. Some fear that serious intellectual impoverishment and over-conservative attitudes will result from this situation, although there are still sufficient lively minds around, in spite of the long history of Irish emigration, to dampen enthusiasm for that view. Nevertheless it does suggest that Ireland may not derive the full share of material benefits from the economic growth that the single market is planned to encourage.

There is also a contrasting, more optimistic view, which sees many of the benefits of European economic growth trickling down to Ireland. Such an interpretation stands the technical position on its head by arguing that information technology offers an escape from a geographically marginal location. Already routine work from the City of London is decanted to Dublin and, on a smaller scale, to Belfast. With the magic of computer technology, insurance payments for a Boston company are processed in Tralee, to be available for printing at head office when it is morning in New England but the end of the working day in Ireland. There is an act of faith involved in assuming that executive decision-making for multinational companies could be similarly located in Ireland, although the operations of the important aircraft-leasing company GPA might be taken as pointing in that direction, in spite of its currently shaky financial position. If the availability of computer technology and fax machines were the only factor involved there would be less cause to be sceptical, but the personal contact and interplay that is involved in the higher

Photo 23 Irish Financial Services Complex, Customs House Quay, Dublin. This complex of new office buildings adjoins James Gandon's famous Customs House which now forms part of the same initiative, designed to encourage international financial services to locate in Dublin. It remains to be seen whether these developments will mainly consist of more routine activities decanted from great financial centres like London, or (perhaps more unlikely) whether some of the major control points of the international financial services industry will eventually find a home here. (Courtesy of the Industrial Development Authority)

levels of business remain difficult to replicate between participants at a physical distance from one another.

The possibility of a common EC currency seems rather more distant than might have been thought a few years ago; but the underlying pressures in that direction remain powerful from those states with strong economies. The easier administration of trade and commerce and an end to destructive currency speculation may prove irresistible incentives towards that goal in the longer run. However, the absence of currency flexibility could be an important problem in Ireland. Already it can be argued that Northern Ireland might have fared better economically (at least in terms of generating employment) if it had been able to operate on a different parity from that of Sterling, although in fact the problem is currently offset by regional aid of various kinds and high direct government spending on employment. The original devaluation of the Irish Punt in relation to Sterling (and even more in relation to the US dollar) proved an advantage for expanding tourism and encouraging exports from the Republic, although it has been argued that it encouraged high inflation as a result of its impact on import prices. The forced detachment of Sterling from the European Monetary System temporarily altered its relationship with the Irish Punt, although there followed an almost inevitable devaluation of the Punt within the EMS. The problems of uncertainty which this has created for producers in the Republic is unfortunate at a time when unemployment is a matter of national crisis.

Such instability may eventually pass with the development of monetary union within the European Community, but from an Irish point of view a common European currency would require a generous and far-reaching European regional policy, which would spread the economic benefits of the richer regions to the poorer, more marginal areas. Certainly the impact of regional subventions from the European Community are increasingly evident in Ireland, but they have an uncoordinated and piecemeal character and they have had little impact so far on the serious unemployment problem in both parts of Ireland. As a result it is possible to speculate that economic contrasts within Europe will increase, rather than decrease, even though overall prosperity may grow. The degree to which these contrasts can be counteracted depends on the preparedness of the electorates of the economically stronger countries to allow subventions to the weaker. Good intentions and high moral stances often evaporate when these have to be translated into high personal taxes which are destined to be spent elsewhere.

Membership of the European Community means that there can be no reversal of the policy of opening up the economy to outside influences. In fact the introduction of firms from outside Ireland has been of the greatest economic significance and will continue to be important in the future. Certainly there have been criticisms of the kind of work brought to Ireland by foreign firms, some of them clearly justified. However, the impact of foreign firms takes on a different light when viewed in comparison with the lack of success of indigenous businesses. In the Irish Republic foreign firms have been the source of nearly 90 per cent of exports going to areas of the European Community outside the United Kingdom; and they currently provide over 60 per cent of net export earnings. Indigenous firms, on the other hand, export less than a third of their output (largely to the United Kingdom) and they produce less than 10 per cent of high technology exports (Foley and Griffith, 1992).

As a result the problem of indigenous firms is more to do with their restricted scale, the limits of the management skills they have at their disposal, and their relatively low level of technology. The single European market is of much less relevance for them and is unlikely to reverse their decline. In fact the stronger points of much Irish industry are largely to do with the branch plants of the multinationals and it is indigenous industry that is relatively weak. In the long run, however, it is unlikely that a branch plant economy will produce the industrial structure of an advanced economy and the relatively high average income levels which accompany it.

Convergence of Northern Ireland and the Irish Republic

Earlier chapters of this book have documented increased similarity between various aspects of the human geography of Northern Ireland and the Irish Republic. That convergence is far from complete, not least because of the different political regimes in the two areas. Because of its independence the government of the Republic has autonomy over its budget, at least in so far as that can be exercised within the framework of the European Monetary System. As has been already noted, the currencies of the two jurisdictions are now different: since 1979 the Irish Punt has been decoupled from what was essentially a monetary union with Sterling. Wage negotiations in Northern Ireland are largely governed by national bargaining in the United Kingdom, while the process in the Republic is much more influenced by domestic considerations, although not completely independent of what is happening in Britain because of the long-standing associations between the two labour markets. Yet the eventual move towards a single European currency is likely to reduce these sources of contrast.

The points of similarity are already considerable. The common problem of peripherality, already described, is coupled with quite similar demographic problems, with high natural increase by European standards (although likely to fall further in the future) and a large flow of young adults into the labour force. Severe overall levels of unemployment in both political units is accompanied by high levels of long-term unemployment and endemic emigration. Inevitably economic growth has been linked in both economies with overseas investment (particularly from Britain in Northern Ireland and from a wider variety of sources in the Republic) with the result that growth has been export-led. Such investment has brought access to new markets and technology, but has also introduced the problems of a branch-plant economy. Each area benefits from resource transfers from outside the local economy and in each, by EC standards, the public sector makes an above average contribution to expenditure and employment. In each area a high proportion of the population does not form part of the workforce either because it is too young or over retirement age and GDP per capita is lower than in many other areas of Europe; but the general public expects standards of living and of public services which match those on offer elsewhere.

Even some of the contrasts between the two areas are becoming less marked. The birth rate is now falling in the Irish Republic and there is evidence of a similar reduction among some of the Roman Catholic population in Northern Ireland, moving gradually towards Protestant levels. In recent years patterns of emigration have been quite similar, in contrast to the 1970s, when a divergent course was established for a number of years. Manufacturing industry, measured as a percentage of the GDP, has increased greatly in the South and in fact is now more important than in the North, although the levels are really quite similar. Unlike the situation earlier in the twentieth century the broad structure of

Photo 24 Killybegs, county Donegal. Killybegs is the most important fishing port in the Irish Republic and has developed associated industries, in particular frozen food. Formal cooperation between the governments of Northern Ireland and the Irish Republic has avoided problems over fishing rights in each other's territorial waters. (Courtesy of Jean Johnson)

manufacturing industry in Northern Ireland and the Irish Republic is now not dissimilar. Agriculture is still an important source of income in both the North and the South, but its share of both economies has fallen noticeably during the last two decades. Again, for both parts of Ireland tourism is of actual and potential importance.

Economic benefits of cooperation

Not surprisingly in these circumstances there are also various areas of mutual concern where cooperation between the two parts of Ireland would make considerable sense. Cooperation has been going on quietly in a number of ways; for example, a formal agreement allows the fishing fleets of Northern Ireland and the Republic to fish in each other's territorial waters, and informal arrangements concerned with animal health, river management and the exchange of non-political criminals have operated for many years. Yet, the political situation in Ireland clearly limits the scope for all-out collaboration. Considerable cooperation in dealing with terrorism has developed although some would argue that it is not yet as effective as could be envisaged. There are also other, less politically charged fields where highly useful benefits could be derived.

For example, the coming of the single market points to some immediate benefits for efficient firms on both sides of the Irish border, which do not need to await the agreement of politicians, and merely require administrative good-will and an adherence to EC agreements already reached. Cross-border trade is currently relatively unimportant for both political areas. Only five per cent of the Republic's total exports go to Northern Ireland and only four per cent of its imports come from Northern Ireland. This perhaps emphasizes the fact that, overall, the two economies are basically not complementary, but there still remains scope for individual firms to expand their markets across the Irish border. Manufacturers in the Republic sell only one-third as much per capita in Northern Ireland as they do in their home market. Similarly manufacturers in Northern Ireland sell only one-sixth as much per capita in the Republic as they do in Northern Ireland (Gray, 1992, Table 1.3). The businesses involved are likely to be predominantly indigenous firms; and what is on offer for Northern Ireland is effectively a 'home' market of five million, rather than 1.5 million.

Tourism represents another obvious area where formal cooperation would

Photo 25 Ladies View, Lakes of Killarney, county Kerry. One important Irish resource is its attractive landscapes. Around Killarney the pressure of tourism is considerable and will certainly grow further in the future. The preservation of unspoilt landscapes like this is essential if their real economic value is to be maintained, but this will require considerable attention to landscape planning in the future. (Courtesy of Bord Failte)

offer benefits. Clearly civil disruption in Northern Ireland has meant that the tourist industry there is labouring under great difficulties and is largely but not exclusively dominated by business visitors and people of local origin returning for a visit to their roots. There is no doubt that tourism in the Republic has also been adversely affected, but not so severely as in Northern Ireland, and a more diversified range of tourists, from mainland Europe as well as North America make important contributions to the industry. But visitors from a distance wish to deal with one source of information and in normal times would probably want to visit all of Ireland. In fact senior officials of the Northern Ireland Tourist Board and of the Irish Tourist Board (*Bord Failte*) already meet regularly to discuss broad policy issues and the beginnings of more formal cooperation in overseas marketing and in the distribution of each other's promotional literature has begun. Recently a joint computerized information and reservation database has been established (Fitzpatrick and McEniff, 1992). What is now needed are more settled political conditions in the North which would lead to the wholehearted cooperation in tourist promotion which would then make obvious sense.

The increasing similarity in the types of manufacturing industry which can be attracted to Northern Ireland and the Irish Republic can be interpreted in two ways. On the one hand it can be seen as wasteful for the two areas to be competing with one another to attract new industry. Cooperation would prevent unnecessary bidding against one another for new employment. This argument can obviously be reversed. Because similar types of new employment are available there is no complementarity between the needs of the two areas and the exigencies of politics would mean that the agencies promoting new employment could not stand aside and see a potential new source of employment go to its rivals within Ireland. Closer political union might resolve that difficulty, but that is not on offer in the foreseeable future, although a longer-term possibility in the context of the European Community might be some form of joint agency which could share out new developments. If that agency were able to increase the total amount of new employment brought to Ireland as a whole then it might have the possibility of success.

Energy supplies also offer potential for cooperation. Piped gas supplies are no longer available in Northern Ireland because of the cost of production from oil. However, natural gas is now being produced off the south coast of Ireland and a grid involving both parts of Ireland would spread the costs of production and at the same time make a valuable heating fuel available in the North, with the greatest practical importance in the Belfast region where town gas was formerly an important fuel. Such a development has run into political problems over appropriate charges. Recent suggestions have argued that a gas connection to Scotland, linking with the system in the Republic but with a spur to serve Belfast, would be economically more viable, although this alternative also highlights the need for trans-border cooperation.

At the same time massive lignite finds in Northern Ireland, near Lough Neagh, have yet to be exploited, with power generation being probably the most logical way forward (Northern Ireland Economic Council, 1987). The large reserves are sufficient for more than the Northern Irish market, so that again a power grid would seem to make sense. Such would not be a new experiment, as power supplies were exchanged earlier between the two jurisdictions until the necessary link, originally installed in 1970, was blown up on a number of occasions by the IRA – a perverse target surely for an organization which purports to seek a unified Ireland. Nevertheless, the economies of scale suggest that given the restricted local markets of both countries there are considerable advantages for both in producing cheaper gas and electricity than would otherwise be possible without cooperation. The limitation is now to do with problems of security than with the scale of the economic advantages that would be produced.

The benefits which closer association between North and South can offer in the economic environment of the 1990s have yet to make an impact on formal political attitudes, particularly in the North. It would be foolish to think that the economic and political logic, which to an outsider would seem to be drawing the two Irelands closer together, will in fact bring about that result. Terrorist organizations, although they are supported by an insignificant proportion of the electorate in the Irish Republic and by a small minority in Northern Ireland, are still able to fan the embers of communal discord and thus distract the attention of politicians from what is happening in the wider world. On that broader stage the real independence of individual states is being reduced, new loyalties are being created and the problems of regions are likely to be assessed more at a European than at a national scale. Yet the pressures of outside realities cannot be resisted indefinitely. Modern Northern Ireland remains economically viable because of the transfer payments currently being made by the United Kingdom. Like other less fortunate regions within the United Kingdom its current tax revenues do not cover local costs and its GDP could not support the average income per head which is made available within its boundaries. Yet there must be doubts about how long politicians in London will allow that situation to continue in a context in which local politicians seem powerless to conjure up some sort of workable political settlement.

That political settlement would be easier to achieve in a context of economic growth and reduced unemployment in both parts of Ireland. In the last resort this demands, as a basic requirement, an expansion of international demand, particularly in Europe, although a favourable outcome cannot be guaranteed. Certainly, greater integration in Europe offers the possibility of increased markets as well as increased competition. The future depends on exploitation of the physical and human environmental advantages of Ireland, which are not inconsiderable.

For a start, the island is perceived as relatively free of pollution. Air quality in Dublin leaves something to be desired, although heating by natural gas may improve this situation quite rapidly. However, the perception of Ireland as an island with clean air and unpolluted rivers is widely held and must be energetically sustained, not least by seeing that image and reality continue to coincide.

Linked to this perception, Irish agricultural products are widely thought of as being of high quality, a characteristic with potential spin-offs for the food processing industry as well as for farming. Irish handicrafts are also well thought of, giving the possibility of moving further into the high-quality consumer goods area. International niche markets of this kind offer some possibility of economic growth, although a headlong attack on mass markets is unlikely to be successful. More mundane products suffer from the problem of establishing a recognized presence on the world market from a comparatively small industrial base and in the face of international competition. One useful strategy may be for smaller firms to act as subcontractors for international suppliers: Shorts in Belfast, producing component aircraft parts for American airframe manufacturers, already offers a notable example.

An overall conclusion has to be that considerable brain-power will have to be applied to the economic problems of Ireland and in that context cooperation between the two states is not only desirable, but is essential for future prosperity. A recent report commissioned by the Government of the Irish Republic has spelt out some of the forms that this could take (Gray, 1992, pp. 61–63). These include among other things using government support for industry to encourage firms cooperating on an all-Ireland market; exploiting EC regional policy to improve the infrastructure in both parts of Ireland on an integrated basis; joint approaches to encourage the location of employment by EC institutions in Ireland; joint research on market developments; increased resources to be found to set up a new all-Ireland venture capital fund; extending different skill-training programmes in Northern Ireland and the Republic so that, if appropriate, they could be made available on an all-Ireland basis; developing joint product-testing facilities; and sharing the services of research and development establishments of various kinds. Similar initiatives are seen as possible in agriculture, particularly the marketing of agricultural products, and in transport.

Conclusion

These somewhat random observations about current processes that may have future importance lead to a mixed conclusion. Are we to look forward with ambitious hope or fear future shock? The pessimistic view is probably easiest to outline. A political settlement in Northern Ireland is clearly of the greatest importance, but it is something that politicians (probably reflecting rather accurately the views of their various electorates) have been unable to deliver. Even if some form of power-sharing agreement could be reached, there is no guarantee that a longer-term stable government would be created, acceptable to the great majority of the population. People of violence (of all viewpoints) are unlikely to accept any likely outcome, and in the light of the history of the last 25 years it would be easy for them to disrupt any settlement. In reality, violence in Northern Ireland is currently very modest compared with what has been occurring elsewhere, but it could easily deepen into genuine inter-community strife. Such a situation would spill over almost automatically into the Republic, with drastic results for an already precarious economy. Civil discontent has not been eased by high unemployment, now marginally worse in the Republic than in Northern Ireland. It is easy to see a more integrated European market bringing greater contrasts in prosperity, with Ireland gaining only a fraction of its proportionate share of economic growth and perhaps an even worse unemployment problem than at present, as competition from lower wage economies in southern Europe bites harder. Such an unpalatable path of events need not be spelt out further.

Fortunately there is a brighter picture which can also be constructed. If some sort of settlement can be achieved which restores a more normal political process in Northern Ireland, the politicians who currently find great difficulty in agreeing may find it possible to work together effectively when released from the stress of bitter negotiation. An upswing in prosperity would make their task easier and those who look to violence would find the basis of their support eroded. Reduced local tension would also make cooperation with the government of the Irish Republic smoother.

Intense national fervour may make less sense in the Europe of the future; and that future may include a distinctive niche for the qualities of people and environment which Ireland has to offer. The formal political division of the island is unlikely to go away, but its functional significance in everyday life may quietly disappear. In spite of appearances cooperation goes on, both between members of the different communities in Northern Ireland and between Northern Ireland and the Irish Republic. At the moment attitudes within Northern Ireland are uncompromising, but given a favourable run of events it would not be impossible for the political climate to change remarkably quickly.

Elsewhere in Ireland the lasting stability which was established in the late 1920s may well continue, but it will nevertheless be a new Ireland. Economic and political change in the Republic of Ireland has brought a new openness among young people to the social influences of the outside world, with many eager for an active European role and holding traditional values less tenaciously than in the past. For some this incipient trend is a matter for worry and regret. For others it is a realistic expression of where the future lies and offers an escape from those older obsessions which have masked the basic truth that what is most important is not the form of government but the quality of personal life which can be enjoyed within political boundaries – an observation which is equally relevant for both parts of Ireland.

Further reading

An excellent series of progress reports on the Northern Ireland economy and a series of analyses of future developments is provided by the regular reports issued by the Northern Ireland Economic Council (Northern Ireland Economic Development Office, Belfast). The Government of the Irish Republic has commissioned a series of short reports on the necessity for North/South cooperation in a variety of fields in order to exploit new opportunities in the European Community in, *Ireland in Europe, a Shared Challenge: Economic Co-operation on the Island of Ireland in an Integrated Europe* (Stationery Office, Dublin, 1992). An analysis of the effects of the single European market is provided in A. Foley and M. Mulreany, *The Single European Market and the Irish Economy* (Institute of Public Administration, Dublin, 1990).

Bibliography

Aalen, F.H.A. (1970), 'The origin of enclosures in eastern Ireland', in N. Stephens and R.E. Glasscock (eds), *Irish Geographical Studies*, 209–23.

Aalen, F.H.A. (1978), *Man and the Landscape of Ireland*, London, Academic Press.

Aalen, F.H.A. (1986), 'The rehousing of rural labourers in Ireland under the Labourers (Ireland) Acts, 1883–1919', *Journal of Historical Geography* 12, 287–306.

An Foras Forbartha (1987), *Regional Planning in the 1990s: a Discussion of the Issues*, Dublin, An Foras Forbartha.

An Foras Forbartha (1987), *Regional Planning: a Review of Regional Studies*, Dublin, An Foras Forbartha.

Andrews, J. (1960), 'The Morning Post line', *Irish Geography* 4, 99–106.

Andrews, J. and Simms, A. (eds) (1966–), *Irish Historic Towns Atlas*, Dublin, Royal Irish Academy.

Armstrong, J.A., *et al.* (1980), *A Policy for Rural Problem Areas in Northern Ireland*, Belfast, Ulster Polytechnic.

Atlas of Ireland (1979), Dublin, Royal Irish Academy.

Bannon, M.J. (ed.) (1989), *Planning: the Irish Experience, 1921–1988*, Dublin, Wolfhound Press.

Barbour, M. (1977), 'Rural road lengths and farm-market distances in north-east Ulster', *Geografiska Annaler* 59B, 14–27.

Barritt, D. and Carter, C. (1972), *The Northern Ireland Problem: a Study in Group Relations*, London, Oxford University Press.

Beckett, J.C. and Glasscock, R.E. (eds) (1967), *Belfast: the Origin and Growth of an Industrial City*, London, BBC.

Boal, F.W. and Royle, S. (1986), 'Belfast: boom, blitz and bureaucracy', in G. Gordon, (ed.), *Regional Cities in the United Kingdom, 1890–1980*, London, Harper and Row, 191–216.

Boyle, P. and O'Grada, C. (1986), 'Fertility trends, excess mortality and the great Irish Famine', *Demography* 23, 542–62.

Brady, J. and Parker, A. (1986), 'The socio-demographic spatial structure of

Dublin in 1981', *Economic and Social Review* 17, 229–52.

Breathnach, P. (1982), 'The demise of growth-centre policy: the case of the Republic of Ireland', in R. Hudson and J.R. Lewis (eds), *Regional Planning in Europe*, London, Pion, 35–56.

Breathnach, P. and Cawley, M. (eds) (1986), *Change and Development in Rural Ireland*, Maynooth, Geographical Society of Ireland, Special Publication 1.

Breen, R. (1984), 'Population trends in later nineteenth and early twentieth century Ireland: a local study', *Economic and Social Review* 15, 95–108.

Brett, C. (1967), *Buildings of Belfast, 1700–1914*, London, Weidenfeld and Nicolson.

Brett, C. (1986), *Housing a Divided Community*, Dublin, Institute of Public Administration in association with Institute of Irish Studies, Queen's University Belfast.

Brown, S. (1990), 'Twenty years of change: retailing in the Belfast Region 1969–1989', in J. Doherty (ed.), *Geographical Perspectives on the Belfast Region*, 54–67.

Brunt, B. (1988), *The Republic of Ireland*, London, Chapman.

Bruton, R. and Convery, F. (1982), *Land Drainage Policy in Ireland*, Dublin, Economic and Social Research Institute.

Buchanan, C. and partners (1968), *Regional Studies in Ireland*, Dublin, Stationery Office.

Buchanan, R.H. (1958), 'Rural change in an Irish townland, 1890–1955', *Advancement of Science* 14, 291–300.

Buchanan, R.H. (1970), 'Common fields and enclosure: an eighteenth century example from Lecale, county Down', *Ulster Folklife* 25/26, 99–118.

Buchanan, R.H. (1973), 'Field systems of Ireland', in A. Baker and R. Butlin (eds), *Studies of Field Systems in the British Isles*, Cambridge, University Press, 580–618.

Buchanan, R.H. (1986), 'Towns and Plantations, 1500–1700', in W. Nolan (ed.), *The Shaping of Ireland*, 84–98.

Buchanan, R.H. and Walker, B.M. (eds) (1987), *Province, City and People: Belfast and its Region*, Antrim, Greystone Books.

Burke, W. (1968), 'Growing degree-days in Ireland', *Irish Journal of Agricultural Research* 7, 61–71.

Butlin, R. (1977), 'Urban and proto-urban settlement in pre-Norman Ireland', in R. Butlin, (ed.), *The Development of the Irish Town*, London, Croom Helm, 11–27.

Cabot, D. (1985), *The State of the Environment*, Dublin, An Foras Forbartha.

Caldwell, J.H. and Greer, J.V. (1984), *Physical Planning in Rural Areas of Northern Ireland*, Belfast, Queen's University, Department of Town and Country Planning, Occasional Paper 5.

Carter, R. and Parker, A.L. (eds) (1989) *Ireland – a Contemporary Geographical Perspective*, London, Routledge.

Cawley, M. (1980), 'Aspects of rural–urban migration in western Ireland', *Irish Geography* 13, 20–32.

Cawley, M. (1986), 'Disadvantaged areas and groups: problems of rural service provision', in P. Breathnach and M. Cawley (eds), *Change and Development in Rural Ireland*, 48–59.

Cawley, M. (1989), 'Problems of rural Ireland', in R. Carter and A.L. Parker (eds), *Ireland: a Contemporary Geographical Perspective*, 145–70.

Cawley, M. (1990), 'Population change in the Republic of Ireland, 1981–1986', *Area* 22, 67–74.

Cawley, M. (1991), 'Town population change 1971–1986', *Irish Geography* 24, 106–16.

Clarke, H.B. and Simms, A. (eds) (1985), *The Comparative History of Urban Origins in Non-Roman Europe: Ireland, Wales, Denmark, Germany, Poland and Russia from the 9th to the 13th Century*, Oxford, British Archaeological Reports, International Series.

Compton, P. (1978), *Northern Ireland: a Census Atlas*, Dublin, Gill and Macmillan.

Compton, P. (1986) *Demographic Trends in Northern Ireland*, Belfast, Northern Ireland Economic Development Office, Report no. 57.

Compton, P. (1990), 'Demographic trends in the Belfast region with particular reference to the changing distribution of population', in P. Doherty (ed.), *Geographical Perspectives on the Belfast Region*, 15–27.

Connell, K.H. (1950), *The Population of Ireland, 1750–1845*, Oxford, Clarendon Press.

Connell, K.H.(1962), 'Peasant marriage in Ireland: its structure and development since the Famine', *Economic History Review* 14, 501–62.

Connell, K.H. (1968), *Irish Peasant Society: Four Historical Essays*, Oxford, Clarendon Press.

Conry, M. (1971), 'Irish Plaggen soils – their distribution, origin and properties', *Journal of Soil Science* 22, 401–16.

Coward, J. (1980), 'Recent characteristics of Roman Catholic fertility in Northern and Southern Ireland', *Population Studies* 34, 31–44.

Coward, J. (1989), 'Irish population problems', in R. Carter and A.L. Parker (eds), *Ireland – a Contemporary Geographical Perspective*, 55–86.

Craig, M. (1980), *Dublin, 1660–1860*, Dublin, Allen Figgis.

Daly, M.E. (1984), *Dublin the Deposed Capital: A Social and Economic History, 1860–1914*, Cork, University Press.

Daly, M.E. (1985), 'An alien institution? Attitudes towards the city in nineteenth and twentieth century Irish society', *Etudes Irlandaises* 10, 181–94.

Davies, G.L.H. and N. Stephens (1978), *The Geomorphology of the British Isles: Ireland*, London, Nelson.

De Paor, L. (1971), *Divided Ulster*, Harmondsworth, Penguin Books.

Department of the Environment for Northern Ireland (1975), *Regional Physical Development Strategy, 1975–95*, Belfast, HMSO.

Department of the Environment for Northern Ireland (1988), *Belfast Urban Area Plan 2001*, Belfast, HMSO.

Doherty, P. (1978), 'A social geography of the Belfast Urban Area, 1971',

Irish Geography 11, 68–87.

Doherty, P. (1988), 'Socio-spatial change in the Belfast Urban Area, 1971–1981', *Irish Geography* 21, 11–19.

Doherty, P. (1989), 'Ethnic segregation levels in the Belfast Urban Area', *Area* 21, 151–59.

Doherty, P. (ed.) (1990a), *Geographical Perspectives on the Belfast Region*, Jordanstown, Geographical Society of Ireland, Special Publication 5.

Doherty, P. (1990b), 'Social contrasts in a divided city', in P. Doherty (ed.), *Geographical Perspectives on the Belfast Region*, 28–36.

Donnelly, J. Jr. (1975), *The Land and People of Nineteenth-Century Cork*, London, Routledge and Kegan Paul.

Duffy, P.J. (1983), 'Rural settlement change in the Republic of Ireland – a preliminary discussion', *Geoforum* 14, 185–91.

Duffy, P.J. (1986), 'Planning problems in the countryside', in P. Breathnach and M. Cawley (eds), *Change and Development in Rural Ireland*, 60–68.

Duffy, P.J. (1987), 'The Dublin region: a perspective on the fringe', in A.A. Horner and A.J. Parker (eds), *Geographical Perspectives on the Dublin Region*, 113–25.

Eastern Regional Development Organization (1985), *Eastern Region Settlement Strategy 2011*, Dublin, ERDO, 2 vols.

Edwards, C. (1974), 'Farm enterprise systems in east county Londonderry', *Irish Geography* 7, 29–52.

Edwards, C. (1986), 'Changes in agricultural labour efficiency in Northern Ireland, 1975–1984', *Irish Geography* 19, 74–82.

Evans, E.E. (1942), *Irish Heritage*, Dundalk, Tempest.

Evans, E.E. (1944), 'Belfast, the site and the city', *Ulster Journal of Archaeology* 7, 5–29.

Evans, E.E. (1957), *Irish Folkways*, London, Routledge and Kegan Paul.

Evans, E.E. (1973), *The Personality of Ireland: Habitat, Heritage and History*, Cambridge, University Press.

Eversley, D. (1989), *Religion and Employment in Northern Ireland*, London, Sage.

Fennell, R. (1968), 'Structural change in Irish agriculture', *Irish Journal of Agricultural Economics and Rural Sociology* 1, 171–93.

Fitzpatrick, J. and McEniff, J. (1992), 'Tourism', in Government of Ireland, *Ireland in Europe*, 119–52.

Flatrès, P. (1957), *Geographie Rurale de Quatre Contrées Celtiques: Irlande, Galles, Cornwall et Man*, Rennes, Plihon.

Foley, A. and Mulreany, M. (1990), *The Single European Market and the Irish Economy*, Dublin, Institute of Public Administration.

Foley, A. and Griffith, B. (1992), 'Indigenous manufacturing enterprises in a peripheral economy and the single market: the case of the Republic of Ireland', *Regional Studies* 26, 375–86.

Forbes, J. (1970), 'Towns and planning in Ireland', in N. Stephens and R.E. Glasscock (eds), *Irish Geographical Studies*, 291–311.

Freeman, T. (1957), 'Galway: the key to west Connacht', *Irish Geography* 3, 194–205.

Gaffikin, E., Mooney, S. and Morrissey, M. (1991), 'Planning for a change in Belfast: the urban economy, urban regeneration and the Belfast Urban Area Plan 1988', *Town Planning Review* 62, 415–30.

Gardiner, M. (1979), 'Soils', in D.A. Gillmor (ed.), *Irish Resources and Land Use*, 91–108.

Gardiner, M.J. and Radford, T. (1980), *Soil Associations of Ireland and their Land Use Potential*, Dublin, An Foras Taluntais.

Gerald of Wales (1982), *The History and Topography of Ireland*, translated J.J. O'Meara, Harmondsworth, Penguin Books.

Gillmor, D.A. (1967), 'Cattle marketing in Ireland', *Administration* 15, 308–327.

Gillmor, D.A. (1969), 'Cattle movements in the Republic of Ireland', *Transactions Institute of British Geographers* 46, 143–54.

Gillmor, D.A. (1970), 'Spatial distribution of livestock in the Republic of Ireland', *Economic Geography* 46, 587–97.

Gillmor, D.A. (1977), *Agriculture in the Republic of Ireland*, Budapest, Akademiai Kiado.

Gillmor, D.A. (ed.) (1979a), *Irish Resources and Land Use*, Dublin, Institute of Public Administration.

Gillmor, D.A. (1979b), 'Agriculture', in D.A. Gillmor (ed.), *Irish Resources and Land Use*, 109–36.

Gillmor, D.A. (1987), 'Concentration of enterprises and spatial change in agriculture in the Republic of Ireland', *Transactions Institute of British Geographers* 12, 204–16.

Gillmor, D A. (ed.) (1989a), *The Irish Countryside: Landscape, Wildlife, History, People*, Dublin, Wolfhound Press.

Gillmor, D.A. (1989b), 'Agricultural development', in R. Carter and A.L. Parker (eds), *Ireland – a Contemporary Geographical Perspective*, 171–99.

Goodyear, P. and Eastwood, D. (1978), 'Spatial variations in the level of living in Northern Ireland', *Irish Geography* 11, 54–67.

Government of Ireland (1992), *Ireland in Europe, a Shared Challenge: Economic Co-operation on the Island of Ireland in an Integrated Europe*, Dublin, Stationery Office.

Gray, A. (1992), 'Industry and trade', in Government of Ireland, *Ireland in Europe*, 35–63.

Green, E.R.R. (1949), *The Lagan Valley, 1800–1850: a Local History of the Industrial Revolution*, London, Faber.

Greenwood, G. (1992), 'The state of the environment in Ireland', *European Environment* 2, 8–9.

Greer, J. and Jess, P. (1987), 'Town and country planning', in R.H. Buchanan, and B.M. Walker (eds), *Province, City and People: Belfast and its Region*, 101–124.

Grimes, S. (1988), Agricultural policy and land tenure in an Irish marginal county, *Irish Geography* 21, 33–40

Harrison, R. (1986), 'Industrial development policy and the restructuring of the Northern Ireland economy', *Environment and Planning C* 4, 53–70.

Haughton, J. (1946), 'The site of Dublin', *Irish Geography* 1, 53–56.

Heslinga, M. (1962), *The Irish Border as a Cultural Divide: a Contribution to the Study of Regionalism in the British Isles*, Assen, Van Gorcum.

Hoare, A.R. (1977), *Spheres of Influence of Location Factors*, SSRC, Final Report on grants no. HR 3107/1 and 2.

Hoare, A.R. (1978), 'Industrial linkages and the dual economy: the case of Northern Ireland', *Regional Studies* 12, 167–80.

Hoare, A.R. (1981), 'Why they go where they go: the political imagery of industrial location', *Transactions Institute of British Geographers* 6, 153–75.

Horner, A.A. (1986), 'Rural population change in Ireland', in P. Breathnach and M. Cawley (eds), *Change and Development in Rural Ireland*, 34–47.

Horner, A.A. (1990), 'Changes in population and in the extent of the built-up area in the Dublin city-region', *Irish Geography* 23, 50–55.

Horner, A.A. and Daultry, S. (1980), 'Recent population changes in the Republic of Ireland', *Area* 12, 129–35.

Horner, A.A., Walsh, J.A. and Williams, J.A. (1984), *Agriculture in Ireland: a Census Atlas*, Dublin, University College.

Horner, A.A., Walsh, J.A. and Harrington, V.P. (1987), *Population in Ireland: a Census Atlas*, Dublin, University College.

Horner, A.A. and Parker, A.J. (eds) (1987), *Geographical Perspectives on the Dublin Region*, Dublin, Geographical Society of Ireland, Special Publication 5.

Hourihan, K. (1978), 'Social areas in Dublin', *Economic and Social Review* 9, 301–18.

Hourihan, K. and Spillane, N. (1989), 'Manufacturing change in Cork city centre', *Irish Geography* 22, 13–21.

Huff, D. and Lutz, J. (1979), 'Ireland's urban system', *Economic Geography* 55, 196–212.

Industrial Development Authority (1972), *Regional Industrial Plans*, 1973–77, Dublin, IDA.

Industrial Development Authority (1979), *Industrial Plans*, 1978–82 , Dublin, IDA.

Jefferson, C. (1987), 'Economy and employment', in R.H. Buchanan, and B.M. Walker (eds), *Province, City and People: Belfast and its Region*, 191–214.

Jefferson, M. (1939), 'The law of the Primate City', *Geographical Review* 29, 226–32.

Johnson, J.H. (1957–58), 'The age of marriage in nineteenth century Londonderry', *Journal of the Statistical and Social Enquiry Society of Ireland* 21, 99–117.

Johnson, J.H. (1958), 'Studies of Irish rural settlement', *Geographical Review* 48, 554–66.

Johnson, J.H. (1961), 'The development of the rural settlement pattern of Ireland', *Geografiska Annaler* 43, 165–73.

Johnson, J.H. (1962), 'The political distinctiveness of Northern Ireland', *Geographical Review* 53, 78–91.

Johnson, J.H. (1963a), 'Partnership and clachans in mid-nineteenth century Londonderry', *Ulster Folklife* 9, 20–29.

Johnson, J.H. (1963b), 'The disappearance of clachans from county Derry in the nineteenth century', *Irish Geography* 4, 404–14.

Johnson, J.H. (1963c), 'Population changes in Ireland, 1951–1961', *Geographical Journal* 129, 167–74.

Johnson, J.H. (1970a), 'The two "Irelands" at the beginning of the nineteenth century', in N. Stephens and R.E. Glasscock (eds), *Irish Geographical Studies*, 224–44.

Johnson, J.H. (1970b), 'Rural population changes in nineteenth century Londonderry', *Ulster Folklife* 15/16, 119–36.

Johnson, J.H. (1987), 'Republic of Ireland', in H.D. Clout (ed.), *Regional Development in Western Europe*, London, Fulton, 285–305.

Johnson, J.H. (1988), 'The distribution of Irish emigration in the decade before the Great Famine', *Irish Geography* 21, 78–87.

Johnson, J.H. (1990), 'The context of migration: the example of Ireland in the nineteenth century', *Transactions of the Institute of British Geographers* 15, 259–276.

Jones, E. (1960), *A Social Geography of Belfast*, London, Oxford University Press.

Kearns, K.C. (1982), 'Preservation and transformation of Georgian Dublin', *Geographical Review* 72, 270–90.

Kearns, K.C. (1984), *Georgian Dublin: Ireland's Imperilled Architectural Heritage*, Newton Abbot, David and Charles.

Kennedy, K.A., Giblin, T. and McHugh, D. (1988), *The Economic Development of Ireland in the Twentieth Century*, London, Routledge.

Kennedy, L. (1989), *The Modern Industrialization of Ireland, 1940–1988*, Dublin, Economic and Social History Society of Ireland.

Kennedy, L. (1991), 'Farm succession in modern Ireland: elements of a theory of inheritance', *Economic History Review* 44, 477–99.

Kennedy, R.E. (1973), *The Irish: Emigration, Marriage and Fertility*, Berkeley, University of California Press.

King, R. (ed.) (1991), *Geographical Perspectives on Contemporary Irish Migration*, Dublin, Geographical Society of Ireland, Special Publication 6.

Lee, R. (1985), 'Intermarriage, conflict and social control in Ireland: the decree *ne temere*', *Economic and Social Review* 17, 11–27.

Lichfield, N. (1966), *Report and Advisory Outline Plan for the Limerick Region*, Dublin, Stationery Office.

Lynch, P. and Vaizey, J. (1960), *Guinness's Brewery in the Irish Economy, 1759–1876*, Cambridge, University Press.

MacAodha, B. (1956), 'Souming in the Sperrins', *Ulster Folklife* 2, 19–21.

MacAodha, B. (1965), 'Clachan settlement in Iar-Connacht', *Irish Geography* 5, 20–28.

MacAodha, B. (1967), *Conacre in Ireland: the Distribution of Conacre in the Twenty-Six Counties*, Dublin, Scepter Publishers.

McCourt, D. (1955), 'Infield and outfield in Ireland', *Economic History Review* 7, 369–76.

McCourt, D. (1970), 'The dynamic quality of Irish rural settlement', in R.H. Buchanan, E. Jones and D. McCourt (eds), *Man and his Habitat*, London, Routledge and Kegan Paul, 128–64.

McCullough, N. (1989), *Dublin: An Urban History*, Dublin, Anne Street Press.

McDowell, R. (1957), 'The growth of Dublin', in J. Meenan and D. Webb (eds), *A View of Ireland*, Dublin, British Association.

MacLaran, A. (1993), *Dublin* (World Cities Series), London, Belhaven Press.

Matthew, R. (1964), *Belfast Regional Survey and Plan*, Belfast, HMSO.

Mitchell, F. (1976), *The Irish Landscape*, London, Collins.

Mitchell, F. (1986), *Shell Guide to Reading the Irish Landscape*, Dublin, Country House.

Mokyr, J. (1980), *Why Ireland Starved: a Quantitative and Analytical History of the Irish Economy, 1846–1851*, London, Allen and Unwin.

Mokyr, J. and O'Grada, C. (1988), 'Poor and getting poorer? living standards in Ireland before the Famine', *Economic History Review* 41, 209–35.

Murray, M. (1990), 'Single dwelling planning control in Belfast's rural fringe', in P. Doherty (ed.), *Geographical Perspectives on the Belfast Region*, 68–79.

Murray, M. (1991), *The Politics and Pragmatism of Urban Containment: Belfast since 1940*, Aldershot, Avebury.

Newman, J. (1967), *New Dimensions in Regional Planning*, Dublin, Stationery Office.

Nolan, W. (ed.) (1986), *The Shaping of Ireland: the Geographical Perspective*, Cork, Mercier Press.

Nolan, W. (1988), 'New farms and fields: migration policies of state land agencies', in W. Smyth and K. Whelan (eds), *Common Ground: Essays on the Historical Geography of Ireland*, 296–319.

Northern Ireland Development Programme 1970–75 (1970), Belfast, HMSO.

Northern Ireland Economic Council (1987), *Economic Strategy: Impact of Lignite*, Belfast, Northern Ireland Economic Development Council, Report 65.

Northern Ireland Economic Council (1990), *The Industrial Development Board for Northern Ireland: Selective Financial Assistance and Economic Development Policy*, Belfast, Northern Ireland Development Council, Report 78.

O'Farrell, P.N. (1969), 'Continuous regularities and discontinuities in the central place system', *Geografiska Annaler* 52B, 104–14.

O'Grada, C. (1988), *Ireland before and after the Famine, Explorations, 1800–1925*, Manchester, University Press.

O'Grada, C. (1989), *The Great Irish Famine*, Basingstoke, Macmillan.

Osborne, R.D. and Cormack, R.J. (1986), 'Unemployment and religion in Northern Ireland', *Economic and Social Review* 17, 215–25.

Osborne, R.D. and Cormack, R.J. (1991), *Discrimination and Public Policy in Northern Ireland*, Oxford, Clarendon Press.

Parker, A.L. (1987), 'The changing nature of retailing', in A.A. Horner and A.L. Parker (eds), *Geographical Perspectives on the Dublin Region*, 27–40.

Patrick, S. (1987), 'The *per capita* output of phosporous from domestic detergents in Ireland, 1950–1982', *Irish Geography* 20, 89–94.

Pringle, D. (1990), 'The 1990 Presidential election', *Irish Geography* 23, 136–41.

Pringle, D. (1991), 'Urban growth and economic change in the Republic of Ireland, 1971–1981', in M.J. Bannon, L.S. Bourne and R. Sinclair (eds), *Urbanization and Urban Development: Recent Trends in a Global Context*, Dublin, Service Industries Research Centre, University College, 151–62.

Proudfoot, V.B. (1956), 'Studies in conacre', *Irish Geography* 3(3), 162–67.

Proudfoot, V.B. (1959), 'Clachans in Ireland', *Gwerin* 2, 110–22.

Report of the Departmental Committee (1914) *[on]* . . . *the Housing Conditions of the Working Classes in the City of Dublin*, British Parliamentary Papers, 1914 XIX (cd 7273), appendix xxv.

Report of the Irish Boundary Commission 1925, with an introduction by G. Hand, Shannon, Irish Universities Press, 1969.

Rohan, P.K. (1975), *The Climate of Ireland*, Dublin, Stationery Office.

Ryan, D. (ed.) (1948), *Socialism and Nationalism: a Selection from the Writings of James Connolly*, Dublin, Three Candles.

Salt, J. and Johnson, J.H. (1975), 'Recent trends in the level and distribution of unemployment in Northern Ireland', *Tijdschrift voor Economische en Sociale Geografie* 66, 225–33.

Simms, A. (1979), 'Medieval Dublin: a topographical analysis', *Irish Geography* 12, 25–41.

Simms, A. and Simms, K. (1990), *Kells*, Dublin, Irish Historic Towns Atlas, folio 4, Royal Irish Academy.

Smyth, W. and Whelan, K. (eds) (1988), *Common Ground: Essays on the Historical Geography of Ireland*, Cork, University Press.

Stephens, N. and Glasscock, R.E. (eds) (1970), *Irish Geographical Studies in Honour of E. Estyn Evans*, Belfast, Queen's University.

Stockdale, A. (1991), 'Recent trends in urbanisation and rural repopulation in Northern Ireland', *Irish Geography* 24, 70–80.

Sweeney, J. (1982), 'Air pollution and morbidity in Dublin', *Irish Geography* 15, 1–10

Sweeney, J. (1989), 'Air pollution problems in Ireland', in R. Carter and A.L. Parker (eds), *Ireland – a Contemporary Geographical Perspective*, 421–39.

Symons, L. (ed.) (1963), *Land Use in Northern Ireland*, London, University of London Press.

Synge, F. and Stephens, N. (1960), 'The Quaternary Period in Ireland – an assessment', *Irish Geography* 4, 121–30.

Telesis Consulting Group (1982), *A Review of Industrial Policy*, National Economic and Social Council report no. 64, Dublin, Stationery Office.

Walsh, B.M. (1970a), 'Marriage rates and population pressure in Ireland, 1871 and 1911', *Economic History Review* 23, 148–62.

Walsh, B. (1970b), *Religion and Demographic Behaviour in Ireland*, Dublin, Economic and Social Research Institute, Paper no. 55.

Walsh, J.A. (1986), 'Agricultural change and development', in P. Breathnach and M. Cawley (eds), *Change and Development in Rural Ireland*, 11–33.

Walsh, J.A. (1991), 'The turn-around of the turn-around in the population of the Republic of Ireland', *Irish Geography* 24, 117–25.

Whelan, K. (1983), 'The Catholic parish, the Catholic chapel and village development in Ireland', *Irish Geography* 16, 1–15.

Whittow, J. (1973), *Geology and Scenery in Ireland*, Harmondsworth, Penguin Books.

Whyte, J. (1988), Interpretations of the Northern Ireland problem, in C. Townshend (ed.), *Consensus in Ireland: Approaches and Recessions*, Oxford, Clarendon Press, 24–46.

Whyte, J. (1991), *Interpreting Northern Ireland*, London, Oxford University Press.

Wilcock, D. (1979), 'Post-war land drainage, fertilizer use and environmental impact in Northern Ireland', *Journal of Environmental Management* 8, 137–49.

Wilcock, D. (1989), 'Water resource management', in R. Carter and A.L. Parker (eds), *Ireland – a Contemporary Geographical Perspective*, 359–93.

Wilson, T. (1965), *Economic Development in Northern Ireland*, Belfast, HMSO.

Wright, M. (1967), *The Dublin Region: Advisory Plan and Final Report*, Dublin, Stationery Office.

Index